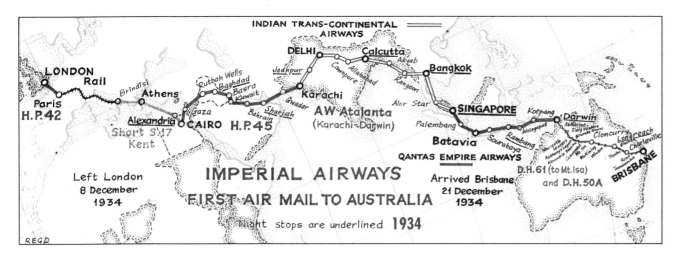

INDIAN TRANS-CONTINENTAL AIRWAYS

LONDON Rail
Paris H.P.42
Brindisi
Athens
Alexandria
Short S.17 Kent
CAIRO H.P.45
Gaza
Rutbah Wells
Baghdad
Basra
Kuwait
Bahrain
Sharjah
Gwadar
Karachi
Jodhpur
DELHI
Cawnpore
Allahabad
Calcutta
Akyab
AW Atalanta (Karachi-Darwin)
Rangoon
Alor Star
Bangkok
SINGAPORE
Palembang
Batavia
Sourabaya
Koepang
Rambang
Waingapoe
Darwin
Katherine
Daly Waters
Cloncurry
Camooweal
Longreach
Charleville
BRISBANE
D.H.61 (to Mt.Isa)
and D.H.50A

IMPERIAL AIRWAYS
FIRST AIR MAIL TO AUSTRALIA

Left London 8 December 1934

QANTAS EMPIRE AIRWAYS

Arrived Brisbane 21 December 1934

Night stops are underlined **1934**

REGD

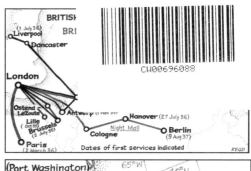

BRITISH BRI
Liverpool (1 July 36)
Doncaster
London
Ostend LeZoute (1 Oct 36)
Lille (5 July 36)
Brussels
Antwerp (1 Nov 36)
Hanover (27 July 36)
Cologne
Night Mail
Berlin (9 Aug 37)
Paris (2 March 36)
Dates of first services indicated
REGD

(Port Washington)
New York
65°W 40°N
SERVICE TO **BERMUDA** 1937
35°N
Baltimore
16 June 1937
17 November 1937 (winter service)
Bermuda
REGD 75°W 70°W 30°N 60°W

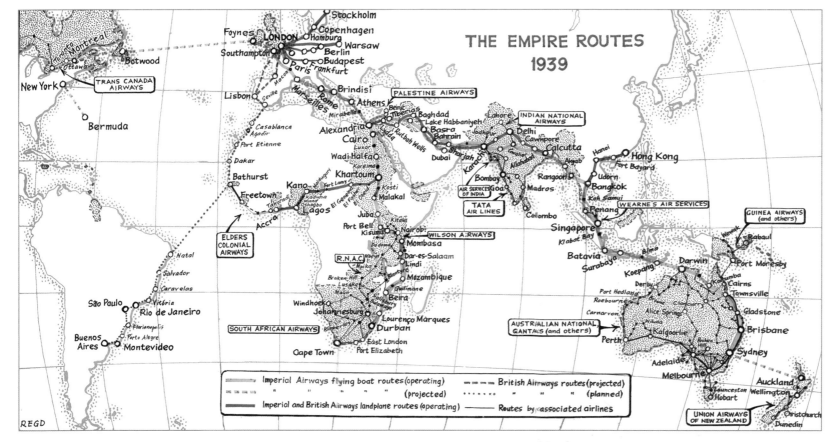

THE EMPIRE ROUTES 1939

Stockholm, Foynes, Copenhagen, Hamburg, LONDON, Warsaw, Southampton, Berlin, Budapest, Paris, Frankfurt, Montreal, Ottawa, Botwood, New York, Bermuda, Lisbon, Seville, Macon, Marseilles, Rome, Brindisi, Athens, Mirabella, PALESTINE AIRWAYS, Casablanca, Agadir, Port Etienne, Dakar, Bathurst, Alexandria, Cairo, Luxor, Wadi Halfa, Beirut, Damascus, Baghdad, Lake Habbaniyeh, Basra, Bahrain, Rutbah Wells, Dubai, Sharjah, Lahore, Delhi, INDIAN NATIONAL AIRWAYS, Cawnpore, Calcutta, Gwalior, Allahabad, Akyab, Hanoi, HONG KONG, Fort Bayard, Karima, Khartoum, Kosti, Malakal, Kano, El Geneina, Bombay, Goa, AIR SERVICES OF INDIA, TATA AIR LINES, Madras, Rangoon, Udorn, Bangkok, Colombo, Koh Samui, WEARNE'S AIR SERVICES, Penang, Klabat Bay, Singapore, GUINEA AIRWAYS (and others), Rabaul, Port Moresby, Freetown, Accra, ELDERS COLONIAL AIRWAYS, Lagos, Juba, Port Bell, Kisumu, Nairobi, WILSON AIRWAYS, Mombasa, Dar-es-Salaam, Lindi, Mozambique, R.N.A.C., Batavia, Surabaya, Koepang, Bima, Darwin, Wyndham, Derby, Port Hedland, Roebourne, Carnarvon, Cairns, Townsville, Gladstone, Broken Hill, Lusaka, Windhoek, Quilimane, Beira, Salisbury, Johannesburg, Lourenço Marques, Durban, SOUTH AFRICAN AIRWAYS, East London, Port Elizabeth, Cape Town, Alice Springs, AUSTRALIAN NATIONAL QANTAS (and others), Perth, Kalgoorlie, Adelaide, Brisbane, Sydney, Melbourne, Launceston, Hobart, UNION AIRWAYS OF NEW ZEALAND, Auckland, Wellington, Christchurch, Dunedin, São Paulo, Natal, Salvador, Caravelas, Vitória, Rio de Janeiro, Florianopolis, Porto Alegre, Buenos Aires, Montevideo

TRANS CANADA AIRWAYS

Imperial Airways flying boat routes (operating)
" " " " (projected)
Imperial and British Airways landplane routes (operating)
British Airways routes (projected)
" " " (planned)
Routes by associated airlines

REGD

BRITISH AIRWAYS

AN AIRLINE AND ITS AIRCRAFT

VOLUME 1: 1919–1939

THE IMPERIAL YEARS

Other Books by R.E.G. Davies

Standard References

A History of the World's Airlines
Airlines of the United States Since 1914
Airlines of Latin America Since 1919
Airlines of Asia Since 1920
Commuter Airlines of the United States
(with Imre Quastler)

Airline Histories

Continental Airlines—The First Fifty Years
Pan Am: An Airline and Its Aircraft
Lufthansa: An Airline and Its Aircraft
Delta: An Airline and Its Aircraft
Aeroflot: An Airline and Its Aircraft
Saudia: An Airline and Its Aircraft
TransBrasil: An Airline and Its Aircraft
TWA: An Airline and Its Aircraft
Eastern: An Airline and Its Aircraft

Specials

Berlin Airlift: The Greatest Humanitarian Airlift
(with John Provan)
Comet: The World's First Jetliner
(with Phil Birtles)
Fallacies and Fantasies of Air Transport History
Lindbergh: An Airman, his Aircraft, and his Great Flights
Rebels and Reformers of the Airways
Supersonic Nonsense
The Chelyuskin Adventure
(with Yuri Salnikov)

Titles in bold type are available through Paladwr Press

BRITISH AIRWAYS

AN AIRLINE AND ITS AIRCRAFT

VOLUME 1: 1919–1939
THE IMPERIAL YEARS

by R.E.G. Davies

Special Consultant: John Stroud

Art Direction by Mike Machat

Paladwr Press

To the memory of
George Woods Humphery

Published by Paladwr Press, 1906 Wilson Lane, #101, McLean, Virginia 22102-1957, USA

Manufactured in Singapore

Aircraft Drawings, Maps, and Charts by R.E.G. Davies

Special Consultant: John Stroud

Art Direction by Mike Machat

Detailed Layout by Liz Weaver

ISBN 1-888962-24-0

Contents

Foreword, by Lord Marshall of Knightsbridge

Today's world-wide British Airways traces its heritage back for more than eight decades. The first twenty of the pioneering years of the airline's predecessors are chronicled in this wonderfully evocative illustrated history of people, aircraft, and early flying routes. As will be seen on the pages that follow, this is the story of struggling airlines (many short-lived and operating but a handful of aeroplanes), occasional tragedy, changing and sometimes conflicting government policies, developing airfields, and steadily improving technology. And let us not forget the intrepid passengers, for whom a flight was, in the early years, often an adventure — for if possible they had to be looked after in comfort, and safely. But unlike today, until the early 1930s at least, neither could be guaranteed.

Over the years, several books have told the story of Britain's developing airlines between the world wars. John Pudney's *The Seven Seas* (1959), for example, focussed on the people who made both Imperial Airways and B.O.A.C., while Robin Higham's *Britain's Imperial Air Routes* (1960) described the technical and political story of building the world's international air routes before 1940. Several of the classic interwar airliners have been the subject of books as well — especially those dealing with the majestic flying boats with their promenade decks.

This newest history, *The Imperial Years*, by historian Ron Davies, now provides a comprehensive overview in a combination of concise and informed text, detailed reference information on the aircraft fleets, colour profiles, photographs and paintings, as well as specially-drawn maps and charts. All these shed light, in an attractive format, on all the multiple facets of a fascinating and fast-changing era of dynamic airline development.

Dynamic it certainly was, and the extraordinary aspect of the eventful period covered by the book, from the end of the First World War to the beginning of the Second, is that it lasted only 20 years. The progress made was truly amazing. Wood-and-fabric, single-engined, open-cockpit biplanes, with fixed undercarriages, gave way, all within 20 years, to four-engined comfortable airliners with retractable landing gears. The slow and flimsy aircraft inherited from the First World War were unrecognizable from the fast and elegant airliners that served the country during the Second.

Many generations of aircraft technology and several advancing steps in managerial and operating practice are thus covered in Davies's *The Imperial Years*. And to emphasize the remarkable progress and changes made in those 20 years, I reflect that my own tenure with British Airways, from 1983 to 2004, was longer than that whole period. But in contrast, at least on the technical side, the changes were only of modification and size. The Boeing 747 was our intercontinental workhorse when I joined the airline, and it was still earning its keep when I left. The severely-demanding operational life of our flagship Concorde was twice as long as that of the pre-war Handley Page 42, then regarded as long-lived.

This book, then, has the best qualities of a well-written history, enhanced by handsome illustrations and layout that together relate the complex story of British airlines, from their first faltering steps in 1918 to the continent-spanning air services that began to replace the ocean liners two decades later. Davies's half-century of airline historical research is complemented by collaboration with consultant John Stroud, who first worked for Imperial Airways in 1933 — before I was born — and whose knowledge and records have ensured the accuracy of the facts and figures that make this book a reliable reference as well as an enjoyable one to peruse.

This is the thirteenth book in Paladwr Press's pictorial "An Airline and its Aircraft" series. It may come to be regarded as the jewel in the publisher's crown.

Marshall
October 2005

Author's Preface and Acknowledgements

Of all the books that I have written and published, none has been more challenging than this pictorial volume on the early history of the airlines that were the ancestors of the present-day British Airways. The objective of Paladwr Press's books in this series about airlines and air transport history is to combine a well-researched narrative with good illustrations, to complement each other, and collectively condense a wealth of information into an economical presentation. These books aim to be useful references for the student of commercial airline history, providing a broad background of technology, pioneering enterprise, and politics. If there is a preponderance of itemized facts and figures, and a generous provision of photographs, pictures, charts, and maps, this is quite deliberate. Together they serve to condense material that could otherwise need hundreds of pages of library-type text, not to mention the footnotes, into a standard volume.

To accomplish this daunting task, I have been well aware of the old saying that to copy someone else's work is plagiarism, but to copy several other people's work is research. I do not plead guilty to either of these literary indiscretions; but I do wish, with great respect, to acknowledge the help that I have so generously received from many other authors who have specialized in the fascinating subject of British airline history between the two World Wars.

Head and shoulders above all others, John Stroud, whom I regard as the doyen of British commercial aviation historians, has given me the encouragement, technical advice, and contributions from his own writings and archives, without which the Imperial Years chronicled within these pages would have been seriously deficient. I have been fortunate to have been able to draw upon his almost infallible memory of details that could only have come from someone who joined Imperial Airways in 1933, and subsequently kept detailed notes of his sojourn with Britain's flag carrier.

In particular, John was a technical artist and I was able to refer to his notes on the colour schemes of the early transport aircraft (they were not called airliners then) of the inter-war years. These were priceless records, compiled before the wide use of colour photography. His immaculate editorship that was the hallmark of no less than seventy of the comprehensive Putnam series of aviation books was available to me. He checked every fact and figure and supplied essential material for the many fleet lists.

These lists, incidentally, may seem to be of use only to dedicated collectors. But they serve a purpose, emphasizing the short-lived careers of pre-war aeroplanes, and the hazardous nature of air transport during its adolescent years. The term "crashed" is all too frequent an entry in the Remarks column of the tabulations, whereas today the airlines fly for years without reporting a single injury, much less a fatality, of its passengers. Air transport has come a long way.

A long way indeed, from open-cockpit stick-and-string biplanes in 1919 to comfortable all-metal airliners and flying boats with promenade decks in 1939. And is it not a neat irony that, in the beginning, George Holt Thomas used machines that were built for the military, and at the end of this two-decade period, the British airliners were requisitioned for wartime use? The original debt was repaid handsomely.

I have also drawn from many other published sources, listed in the bibliography. An outstanding reference, which I commend to every serious student of the subject, is Arthur Ord-Hume's *British Commercial Aircraft*. His truly encyclopaedic tome contains many anecdotes to remind us of the diverse personalities of the individuals who collaborated (or conspired) to lay the foundations of the British airline industry. I am indebted too to Peter Clegg, who has chronicled so well the lives and achievements of Scotland's pioneers in his own delightful series of books. Peter also arranged for me to include a selection of Ed Miller's wonderfully artistic depictions of the embryo years north of the Border. These carefully-drawn portraits bring those bold initiatives vividly back to life.

I must thank Neville Doyle for being able to refer to his detailed and almost intimate account of *The Triple Alliance*, the amalgamation that formed the pre-war British Airways; and John Hamlin, for the complete record of *The de Havilland Dragon/Rapide Family*, without which the internal development of airlines in the United Kingdom would have been found wanting. Books like these — and I consulted many others — leave no historical stone unturned, and I was fortunate not to have to turn those stones myself.

The great Short flying boats restored some dignity, and invoked a sense of romance, to the image of Imperial Airways in its competitive efforts against the speed and efficiency of K.L.M.'s Douglases. Their late-1930s excursions have been superbly portrayed by marine artist Ian Marshall in his incomparable compendium of water-colours, *Flying Boats — The J-Class Yachts of Aviation*. Ian graciously permitted me to include a two-page spread of his paintings that bring back memories of those bygone years, when flying to India or Africa was as much an adventure as simply going from one place to another. In those days, I should note, they were POSH — Port Out, Starboard Home — people, just as they were in the ships that plied the Suez Canal and the Red Sea to India.

The Short boats have often been compared to the big American flying boats — not always to their credit, because at first they lacked trans-Atlantic range. Nevertheless, of all the 1,266 large flying boats built, world-wide, 821 were commercial or C-Class Empire types, most of them military developments, serving as reconnaissance squadrons throughout the Second World War and afterwards converted back to civilian use, as interim capacity for B.O.A.C.

The work of the oft-maligned bureaucrats has been essential. Every year, following the end of the Great War of 1914-18, the Air Ministry published its annual reports on the progress of civil aviation, which remain today as models of disciplined accounting by conscientious, but sadly anonymous, civil servants. When I first started work at the Ministry of Civil Aviation in 1946, I believe I once met the un-named editor, a Mr. Pike, and I hope that this book reflects his constant attention to accuracy.

Finally, I must thank British Airways for its support for my work. David Hyde and Martin George showed faith in my ambition, while Jack Ligterwood and his successor Paul Jarvis lent their support and encouragement from the British Airways archives. To have been assigned to write this book has been a privilege and I hope that these pages will provide enjoyable reading to all its employees, past and present. Even by the exhibits and illustrations alone, neatly arranged by graphic designer Liz Weaver, they may savour a glimpse of the flying heritage that laid the foundations of the great airline that it is today.

R.E.G. Davies, *August 2005*

The First Airlines

Perspectives

Any narrative or chronology about the pioneering years of air transport inevitably calls to question the familiar subject of "who was first?" As with many such discussions, the precise definitions are always essential to recognize. To put the first British airlines in their true historical place in the annals of airline history, some of the early efforts must therefore be mentioned.

Prelude: Air Mail in India

On 18 February 1911, the French aviator, Henri Pequet, using a Humber biplane, flew a small parcel of mail from Allahabad,, India, to Naini, in connection with the **United Provinces Exhibition** held at the time. This event is accepted by air mail philatelists as the world's first aerial post.

The "Coronation Aerial Post"

During the same year, from 9 to 26 September, the Grahame-White Aviation Company operated a series of flights from Hendon aerodrome in north London to Windsor, to commemorate the Coronation of King George V. Flown by the well-known pilot, Gustav Hamel, 25,000 letters and 90,000 postcards were delivered to the Castle, postmarked **"Coronation A.D. 1911. First U.K. Aerial Post by Sanction of H.M. Postmaster-General."** Though short-lived, it was an impressive demonstration of what the aeroplane could do to speed up the mail.

Gustav Hamel's route to deliver the Coronation Air Mail.

Other Early Air Mail Experiments

Other countries began to realize the potential of the fast aeroplane to speed up the mails. In Italy, on 19 September 1919, letters were carried by air mail between Bologna and Venice and between Venice and Rimini. And in the United States, Earle Ovington gained attention when he made a few flights on Long Island, between Nassau Boulevard and Mineola.

Pre-War German Airship Activity

Since the end of the 19th Century, the German Count Zeppelin had developed the rigid airship, and by 1909 he was ready to demonstrate the practicality of his lighter-than-air craft for carrying passengers as well as mail. On 16 October of that year, with the financial support of the Hamburg-Amerika shipping line, he formed **Die Deutsche Luftschiffahrt Aktien Gesellschaft (DELAG).** Zeppelin supplied the airships and the shipping company did the marketing. Between 22 June 1910 and 31 July 1914 (just before the outbreak of the Great War) seven airships carried more than 30,000 passengers on special inter-city flights and for sightseeing

Contrary to some claims, the airships did not offer regular air services; but undoubtedly the efforts of DELAG popularized aviation as a whole. This created a level of enthusiasm on a nation-wide scale that was to emerge again after the conflict, in government, state, and city organizations and agencies. Such encouragement created a mood of airmindedness in Germany which led to its national airline dominating the airways of Europe until the outbreak of the Second World War in 1939.

One of DELAG's airships, the Viktoria Luise

A Post office waybill, dated 9 September 1911.

Igor Sikorsky's historic flight in the Il'ya Muromets in 1914

The World's First Airline

Pride of place for claiming the world's first (without qualifying criteria, except regularity and public availability) must go to the United States. On 1 January 1914, founded by Percy Fansler, the **St. Petersburg-Tampa Airboat Line** began to carry passengers across Tampa Bay, in a 20-minute journey in a Benoist flying boat. This was preferable to a two-hour boat trip or a 12-hour cicuitous rail journey around the Bay. The service lasted for only three months, but Fansler had proved a point.

The Benoist XIV flying low across Tampa Bay

The World's First Transport Aircraft

By an extraordinary coincidence, during the very same months, in the Russian St. Petersburg, the great aircraft designer, **Igor Sikorsky**, was successfully demonstrating his new four-engined transport aircraft. On 30 June 1914, he flew the *Il'ya Muromets*, with a crew of three, from St. Petersburg to Kiev, with only one stop. This remarkable aeroplane could carry as many as 16 passengers, in wicker chairs, and it had electric lighting and a toilet. It was the greatest advance in aviation technology since the Wright brothers. But like Zeppelin's airships, all development ceased as the Lights Went Out in Europe in August.

Igor Sikorsky's great Il'ya Muromets, the world's first transport aircraft

The Vision of George Holt Thomas

An Early Visionary

The industrialist **George Holt Thomas** made his first aeroplane flight in 1909, and was a strong advocate for aircraft as a weapon of war. Yet as early as 1916, he realized their commercial potential as well. On 5 October 1916, he founded Aircraft Transport & Travel (A.T.& T.) as a subsidiary of his **Aircraft Manufacturing Company, Ltd. (Airco)** (see page 5).

Shrewd Predictions

He explained his enthusiasm for this new form of travel in an historic book, *Aerial Transport,* published in 1920, with an introduction by the newspaper and publishing magnate (also an aviation advocate), Lord Northcliffe. Some of his observations and predictions were remarkably farsighted, even though aeronautical technical knowledge at that time was in its infancy, railways predominated over land, and ocean liners ruled the seas. At the beginning of his book, he claimed: "London to New York by air will certainly become a commercial proposition, but only in stages; probably, as far as possible, by long-distance machines and the practical flying boat."

This is not to suggest that all his predictions were exactly right —but his approach to lighter-than-air possibilities were more cautious than the confident promotion of airships by others. He warned about the problems of hangarage for such large machines, and of the need for precision-built mooring masts; and he foresaw the problem of "hundreds of men required to manipulate (airships) at the time of ascent or descent." This was still a problem when the *Graf Zeppelin* and the ill-fated *Hindenburg* were still operating in 1937.

He identified the advantage of the aeroplane's speed, compared to that of the fastest trains, and considered the higher costs involved in a matter-of-fact but nonetheless logical way. He pointed out that telegrams cost one halfpenny per word but a thousand-word letter cost only three-halfpence; and that a taxi ride at two shillings was sometimes necessary in preference to an omnibus at twopence. And he quoted an amusing anecdote from the early weeks of A.T.& T. when two foreign diplomats arrived in Paris some time before the cable was delivered to announce their arrival.

Mr. G. Holt Thomas

The son of the founder of Britain's first newspaper to include pictures, Holt Thomas presented his ideas on the future of commercial aviation to the Royal Aeronautical Society on 30 May 1917. While politicians and other industrialists debated the subject, Holt Thomas backed his words with deeds and, in the middle of the First World War, founded Aircraft Transport and Travel with a capital of £50,000—a substantial declaration of faith.

He correctly recognized the fragile nature of the aeroplanes themselves and the consequent need to amortize their cost. In 1920, the "stick-and-string" wooden-framed and fabric-covered aircraft did not last more than a year or two; and he was aware of the uncertainty of maintaining regularity because of the need for perfect engine maintenance, and the ever-present danger caused by bad weather and the inadequacy of contemporary weather-forecasting.

He also identified the "universally important" aspect that would govern the development of the air transport industry world-wide for the next half-century: "it is not a matter for private enterprise alone but for private enterprise going hand-in-hand with the Governments of the world."

An Air Map for the World

Four maps, in two colours, were folded in at the end of *Aerial Transport*, and are reproduced on the opposite page.

The first shows Captain Ross Smith's Vickers Vimy flight to Australia in the closing months of 1919, and it differs only slightly from that followed by Imperial Airways when it began its flying boat services in 1934 (see page 34).

The second maps the 1919 trans-Atlantic flights of Alcock and Brown, the R.34 airship, and the American NC-4. Again, the map bears an uncanny resemblance to the routes taken by Pan American Airways when it inaugurated North Atlantic airliner services in 1939.

The third map could have served as the plan for the pre-war British Airways of 1936 (see page 88) or even the post-war British European Airways of 1946.

The fourth map illustrates the time-saving on the British Empire routes, as mentioned above.

These maps, drawn in 1920, were truly remarkable in their visionary portrayal of the future development of British air routes during the subsequent decades.

Airline Blueprint for Britain

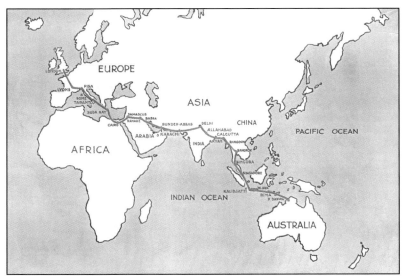

Ross and Keith Smith's flight to Australia, 12 November–10 December 1919

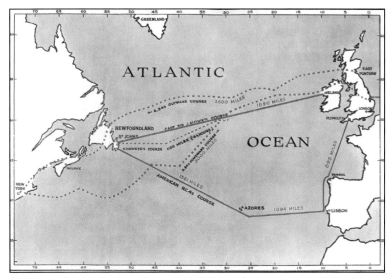

The courses taken by Alcock and Brown, the R.34, the NC-4, and the ill-fated Harry Hawker

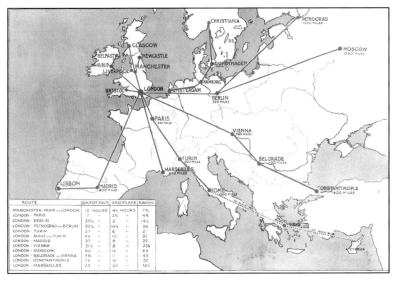

The plan to alter the timetables of Europe

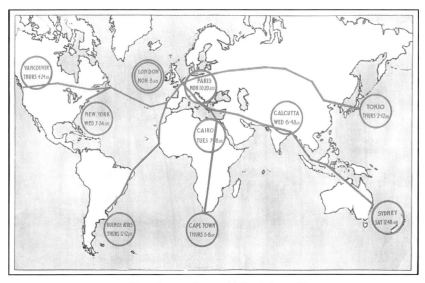

How the aeroplane could shrink the world

The First Cross-Channel Air Services

Swords into Ploughshares

To the relief of the whole of Europe, the Armistice agreement of 11 November 1918 finally ended the hostilities that had killed so many millions of civilians as well as combatants during the Great War of 1914–18. Agreements as to the amount of reparations and the cessations of territories were imposed on the Central Powers by the victorious Allies. The negotiations and discussions to this end were conducted in the Peace Conference in Paris during the early months of 1919, resulting in the Treaty of Versailles, signed by Germany on 28 June.

Before the politicians had finished their work, however, the urge to return to peace-time normality was strong. In aviation, unlike the other weapons of war, the equipment used-aircraft—could be converted to peacetime use; and the pilots, unlike soldiers, could find work to fly them. In Germany, the ancestor airline of Deutsche Luft Hansa, **Deutsche Luft Reederei**, started the first airline service on 22 February 1919, linking Berlin with Weimar, seat of the first post-war German republic. A month later, on 22 March,

the **Lignes Aériennes Farman** started the first international air route, from Paris to Brussels.

The First Military Air Services

Already, on 17 December 1918, barely a month after the Armistice, the **Royal Air Force** began a military air mail service on the Continent with Airco D.H.9s, linking the Army General Headquarters at Hesdin, in northern France, with the Armistice Commission Headquarters at Spa, in eastern Belgium. The service was extended to Cologne on 1 January 1919.

In Great Britain, civilian flying was not permitted until May, although George Holt Thomas's Aircraft Transport and Travel was ready to go (see page 2). But a quasi-airline service was flown in February 1919, by pilots of the R.A.F., using A.T. & T.'s Airco D.H.9As. At the request of the Belgian Government, the operation was from Hawkinge, Kent, to Ghent, carrying supplies to relieve acute food shortages. This was probably the first time that any aeroplanes had been used for humanitarian purposes.

Trail-Blazing for the First Airline

Already, starting on 10 January 1919, the 86th (Communications) Wing of the R.A.F. started a regular service between the airfields at Hendon and Kenley, near London, and Buc, near Paris, carrying delegates and documents to the Paris Peace Conference, and the service continued until September, using 18 Airco D.H.4s, 8 Handley Page O/400s, 2 Martinsyde F.4s, and even some Bristol Fighters. By September, when the service ended, 934 passengers, 1,008 bags of mail, and 46 special despatches had been carried.

Then, on 1 March 1919, Nos. 18, 110, and 120 Squadrons of the R.A.F. expanded the air mail service to Cologne (see above), using D.H.4s, 9s, 9As, and 10s. From Hawkinge, they were routed via Maisoncelle, and later Marquise. By 15 August, when the operation was handed over to A. T. & T., 1,842 flights, of about ten each day, had been made, carrying 90 tons of mail. Holt Thomas's airline carried on until June 1920, by which time it was well under way with its commercial London-Paris service.

The parcel service between Hawkinge and Ghent, started in February 1919 (only 3 months after the Armistice was signed), was flown in Airco D.H. 9s by R.A.F. pilots. Aircraft Transport and Travel's name appeared on stickers beneath the cockpits. A member of the ground crew is about to swing the propeller of the leading aircraft, D 1197, in the foreground.

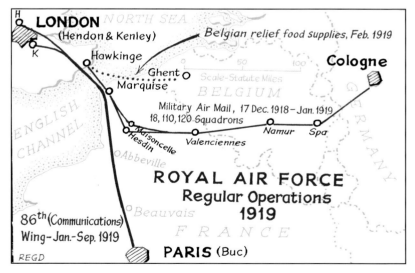

The Royal Air Force's operations during the immediate aftermath of the Great War acted as a trailblazer for the commercial services that began in August 1919. The squadrons used many of the same aircraft, which were flown by many of the same pilots.

Aircraft Transport and Travel

Founded on 5 October 1916 by the visionary George Holt Thomas (see page 2), **Aircraft Transport and Travel (A.T.& T.)** started scheduled air services from London's Hounslow airfield to Paris's le Bourget on 25 August 1919. Its place in airline history is important. There had been other earlier services, but these were mainly experimental or for military support (see page 1), and none was launched with the same flair, nor were they fully comprehensive. In the U.S.A., the Post Office had launched its air mail service on 15 May 1918. In Europe, the Austrians had operated a support service from 20 March 1918 from Vienna to Kiev, to organize food supplied to their beleaguered capital. The German Deutsche Luft Reederei (D.L.R.) began a Berlin-Weimar service on 22 February, to serve the politicians who were creating a new government; and in France, the Farman airline began an international service from Paris to Brussels on 22 March 1919. But the German was a purely local domestic operation, and the Farman was only once a week.

A.T. & T.'s claim to fame was that it was **the first daily international passenger, mail, and parcel service**, i.e., combining all the individual claims of other earlier operators in 1919. The first aircraft used are illustrated below. Holt Thomas's airline operated a total of at least 45 aircraft (see pages 6–7), almost all of them converted military types, light bombers or trainers; but in April 1920, it introduced the first purely civil design, the D.H.18. On 17 May 1920, it started a second route, to Amsterdam, in conjunction with the newly-formed Dutch airline K.L.M., using a D.H.16, piloted by "Jerry" Shaw (see page 7).

Airco's aircraft designer was Geoffrey de Havilland, who started his own company when Airco was purchased by the Birmingham Small Arms (B.S.A.) company in 1920. His line of D.H. aircraft spanned several generations of airliner development, culminating in the world's first jet airliner, the D.H.106 Comet, in 1952, and the world's first tri-jet, the Trident, in 1964.

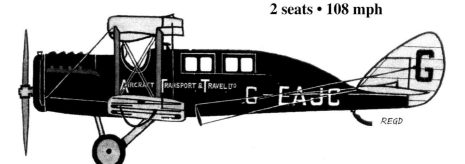

Engine	Rolls-Royce Eagle (375 hp)	Max. Range	400 miles
		Length	30 feet
MGTOW	3,740 lb.	Span	42 feet

Size comparison with the Handley Page H.P.42 (p.37)

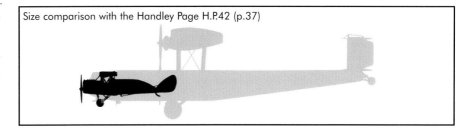

The first air service open to the British public was flown by Major Cyril Patteson in this Airco D.H.16 (K-130) from Hounslow to le Bourget. This picture was taken when giving pleasure flights at Harrogate on Whit-Monday, 9 June 1919.

In open cockpits, the D.H.9B, passengers as well as the crew had to be well wrapped up. This photograph is of the first London-Amsterdam flight by A.T.&T., chartered by KLM. The Paris-London was also by a D.H.9, piloted by Lieut. J. McMullin.

This D.H.4A flew from Hounslow to le Bourget on 25 August 1919, but it was not open to the public. The pilot, Lieutenant E.H. "Bill" Lawford, carried G.M. Stevenson-Reece of the Evening Standard, some newspapers, a brace of grouse, and jars of Devonshire cream.

The First de Havillands

Fragile Equipment

A. T. & T. operated its pioneering cross-Channel air service for only 18 months, using about 45 aircraft (not counting some of those flown by R.A.F. crews before commercial services were authorized. These aeroplanes were built for military use — the D.H.4 was a light bomber — and long life was not expected of it. Its wooden frame, covered with doped canvas, was not robust enough for the more concentrated work demanded of airline scheduling. And as yet, the engines were not reliable enough to guarantee the completion of every flight.

The average operating life was thus measured in months, not years, as the tabulation reveals. Only about a dozen aircraft, most of them D.H.16s, were still in service when Britain's first airline ended service on 17 December 1920.

Rough Fields

When the First (Great) War came mercifully to an end on 11 November 1918, commercial aviation did not exist as an industry. But visionary industrialists such as George Holt Thomas in Great Britain, Hugo Junkers and Claude Dornier in Germany, and Pierre Latécoère in France had realized that heavier-than-air aircraft were capable of carrying mail, goods, and people, as well as guns, bombs, and cameras.

At first the infant airlines had to make do with grass fields, adequate for the light aircraft. **Hounslow Heath**, in London's western suburbs (pictured) was acceptable until heavier aeroplanes were developed. The new London Terminal Airport was opened at Croydon in March 1920, and having served its purpose, Hounslow was closed down.

London's first commercial airfield, Hounslow Heath, about 15 miles west of Piccadilly Circus.

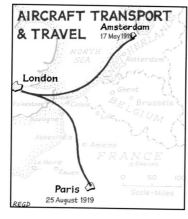

Britain's first airline to the continent, to Paris and Amsterdam, kept the sea crossing to a minimum by a route across the Straits of Dover, so as to be near land for an emergency landing—a not infrequent occurrence in those early pioneering days.

Regn.	Date of C of A or Regn. (R)	Disposal Date	Remarks
Airco D.H.9A (Napier Lion Engine)			
G-EAOF	—	—	ex-E750
G-EAOG	—	—	ex-E752
G-EAOH	—	—	ex-E753
G-EAOI	—	—	ex-E754
G-EAOJ	—	—	ex-E756
G-EAOK	—	—	ex-E757

(See page 4) Liaison with Army of Occupation. Operation begun by R.A.F., taken over by A.T.&T. on 15 August 1919 (D.H.9s), the D.H.9As from November. Terminated in June 1920, aircraft returned to R.A.F.

Regn.	Date of C of A or Regn. (R)	Disposal Date	Remarks
Airco D.H.4 (Rolls-Royce Eagle Engine)			
G-EAEX	—	Apr 20	ex-K-142. Retired.
G-EANK	2 Oct 19 (R)	Apr 20	} Used to replace D.H.4As which were lost.
G-EANL	24 Sep 19 (R)	Apr 20	} Sold overseas.
Airco D.H.4A (Rolls-Royce Eagle Engine)			
G-EAHF	12 Aug 19	11 Dec 19	ex-F2699. Crashed at Caterham
G-EAHG	12 Aug 19	29 Oct 19	ex-F2694. Force-landed in English Channel
G-EAJC	19 Jul 19	Nov 20	ex-F2702. First promotional flight., 25 Aug 19. Scrapped.
G-EAJD	25 Aug 19	Nov 20	ex-F2704. Scrapped
G-EAEW	16 Jun 19 (R)	Jun 20	**(Airco D.H.4R)** ex-K-141. Reg'n cancelled.
Airco D.H.6 (R.A.F. 1A engine)			
G-EAAB	23 Jul 19	Nov 21	ex-K-100. Sold to Marconi. Crashed at Croydon.
Airco D.H.9 (Napier Lion engine)			
G-EAAA	30 Apr 19 (R)	1 May 19	ex-C6054. Made A.T.&T.'s first flight as a commercial service, carrying newspapers to Bournemouth. Capt H.J. Saint and passenger Capt. D. Greig injured in forced landing at Portsdown Hill.
G-EAAD	30 Apr 19 (R)	Sept 19	ex-H9273. Sold overseas.
G-EALJ	26 Aug 19 (R)	Oct 20	ex-D2884. Reg'n cancelled
G-EAMX	15 Sep 19 (R)	Apr 20	ex-D5622 Sold to Major Clayton-Kennedy, Newfoundland
G-EAOP	20 Oct 19 (R)	Sep 20	ex-H5579 Written off

Regn.	Date of C of A or Regn. (R)	Disposal Date	Remarks
Airco D.H.9R (Napier Lion Engine)			
G-EAHT	—	17 Jan 23	ex-K-172 No C of A. Crashed
Airco D.H.9B (Napier Lion, Rolls-Royce Eagle, or Liberty 12 engines)			
G-EAAC	7 May 19	1920	ex-K-109/H9277. To de Havilland—D.H.9J
G-EAGX	7 MAY 19	Aug 20	ex-H9255. Named *Ancuba*. Sold overseas.
G-EAGY	12 Aug 19	Jan 21	ex-H9258. Sold abroad
G-EAOZ	17 Nov 19	Jul 21	MSN P-3AE. To K.L.M. as H-NABF
G-EAPL	28 Nov 19	Jul 21	MSN P-33E. To K.L.M. as H-NABE
G-EAPO	6 Dec 19	Sep 20	MSN P-34E. Written off
G-EAPU	29 Dec 19	Nov 20	MSN P-35E. Written off
G-EAQA	12 Jan 20	Jan 21	MSN P-36E. Crashed
G-EAQL	24 Jan 20	Jul 21	MSN P-38E. Sold Belgium
G-EAQN	28 Jan 20	9 Nov 20	MSN P-37E. Crashed, Le Bourget
G-EAQP	9 Feb 20	1922	MSN P-39E. Sold to de Havilland Aero.
G-EAVK	20 Sep 20	Mar 22	MSN P-60E. Sold overseas. [F.S. Colton]
Airco D.H.10 (Liberty 12 Engine)			
—	—	Oct 19	E 5557. D.H.10 prototype. Used in September–October 1919 during railway strike. Flown between Hendon, Newcastle, and Renfrew
G-EAJO	18 Aug 19	3 Mar 20	ex-E5488. Also used during railway strike. Flown by Capt. Gerald Gathergood. Crashed in the Pyrenees.
Airco D.H.16 (Rolls-Royce Eagle engine)			
G-EACT	25 May 19	Mar 20	MSN DH16/1, ex-K-130. Operated A.T.&T.'s first public service on 25 August 1919, with four passengers. Crashed near Brighton
G-EALM	9 Sep 19	Aug 22	MSN P.1 and 45. To de Havilland
G-EALU	22 Sep 19	Nov 21	MSN P.1 and A/1. Named *Arras*. To de Havilland
G-EAPM	28 Nov 19	Nov 21	MSN P.2. Named *Agincourt*. To de Havilland
G-EAPT	8 Dec 19	9 Dec 19	MSN P.3 and 44. To de Havilland
G-EAQS	29 Mar 20	Dec 20	MSN P.5E. Stored at Croydon. Scrapped 1922
G-EARU	21 May 20	10 Jun 20	MSN P.59. Crashed, Swanley Junction
G-EASW	30 Jun 20	23 Jun 21	MSN P.6. Retired (C of A lapsed)
(G-EAQG	11 Jan 20	Apr 20	This aircraft not used by A.T.&T. It was sold to the Rio Platense de Aviación company in Buenos Aires, and operated to Montevideo)
Airco D.H.18 (Napier Lion engine)			
G-EARI	22 Jul 20	16 Aug 20	MSN 1. Crashed at Wallington

During these early pioneering years, the aircraft were not exactly sturdy. In fact, their wood and fabric construction was flimsy and they did not last long in service, as the tabulated record shows.

Developing the Breed

Geoffrey de Havilland continued to develop his series of single-engined biplanes when he founded his own company on 25 September 1920, with help from George Holt Thomas (see page 2), for whom he had been the chief designer. They were built mainly of wooden frames and plywood, and even after metal became the preferred construction material, de Havilland's wooden technology was invaluable as late as the Second World War with the famous Mosquito light bomber.

A.T. & T.'s fleet consisted almost entirely of Airco aircraft, designated with the initials of their designer, **Geoffrey de Havilland.** It also used a few Avro 504Ks, for mail only. As the fleet list shows, only two survived the demise of Holt Thomas's pioneering airline.

De Havilland D.H.16
4 seats • 105 mph

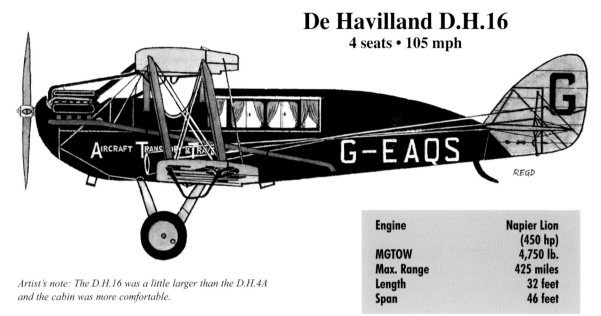

A.T. & T.'S AVRO 504KS (LE RHÔNE ENGINE)

Regn.	Date of C/A	Disposal Date	Remarks
G-EA1O	22 Sep 19	Aug 20	ex-E3359. Withdrawn from use
G-EA1P	7 Aug 19	Aug 19	ex-E4143. C. of A. cancelled
G-EA1Q	28 Aug 19	Nov 20	ex-E4144. Scrapped
G-EA1R	28 Nov 19	Sep 21	ex-E4164. To Surrey Flyng Services
G-EA1S	1919	Apr 20	ex-E4170. Sold overseas

Artist's note: The D.H.16 was a little larger than the D.H.4A and the cabin was more comfortable.

Engine	Napier Lion (450 hp)
MGTOW	4,750 lb.
Max. Range	425 miles
Length	32 feet
Span	46 feet

This picture, taken on 17 May 1920, was of pilot "Jerry" Shaw, about to take off on the inaugural A.T. & T. service from Hounslow to Amsterdam. The D.H.16 did have a cabin for the passengers, but the air stairs were rather precarious, and needed no little agility.

The D.H.18 was the first aircraft built for Airco that was not a modification of a military design. Only six of the series were produced and its service life was short (see also pp. 10 and 12), but it was the predecessor of the more successfull D.H.34.

The D.H.10, a twin-engined bomber design, first flew on 4 March 1918 — too late for service in the Great War. A.T. & T. had two of them and their lives were short. It was not used to carry passengers as the fuselage was not wide enough, even for two-abreast seating.

7

Handley Page Transport

Handley Page Transport was incorporated on 14 June 1919 by **Frederick Handley Page**, whose aircraft had already made a series of flights, dropping newspapers by parachute in various cities. The new airline had acquired some of its maker's **O/400** bombers, which Frederick had described as his "bloody paralysers," and were intended to bomb Berlin. But the Great War ended before they could be put into service and instead were converted for passenger use. The **H.P.O/7** conversion first flew on 5 July 1919, and made a flight to Paris on 25 August; but regular service on the route did not begin until 2 September. This was flown by Lieut.-Col. W. Sholto-Douglas who later, as Lord Douglas of Kirtleside, became chairman of the post-war British European Airways.

On 23 September, an additional route opened to Brussels, flown by an O/400, and from 11 October, lunch baskets were provided, at 3 shillings each (15P today, but worth much more then). The pre-war DELAG Zeppelin sight-seeing flights excepted, these were the first meals ever served aloft. In January 1920, season tickets were introduced, costing £120 for twelve single flights. On 6 July 1920, H.P. Transport started service to Amsterdam, in cooperation with K.L.M., but this ceased on 30 October. Meanwhile, air mail was carried on the Brussels route from 19 July and Rotterdam was added experimentally on the Amsterdam route one week later. The service to Paris was withdrawn on 17 November 1920 because of excessive competition from other airlines on the route.

On 27 May 1921, the London terminal was transferred from Handley Page's factory base at **Cricklewood** to the new

Frederick Handley Page (1885–1962)

(Courtesy: Daniel Kusrow Collection)

airport at Croydon, and the new **H.P. W.8b** was introduced on 4 May 1922. Relief from high cost of operations came on 1 October 1922 when the Government awarded a subsidy of £15,000 for the London-Paris route. Thus, on 16 August 1923, Handley Page began a thrice-weekly service from London to Zurich, via Paris and Basle, subsidized by both the British and the Swiss Governments. The first flight was made by R.H.McIntosh in **H.P. O/10** G-EATH. The airline was one of the four components that combined to become **Imperial Airways** on 31 March 1924.

In the early days of passenger air transport, airlines charged high fares to cover their operating costs. The aircraft seldom lasted more than a year or two in service, and had to be replaced frequently. The clientèle were rich, and the airline had to treat them accordingly.

The little booklet illustrated above is possibly unique in the entire history of air transport, even to the present day. This London Weekly Diary of Social Events (25 June 1923) contained reviews of all the current plays in the West End. Included were sporting events: tennis at Wimbledon, cricket at Lords and the Oval, the Horse Show at Olympia. Arthur Rubinstein was at the Wigmore Hall, Dame Clara Butt at the Albert Hall, and Fay Compton at the Comedy Theatre. All the art galleries and museums were described. There was a map of the Thames at Henley and the advertisements included one for All Breeds of Dogs and Debenham & Freebody's Furs (at 49 guineas). Opposite the one for Cartier (by appointment to royalty of course), the airline courteously trusted "that this Diary of the current Week's events in London will prove of interest and utility to you." It was all very much Upper Class.

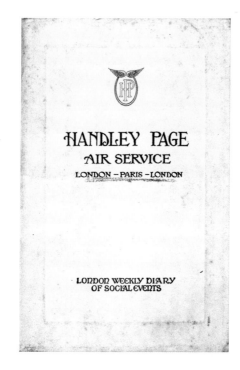

Handley Page Transport's base was its own factory airfield at Cricklewood, in north London, until it transferred to Croydon Airport on 27 May 1921. It was alongside the mainline railway tracks of the L.N.W.R. (later the L.M.S.) and there were still green fields beyond.

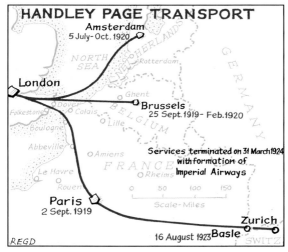

Handley Page O/400

10 seats • 74 mph

THE HANDLEY PAGE TRANSPORT FLEET

Regn. No.	Date of C of A	Fleet No.	Disposal Date	Remarks
Handley Page O/400				
G-EAAE	1 May 19	16	Aug 20	First registered as D8350. Named *Vulture*. Scrapped
G-EAAF	1May 19	13	May 20	First registered as F5414. Rebuilt as O/7, Sent to U.S.A.
G-EAAG	1 May 19	18	Apr 20	First registered as F5418. Named *Penguin*. Crashed.
G-EAAW	1 May 19	14	Apr 20	First registered as F5417. Named *Flamingo*. Withdrawn from use.
G-EAKE	25 Aug 19	22	Jun 20	ex-J2252. Crashed in Sweden
G-EAKF	10 Oct 19	19	Oct 20	ex-J2249. Scrapped
G-EAKG	6 Sep 19	20	Aug 20	ex-J2250. Scrapped
G-EALX	30 Oct 19	21	Apr 21	ex-J2251. Scrapped
G-EALY	17 Oct 19	24	Oct 20	ex-J2247. Scrapped
G-EALZ	17 Dec 19	23	Dec 20	ex-J2243. Withdrawn from use.
G-EAMA	7 Nov 19	25	14 Dec 20	ex-J2248. Crashed near Cricklewood.
Handley Page O/10				
G-EASX	15 Oct 20	34	Apr 21	ex-F308. To India as G-IAAC
G-EASY	23 Jun 20	35	Apr 21	ex-D4614. To India
G-EATG	23 Jun 20	37	Apr 21	ex-D4618. Withdrawn from use
G-EATH	30 Jun 20	38	31 Mar 24	ex-D4631. To Imperial Airways. (broken up, June 1925)
G-EATJ	25 Jun 20	39	Apr 21	ex-F307. Withdrawn from use.
G-EATK	15 Jul 20	40	Aug 22	ex-J2262. Scrapped
G-EATL	30 Aug 20	41	Apr 21	ex-F312. Withdrawn from use.
G-EATM	30 Jul 20	42	30 Dec 21	ex-D4609. Wrecked at Berck, France.
G-EATN	13 Jul 20	43	14 Jan 22	ex-J2261. Crashed at Senlis, France.
Handley Page O/11				
G-EASL	26 Mar 20	30	Apr 20	ex-C9699. Crashed.
G-EASM	26 Mar 20	31	Apr 21	ex-C9731. Withdrawn from use.
G-EASN	23 Jun 20	32	Apr 21	ex-D4611. Withdrawn from use.
G-EASO	15 Apr 20	33	Apr 21	ex-D5444. Withdrawn from use.
G-EASZ	25 Jun 20	36	Apr 21	ex-F310. To India.
Airco D.H.4A				
G-EAVL	11 Nov 20		Apr 21	ex-H5905. Crashed.
G-EAWH	18 Apr 21		1922	ex-F5764. Withdrawn from use.

Regn. No.	MSN	Disposal Date	Remarks
Handley Page W.8			
G-EAPJ	W.8.1	10 Jul 22	Fleet No. 15. Named *Newcastle*, later *Duchess of York*. damaged beyond repair.
Handley Page W.8b			
G-EBBG	W.8.2	31 Mar 24	Named *Bombay*, later *Princess Mary*. To Imperial Airways
G-EBBH	W.8.3	31 Mar 24	Named *Melbourne*, later *Prince George*. To Imperial Airways
G-EBBI	W.8.4	31 Mar 24	Named *Prince Henry*. To Imperial Airways
De Haviland D.H.18B			
G-EAWX	6	Jun 22	On loan from Air Ministry and returned
Bristol Type 62			
G-EAWY	6124	Jun 22	On loan from Air Ministry and returned

Note: In spite of the size of the Handley Pages, the pilots were still exposed to the elements.

Engines	**Rolls-Royce Eagle**
	(360 hp x 2)
MGTOW	**12,050 lb.**
Max. Range	**500 miles**
Length	**63 feet**
Span	**100 feet**

Size comparison with the Handley Page H.P. 42 (p.37)

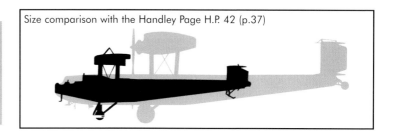

The big Handley Pages were impressive in their time, and were the first British twin-engined airliners — the safety aspects of having more than one engine was emphasized in their promotion. But their performance did not exactly prove the assertion. The first crash by a British commercial airliner was G-EAMA at Golders Green on 14 December 1920, and more significant was the short operating life. The first Certificate of Airworthiness was granted to four aircraft on 1 May 1919, and the last one in service was scrapped in April 1921. Operationally, it was not always reliable. Captain Gordon Olley reported that he once had to make 17 landings en route to Paris, to pump petrol into the tank.

The Instone Air Line

On 13 October 1919, the shipping company, **S. Instone & Co., Ltd.**, began a private air service for the company's documents and staff from Cardiff to London and Paris. Frank Barnard piloted the first de Havilland D.H.4A, and Instone decided to "go public" on 18 February 1920. On 30 April, the **Vickers Vimy Commercial** G-EASI *City of London* entered service and immediately became popular with the travelling public, so that the operating name was changed on 15 May to **The Instone Air Line, Ltd**.

In the face of well-subsidized competition from the French airlines, all British airlines ceased operations on 28 February 1921, but Instone was able to resume on 21 March, following prompt remedial action by the British Government with its own subsidy payments. On 12 December the company was registered with a special capital of £50,000 — the Instones were determined to use their experience with shipping transport and apply it to the new mode. Thus, on 1 January 1922, all staff, including those in the company offices, wore uniforms, and may have been the first to do so. The new de Havilland D.H.34 was introduced on 2 April and opened the new service to Brussels on 8 May.

On 1 October, the Vimy extended this service to Cologne (night-stopping at Brussells because of bad weather), but Instone withdrew from the Paris route because of excessive competition and an agreement between the British airlines on the spheres of interest on routes to the continent.

An experimental service was started to Prague, Czechoslovakia, on 4 August 1923, using a Vickers Vulcan, but problems of over-flight across Germany prevented its continuance. On 31 March 1924, all Instone operations ceased as it became one of the consistent parts in the formation of Imperial Airways.

This picture shows Instone's Chief Pilot F. L. Barnard running up the engine of the D.H.4A, just before take-off (see picture below).

The de Havilland D.H.4A with which S. Instone & Co., Ltd., began its first private service on 13 October 1919.

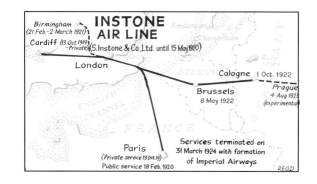

THE INSTONE FLEET

Regn. No.	MSN	Disposal Date	Remarks
Airco D.H.4A			
G-EAMU	–	19 Feb 20	ex-H5939. Named *City of Cardiff*. Rebuilt as D.H.4A, *City of York*. To Imperial Airways, 31 Mar 24
Bristol 47 Tourer			
G-EART	5876	21 Apr 20	Withdrawn from use Feb. 21
Vickers Vimy Commercial			
G-EASI	41	13 May 20	Named *City of London*. To Imperial Airways, 31 Mar 24.
B.A.T. FK 26			
G-EAPK	32	4 Mar 20	Named *City of Newcastle*. Crashed 31 Jul 22.
Westland Limousine			
G-EARE	W.A.C.4	7 Oct 20	(Mark II). Scrapped 19 Jun 23.
G-EARF	W.A.C.5	21 Oct 20	(Mark II). Scrapped 1923.
G-EAWF	W.A.C.9	–	Leased as reserve aircraft. Scrapped Apr 22.
De Havilland D.H.18			
G-EARO	2 and E53	–	(D.H.18A) Named *City of Cardiff*. Loan, Royal Aircraft Establishment.
G-EAUF	3 and E54	–	(D.H.18A) Named *City of Paris*. On loan, crashed 13 May 21.
G-EAWO	4	–	(D.H.18A) To Daimler Airway., 1922.
G-EAWW	5	17 Dec 21	(D.H.18B) Named *City of Brussels*. On loan. Used for ditching test.
G-EAWX	6	23 Jan 22	(D.H.18B) On loan. To Handley Page Transport, Mar 22.
De Havilland D.H.34			
G-EBBR	28	6 May 22	Named *City of Glasgow*. To Imperial Airways, 31 Mar 24
G-EBBT	30	28 Apr 22	Named *City of New York*. To Imperial Airways. (as D.H.34B) 31 Mar 24
G-EBBV	32	19 Jul 22	Named *City of Washington*. To Imperial Airwyas, 31 Mar 24.
G-EBBW	34	25 Aug 23	Named *City of Chicago*. To Imperial Airwyas, 31 Mar 24.
Vickers Type 61 Vulcan			
G-EBBL	1	23 Jun 22	Named *City of Antwerp*. To Imperial Airways, 31 Mar 24
G-EBDH	2	28 Aug 22	Returned to Vickers, June 23
G-EBEA	3	28 Aug 22	Named *City of Brussels*. Returned to Vickers, June 23
Bristol 75 Ten Seater			
G-EBEV	6145	June 22 (Delivery Date)	Named *City of Bristol*. To Imperial Airways, 31 Mar 24. Used only for freight.

Other Instone aircraft, unidentified for details, were named *City of Ghent*, *City of Liège*, *City of Liverpool*.

The Vimy and the D.H.34s continued to fly with Imperial Airways.

Vickers Vimy Commercial
10 seats • 92 mph

Artist's note: The word INSTONE was written along the underside of the fuselage.

Engines	Rolls-Royce Eagle (360 hp x 2)
MGTOW	12,500 lb.
Max. Range	450 miles
Length	43 feet
Span	68 feet

Size comparison with the Handley Page H.P. 42 (p.37)

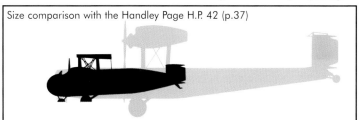

This is the cover of the little booklet by the Aerial Transport Department of S. Instone & Co., Ltd. It extolled the features of its "Vickers Vimy-Rolls Royce Limousine which is the last word in safety, luxury, and comfort." It described the well-ventilated cabin, with mahogany beams, and sliding triplex glass windows, and its upholstered arm-chairs. It mentioned the Vimy's flights across the Atlantic and to Australia, and mentioned that special clothing was unnecessary. "Motor-cars meet all machines on their arrival at both ends."

Instone operated one Bristol Tourer for less than one year.

This historic photograph was taken on 31 March 1924, when Instone paraded its fleet at Croydon before handing over to the newly-constituted Imperial Airways. The standing figures, in front of one of its D.H.34s, are (left to right) Capt. O.P. Jones, Capt. G.R. Hinchliffe, Dennis Handover, Capt. P.D. Robins, S. Baxter, Sir Samual Instone, Theodore Instone, Marcus Davis, Capt G. Powell, C.A. Barnard, Capt. Alfred Instone, Major S.L. Greer, Capt. F.L. Barnard, and Capt. C.F. Wolley Dod.

This photograph of the Vickers Vimy Commercial airliner emphasizes the early attempts to move away from the idea of simply modifying bomber fuselages. In this case the cabin dimensions for the passengers came first, but the pilot was still exposed to the elements—not because of the designer, but because the pilots insisted on it. Instone's City of London was recorded as having flown 108,000 miles when taken over by Imperial, and had carried several thousands of passengers.

The Daimler Airway

On 7 June 1919, the **Daimler Hire** company (owned by the British Small Arms Ltd., (B.S.A.) incorporated **"The Daimler Airway."** This title was used for promotional purposes and advertising, but the aircraft only carried the Hire Company name. It acquired George Holt Thomas's Aircraft Transport and Travel, but did not take over the equipment, relying instead on new aircraft: the **de Havilland D.H.34**, a new nine-seat design, similar to that of the D.H.18, but incorporating features recommended by Daimler and Instone. This was possibly the earliest example of consultation between a commercial user and its manufacturer. Daimler's General Manager was **George Woods Humphery**, who would later direct the fortunes of Imperial Airways.

Daimler began service from London's Croydon Airport to Le Bourget, Paris, on 2 April 1922. The pilot, G.A. Hinchliffe, carried a supply of English newspapers for the local British residents. Only five days later, Daimler's only other aircraft type, a D.H.18A, inherited from Instone, was lost in a head-on collision with a French Farman Goliath between Poix and Beauvais—the disciplines of air traffic control were still in their infancy. Among those killed was the cabin boy in the 18A. But shortly thereafter, on 2 June, the reliability of the D.H.34 was demonstrated when one flew five one-way trips on the London-Paris route in one day.

But such concentration of effort could not be sustained, as five airlines, three British and two French, were competing for the inter-capitals market. The British Government had, by now, recognized the need both to control and to subsidize the infant air transport industry, rationalizing the allocation of routes to comply with the financial assistance. Thus, Daimler abandoned its Paris route in September, by agreement with Handley Page, and on 9 October opened a service to Amsterdam, via Rotterdam. The single fare was £4. The subsidy was £15,000 for six months. Two weeks later, a domestic London-Manchester connection opened up the north of England to the opportunity of flying to Paris.

The following year, on 1 May 1923, with the political atmosphere gradually improving, the Amsterdam service was extended to Berlin, via Bremen and Hamburg, for which the subsidy was £55,000. but on 8 October the service beyond Hamburg was suspended, and through service to Berlin resumed on 4 November via Hanover.

Daimler became one of the constituents of the airline amalgamation to form Imperial Airways on 31 March 1924.

George Woods Humphery started his career with The Daimler Airway and guided Imperial Airways throughout its expansion years of the 1930s.

THE DAIMLER AIRWAY FLEET

Regn.	MSN	Date of C/A	Remarks
De Havilland D.H.34			
G-EBBQ	27	6 May 22	Named *City of Glasgow*. To Imperial Airways, 31 Mar 24
G-EBBS	29	6 May 22	Crashed near Ivinghoe Beacon Bucks, 14 Sep 23
G-EBBU	31	6 May 22	Crashed near Berck, France, 3 Nov 22
G-EBBX	35	19 Sep 22	Modified to D.H.34B. To Imperial Airways, 31 Mar 24
G-EBBY	36	25 Sep 22	To Imperial Airways, 31 Mar 24
G-EBCX	40	30 Dec 22	To Imperial Airways, 31 Mar 24
De Havilland D.H.18A			
G-EAWO	4		Lost in collision with Farman Goliath F-GEAD between Poix and Beauvais, France, 7 Apr 22

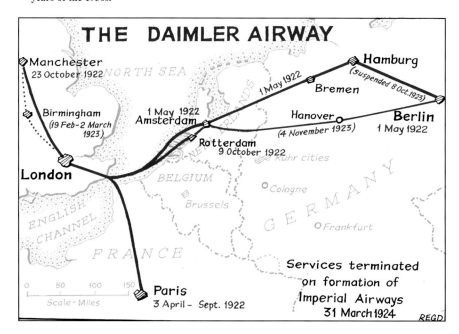

De Havilland D.H.34
9 seats • 100 mph

The cover of the timetable of 8 October 1923 (when the Berlin segment was temporarily suspended) reminds the public of the Daimler Hire Company's royal patronage. It started its joint service with the Dutch K.L.M. and the German Aero Lloyd. Each passenger was allowed 30 lb. of luggage; luncheon baskets or light refreshments were provided; and "The Company attends to all Customs arrangements." Passengers were taken by car from the Hotel Victoria, London, and similar courtesies were available at other stations.

The importance of cooperation between a manufacturer and an operator with commercial experience was demonstrated by Daimler and Instone (page 10). Many of their aircraft, together with the Handley Pages, managed to keep Imperial Airways going until the tri-motored Hercules (p.23) and Argosies (p.25) came along in 1926, to begin the process of creating airliners rather than basic transport aircraft.

Engine	Napier Lion (450 hp)
MGTOW	7,200 lb.
Max. Range	365 miles
Length	39 feet
Span	54 feet

Size comparison with the Handley Page H.P. 42 (p.37)

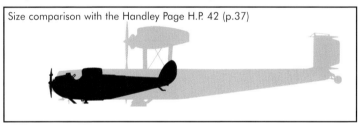

Passengers await boarding the D.H.34 G-EBBS. Unfortunately, this aircraft crashed, near Ivinghoe Beacon on 14 September 1923. The 34's passenger door was enlarged so that a spare engine could be loaded on board in an emergency.

On the D.H.34s, a ladder was fitted for the pilot to climb aboard, and a hinged platform in the nose section allowed engineers to reach the engine for maintenance. The company name, at the rear of the aircraft, was always Daimler Hire Ltd., London.

The Other Pioneer Airlines

During the months immediately following the Armistice of November 1918, by which time tens of thousands of war-planes had been built in Great Britain, there was a nationwide urge to convert the aerial swords into ploughshares. The initiatives to make use of the surplus aeroplanes were wide and varied. The companies in the best position to use them were obviously the manufacturers themselves; and some of them, notably Handley Page and Airco, could be regarded as creating the nucleus of the air transport organization that was to become the national flag-carrier, Imperial Airways. Other Imperial ancestors were already in the business of carrying people, such as Daimler Hire, or goods, such as Instone.

But the directions in which the air transport industry developed into a cohesive entity were not altogether clear during 1919, the first full year of post-war peacetime. The general public regarded the flying machines as dangerous, and were not inclined to patronize the embryo airlines too enthusiastically, particularly as the fares were expensive. To take a joy-ride or a short sight-seeing trip often took a display of bravado, to climb into the open cabin of a biplane trainer. Unlike the situation in Europe, the United States, or Australia, where long distances invited patronage from the post offices, if not the people, Great Britain was still a "tight little island" with excellent rail services. Only the Highlands of Scotland were more than a day's reach from London.

The first domestic air service within Britain was, therefore, less to meet a genuine need than to provide the novelty of flying, as soon as civilian flying was permitted in May 1919. The **Avro Transport Company**, formed by the manufacturer of that name, started a daily service with its Avro 504s on 10 May, flying from Manchester (where the aircraft were built) to the seaside resorts of Southport and Blackpool. The single fare was four guineas, well beyond the weekly wage of the average mill-worker. But it was popular, and set up a praiseworthy record of regularity, and had completed 194 of 222 scheduled flights when the service ended on 30 September. Avro also carried newspapers from Hounslow to Brighton for three weeks in the summer, and operated a sea-plane service from Lake Windermere to Ramsey, in the Isle of Man, for a few days in September. Including sight-seeing flights, Avro had carried more than 30,000 passengers when it ceased flying at the end of 1920.

The other notable operator of substance was the **North Sea Aerial and General Transport**, a subsidiary of the Blackburn aircraft manufacturer, based at Hull. It started a Hull-Leeds-Hounslow service on 30 September 1919, using its twin-engined Blackburn Kangaroo biplanes. But the round-trip fare of £30 was something of a deterrent to possible frequent flyers. It also flew from Leeds to Hull and Scarborough, using Avro 504s, in a Yorkshire echo of the Lancashire enterprise out of Manchester. The company even ventured across the North Sea (to prove the right to its name, perhaps) with an air freight contract to Amsterdam, via Lympne.

A certain incentive for the commercial use of aircraft came in the autumn of 1919, when the railway strike from 27 September to 5 October came close to shutting down the country. Aircraft were used extensively during the emergency, not only by the aspirant airline companies but also by promoters such as the famous aviator Claude Grahame-White.

Another independent during this period of experimental air services was the **British Aerial Transport Company (B.A.T.)**, founded by Samuel Waring, of the Waring & Gillow furniture company. It flew Koolhoven F.K.26 aircraft, designed by Frederick Koolhoven and built in London. It operated to Birmingham during the rail strike, and to Amsterdam from 7 October; but activities were suspended when Koolhoven left B.A.T. in January 1920.

Geoffrey de Havilland founded his own company on 25 September 1920, taking over the activities of Airco, and

he quickly established the **De Havilland Aeroplane Hire Service**, for charter work. But in the summer of 1922, he also operated a short cross-Channel service, with D.H.9s, from Lympne to Ostend. The following year, in September 1923, the Service made experimental flights from Plymouth to Belfast (see map) in cooperation with the Plymouth and Belfast Chambers of Commerce, the Air Ministry, and the Post Office.

Other independent forays into air services in the early 1920s were **Air Post of Banks**, which carried documents from London to Paris, with Westland Limousines, from 13 September to 2 November 1920; and **Northern Air Lines**, which linked Liverpool with Belfast, with D.H.50s from 24 April to 2 June 1924. It also flew from Belfast to Stranraer from March until May 1925, but then terminated all activities. By this time Imperial Airways was established, with government support, and the financial risks involved with using aeroplanes commercially ruled out the spirit of private enterprise over the skies of Britain for almost a decade.

A Blackburn Kangaroo of North Sea Aerial and General Transport.

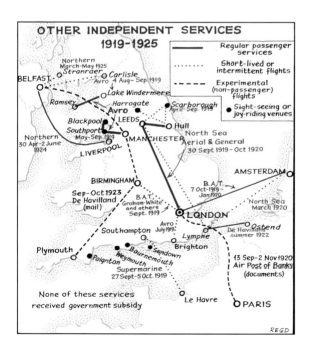

OTHER INDEPENDENT SERVICES 1919-1925

Regular passenger services

Short-lived or intermittent flights

Experimental (non-passenger) flights

● Sight-seeing or joy-riding venues

None of these services received government subsidy

British Marine Air Navigation

On 23 March 1923, Hubert Scott-Paine, of the Supermarine Aviation Works, in cooperation with the Asiatic Petroleum Company, formed the **British Marine Air Navigation Company (B.M.A.N.)**, at Woolston, on the Southampton Water Supermarine base. It had £15,000 of capital, and was promised £10,000 of subsidy to operate an air route to the Channel Islands and the French trans-Atlantic ports. The original idea was for the connection to be made especially to Cherbourg and Le Have for the ocean liners, but B.M.A.N. never operated there. Supermarine would supply the aircraft, and Asiatic would supply the fuel, through the Shell-Mex oil company.

On 14 August, an experimental flight was made to Guernsey with a 6-seat Supermarine Sea Eagle, designed by R.J. Mitchell. Among the passengers was Sir Sefton Brancker, the Director of Civil Aviation, and no doubt this gave the green light to the inauguration of regular services to the Island on 25 September.

On 31 March 1924, B.M.A.N. joined Handley Page, Instone, and Daimler, to form Imperial Airways, which retained the two Sea Eagles in the fleet for a few years.

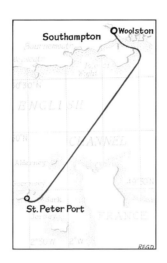

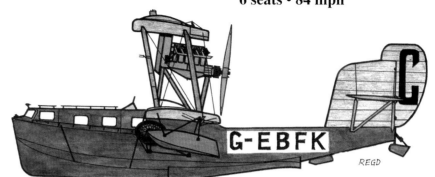

Artist's note: The wood used for the hull was mahogany. After the aircraft was taken over by Imperial Airways, it was painted dark blue, with IMPERIAL AIRWAYS LTD underneath the cabin windows.

During the early years after the Great War of 1914–1918, the British Channel Islands were beginning to become a summer-time vacation destination.

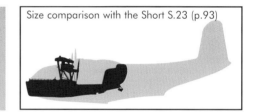

Engine	Rolls-Royce Eagle (360 hp)
MGTOW	5,800 lb.
Max. Range	230 miles
Length	43 feet
Span	46 feet

Size comparison with the Short S.23 (p.93)

THE SUPERMARINE SEA EAGLES

Regn.	MSN	Date of C/A	Remarks
G-EBFK	1163	July 23	Names *Sea Eagle*. Damaged at Alderney, 13 Oct 23 and not repaired
G-EBGR	1164	2 Oct 23	Named *Sarnia*. To Imperial Airways, 31 March 24
G-EBGS	1165	2 Oct 23	To Imperial Airways (rammed and sunk at St. Peter Port, Guernsey, 10 Jan 27)

British Marine Air Navigation's Supermarine Sea Eagle, Sarnia.

The B.M.A.N. base was at Woolston, on Southampton Water. This picture shows two Supermarine Channel flying boats, predecessors of the Sea Eagle, at anchor in front of the slipway. The building on the left is the hangar of the Sopwith Aviation Company.

Foundation of Imperial Airways

A Crisis of Viability

During 1919–1921, the path of the pioneer British airlines had been strewn with obstacles. They were handicapped initially by an apathetic attitude by the Government which at first did not regard air transport as a post-war priority. Winston Churchill's statement to the effect that the airlines should stand on their own feet was quickly seen to be detrimental to British commercial aspirations, and as early as the beginning of 1921, something was done about it.

In the face of generous subsidies by the French Government to their competing cross-Channel airlines, and after the summer services of 1920, the British airlines threw in the towel. Instone severely curtailed its services, A.T. & T. ceased operations altogether on 17 December, and Handley Page did so on 28 February 1921. Recognizing this not only as a desperate situation for the airlines but as a blow to national pride and prestige, the Secretary of State for Air, Sir Samuel Hoare, appointed a committee to examine the problem of cross-Channel routes, with the result that temporary arrangements were made to guarantee a profit of 10 per cent for the carriage of passengers, goods, and mail on the London-Paris route, with a maximum liability of £25,000. The service was re-opened by Handley Page and Instone on 19 March 1921. Not until the following year, on 8 May 1922, was service resumed to Brussels.

The Hambling Committee

Under the chairmanship of **Sir Herbert Hambling**, the committee appointed by Sir Samuel made its report on 15 February 1922. Even under the temporary relief given (see above) the airlines had lost money heavily, and so far-reaching measures were taken. It recommended that a new commercial organization should be created on business principles, and to receive a government subsidy. The initial capital should be £1,000,000 —a generous sum in those days—spread over a period of ten years, with the government appointing some of the directors. An agreement was made on these recommendations on 22 December 1923 with the British, Foreign,and Colonial Corporation to form the Imperial Air Transport Company (the name subsequently changed to **Imperial Airways, Ltd.**), to take effect on 1 April 1924.

Imperial Airways Begins

On that date, the new national airline was to start operations, taking over the routes of Handley Page, Instone, Daimler Hire, and B.M.A.N. (see previous pages). During the past twelve months these four companies had received a total subsidy of £105,000, which may have been the basis for the Hambling recommendations. Imperial's Board of Directors had good credentials. The chairman was Sir Eric Geddes, chairman of Dunlop Rubber, the managing director was Lt.-Col. Frank Searle, who had held that position with Daimler Hire, and the general manager, who was to steer Imperial throughout the 1930s, was George Woods Humphery. Sir Samuel Instone, Hubert Scott-Paine, and Lt.-Col. Barrett-Leonard represented Instone, B.M.A.N., and Handley Page, respectively. The finances seemed to be in good hands, as the government directors were Sir Herbert Hambling himself, who was the deputy chairman of Barclay's Bank, and Major J. Hills, who had been Financial Secretary of the Treasury.

The early weeks of the new airline's existence were fraught with difficulties. The aircraft fleet was not impressive. Imperial inherited fifteen airworthy machines (see tabulation) of which only five were multi-engined, and it immediately planned a multi-engined fleet. Frank Searle was also in favour of replacing biplanes with monoplanes, a choice not generally favoured by everyone then. The route network was not extensive. The route to Berlin was operated only in conjunction with the German Deutscher Aero-Lloyd, while the extension to Zurich had been achieved by Handley Page only with a Swiss subsidy. Assistance had been rendered to Instone by Czechoslovakia for the route to Prague, and over-flying German territory met with objections.

In addition, a pilots' strike over pay and conditions delayed the start of Imperial's regular services until 26 April, when Capt. H. S. Robertson flew D.H.34 G-EBCX to Paris and Capt. A. L. Robertson flew D.H.34 G-EBBY to Cologne on 2 May 1924. Service to Brussels began the next day, to Amsterdam and Berlin on 2 June, and Paris-Basle-Zurich on 17 June.

A Place in Airline History

This was a modest start to what was to become a systematic development that would serve the whole Empire well (except across the Atlantic, frustrated by range limitations of the aircraft until the outbreak of the Second World War). As yet, the United States had not recognized the full potential of air transport, except to carry mail. France and Germany still awaited a national approach, and Italy was slow off the mark. Other European countries were entering the commercial airline arena, but Imperial Airways was leading the way towards a visionary approach to air transport. It was the world's first airline "Chosen Instrument."

A page from Imperial Airways's first winter timetable, 1924/25.

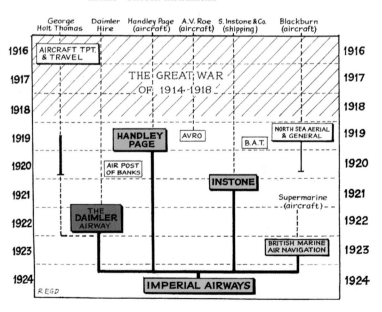

Creation of a British national airline, the world's first "Chosen Instrument".

The First Fleet

A Motley Collection

As the tabulations show, Imperial Airways was severely handicapped by its inheritance of a fleet of six different aircraft types, and its search for equipment better suited for commercial operations yielded seven more. The aircraft and the engines just could not stand up to the rigours of constant use, day-in and day-out. Few of Imperial's initial aircraft lasted more than a year or two. The airline struggled on for two years, using mostly Handley Pages, of which the W.8b was the backbone of the interim fleet. One W.8b was retired in 1932, having flown more than half a million miles, but it was an exception. Under George Woods Humphrey's guidance, and Sir Sefton Brancker's encouragement, help was on the way, with two aircraft types whose specifications were directed exclusively to civil, rather than military use.

IMPERIAL AIRWAYS'S FIRST FLEET — (A) THE INHERITANCE

Regn.	MSN	Previous Operator	Remarks and Disposal
Handley Page W.8b			
G-EBBG	W.8-2	Handley Page	Named *Bombay*, later re-named *Princess Mary*
G-EBBH	W.8-3	Handley Page	Named *Melbourne*, later re-named *Prince George*
G-EBBI	W.8-4	Handley Page	Named *Prince Henry*. Retired in 1932, after more than 5,000 hours of service.
Vickers Vimy Commercial			
G-EASI	41	Instone Air Line	Scrapped, 1926
Supermarine Sea Eagle			
G-EBGR	1164	British Marine Air Navigation	Withdrawn from use in 1928. The hull was preserved until the early 1950s. Wrongly painted as G-EBGS, it was destroyed when used in a fire fighting exercise.
G-EBGS	1165	British Marine Air Navigation	Rammed and sunk at St. Peter Port, Guernsey, 10 January 1927.
De Havilland D.H. 34			
G-EBBR	28	Instone Air Line	Crashed at Ostend, 27 May 24
G-EBBT	30	Instone Air Line	Converted to D.H. 34 B; dismantled March 26
G-EBBV	32	Instone Air Line	Dismantled Mar 26
G-EBBW	34	Instone Air Line	Dismantled Mar 26
G-EBBX	35	Daimler Airway	Dismantled Dec 24
G-EBBY	36	Daimler Airway	Crashed at Purley, 24 Dec 24
G-EBCX	40	Daimler Airway	Dismantled Dec 24
Handley Page O/10			
G-EATH	D4631	Handley Page	Never used, scrapped
Airco D.H. 4A			
G-EAMU	H5939	Instone Air Line	Used only as an engine test-bed

A review of Imperial Airways's inherited equipment emphasizes the difficulties it had to fulfil its mission, handicapped as it was with obsolete or obsolescent aeroplanes.

(B) THE EARLY ACQUISITIONS

Regn.	MSN	Date of Delivery (or C of A)	Remarks and Disposal
Vickers Vulcan			
G-EBFC	8	Dec 24	First flew on 3 March 23. Entered in King's Cup Air Race but retired. Withdrawn from use and dismantled in 1927.
G-EBLB	9	May 25	Crashed and burned, Purley, 13 July 28
De Havilland D.H.50			
G-EBFO	74	Original C/A 12 Nov 23, D.H.50J 14 Nov 25	Use for route surveys by Alan Cobham to India and Burma, 1924–25, and to Cape Town, 1925–26. To West Australian Airways (VH-UMC), January 1929
G-EBFP	75	C/A 12 Nov 23	To Iraq Petroleum, Oct 32; returned to Imperial, May 33; scrapped 23 Oct 24
G-EBKZ	133	C/A 11 June 25	Crashed at Plymouth, 23 Oct 28
Handley Page Hamilton (W.8f/W.8g) (HP26)			
G-EBIX	W.8-7	(W.8f) 27 June 24 (W.8g) 15 Apr 30	Named *City of Washington*. Converted to W.8g in 1930. Crashed at Neufchatel, France, 30 Oct 30

Regn.	MSN	Date of Delivery (or C of A)	Remarks and Disposal
Bristol 75A Ten-Seater			
G-EBEV	6145	July 25	Used only for Cargo evaluation
Avro 563 Andover			
G-EBKW	5097	Summer 25	On loan from the Air Council for cross-Channel proving flights.
Handley Page Hampstead (W.9) (HP27)			
G-EBLE		C/A 20 Jan 26	Named *City of New York*. To New Guinea (YH-ULK) January 1929. Crashed 1930.
Handley Page W.10			
G-EBMM	10-1	C/A 5 Mar 26	Named *City of Melbourne*. ⎫ To Alan Cobham's National
G-EBMR	10-2	C/A 9 Mar 26	Named *City of Pretoria*. ⎬ Aviation Day Displays, ⎭ Nov 33
G-EBMS	10-3	C/A 9 Mar 26	Named *City of London*. Crashed in English Channel, 21 Oct 26.
G-EBMT	10-4	C/A 13 Mar 26	Named *City of Ottawa*. Crashed in English Channel, 17 Jun 29.

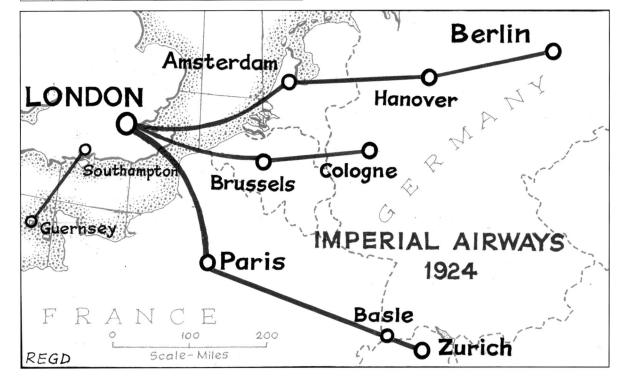

The Inherited Aircraft

The de Havilland D.H.34s were from the Instone and Daimler airlines, and served Imperial for two years, being retired because of the multi-engine policy adopted for safety reasons. Two of them crashed before Imperial's first year was out.

Until the Argosies came into service in 1926, the Handley Page W.8s were the mainstay of the Imperial fleet. Their Great War bomber ancestry is apparent, with almost identical wings and four-wheeled undercarriage.

The sole W.9 Hampstead stayed in service, along with the W.8s, until 1929. As the picture shows, it was a three-engined variant of the series of the large Handley Page biplanes.

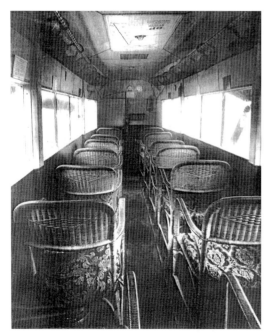

The W.8b had 14 wicker seats, with no structural beams to interfere with the view each side from one long panoramic window. A map on the ceiling illustrated the London-Paris route.

This scene, at the first Croydon Airport, at Plough Lane, and taken on an "Open Day," shows G-EBBI, one of Imperial's initial fleet of Handley Pages. The fuselage was only two feet shorter than that of the modern Douglas DC-3 monoplane, which came into service in the United States ten years later.

An Airport for London

In March, 1920, the R.A.F. field at Hounslow Heath, to the west of London, had become the Empire capital's first commercial aerodrome, with customs clearance facilities, when Aircraft Transport and Travel started Britain's first airline services (see pages 4–5).

These amenities were also provided at Cricklewood, in northwest London, when Handley Page Transport began its services (see pages 8–9). In March 1920, Hounslow was repossessed by the War Office, and the Waddon aerodrome, at Croydon, south of London, was acquired by the Air Ministry. Its location meant that aircraft from the continent did not have to fly over densely-populated city areas, which was rightly considered to be a hazard during the infant years of the airlines, when their safety record was not encouraging.

Nevertheless, the new airport's dimensions were no great improvement on the previous fields. The longest take-off or landing run was only 4,000 feet, and with new and larger aircraft on order by Imperial Airways, this needed improvement, but at least, as a temporary measure, it was adequate for the Handley Pages. Within a few years the grass area was extended and all the buildings were demolished. A handsome new terminal was built on the other side of the field (see page 26).

The welcome sign to Croydon Aerodrome in the early 1920s.

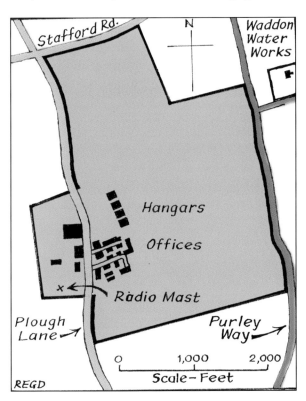

This aerial view of Croydon Airport was photographed before Imperial Airways was formed. Instone's office, and that of the French airline Air Union, can be seen in the centre of the picture, and a Handley Page W.8b is in the foreground. The "level crossing" on Plough Lane, for aircraft to reach the maintenance hangar, is in the upper right.

Survey to India

The infant "chosen instrument" wasted no time in demonstrating that its mission to link the Empire by air service was a prime objective, and that its horizons reached far beyond Berlin and Zurich. While the public and the press were impressed by new records of speed, or height, or endurance, Imperial Airways was concerned with the preparation of airfields, climate and meteorological forecasts, installations, and personnel requirements, along the thousands of miles of routes throughout Asia and Africa.

For the necessary survey work, the airline was fortunate in obtaining the services of a superb pilot. **Alan Cobham** had already shown his interest in commercial aviation. On 30 April 1924, he had flown the first service from Belfast to Liverpool for the short-lived Northern Air Lines (see page 14) and on 19–20 September, whilst with the de Havilland Aeroplane Hire Service (see also page 14) he had made a round trip from Croydon to Tangier—the nearest point in the African continent. In both cases, his aircraft was a D.H. 50, a type that was to serve him well in far more ambitious sorties during the next couple of years or so.

From 10 November 1924 to 17 March 1925, barely six months after Imperial Airways made its inaugural flight (little more than 200 miles, to Paris) Alan Cobham made an 18,000-mile survey flight to the Indian sub-continent. In the D.H. 50 G-EBFO, accompanied by the Director General of Civil Aviation, A.V.M. Sir Sefton Brancker, and engineer A.B.Elliott, the flight (see map on this page) was financed by Imperial Airways, the Air Ministry, the Aircraft Disposal Company, the Society of British Aircraft Constructors, and the Anglo-Persian Oil Company.

A year later, from 16 November 1925 to 13 March 1926, Cobham pioneered another memorable survey flight, with G-EFBO, once more with Elliott, but with B.W.G.Emmott as cameraman, who was assisted in his work by a special hatch cut into the side of the fuselage (see photo, page 22). This journey (map on page 21) was a true trail-blazer as it would map out the Imperial Airways route to South Africa. Cobham received a well-deserved Air Force Cross for this pioneer work.

Losing no time, Cobham was off again on 30 June 1926, yet again with the same D.H.50, this time all the way to Australia and back. This epic flight lasted until he landed spectacularly on the River Thames on 1 October, after 28,000 miles of flying. Cobham was knighted by King George V, but tragically, engineer Elliott was fatally wounded by a bullet fired at the aircraft near Basra.

Sir Alan's survey work was invaluable for Imperial Airways—and he was to make further contributions in the following years. He was more than a pioneer for British air routes; he set an example of laying the foundations for long-distance air transport that would be followed by Charles Lindbergh's trans-ocean surveys for Pan American Airways, Wolfgang von Gronau's North Atlantic flights for Deutsche Luft Hansa, Jean Mermoz's for Air France, and Vasily Molokov's Siberian surveys for Aeroflot. As aerial pathfinders for their respective national airlines, they had no equals.

Alan Cobham, in the cockpit of his D.H.50, talking to Sir Sefton Brancker, then Director General of Civil Aviation. Note that this was for the official Imperial Airways Air Route Survey, and (center) an indication of early sponsorship (by B.P. and Wakefield Castrol).

This picture shows (left to right) Alan Cobham, photographer Emmott, and the flight engineer A.B. Elliott. By today's standards, the camera looks old-fashioned, but Emmott took some superb aerial photographs.

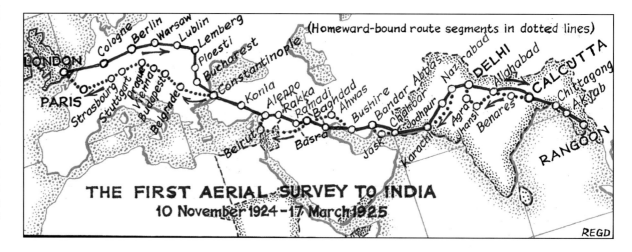

THE FIRST AERIAL SURVEY TO INDIA
10 November 1924 – 17 March 1925

(Homeward-bound route segments in dotted lines)

Cobham Blazes an Empire Trail

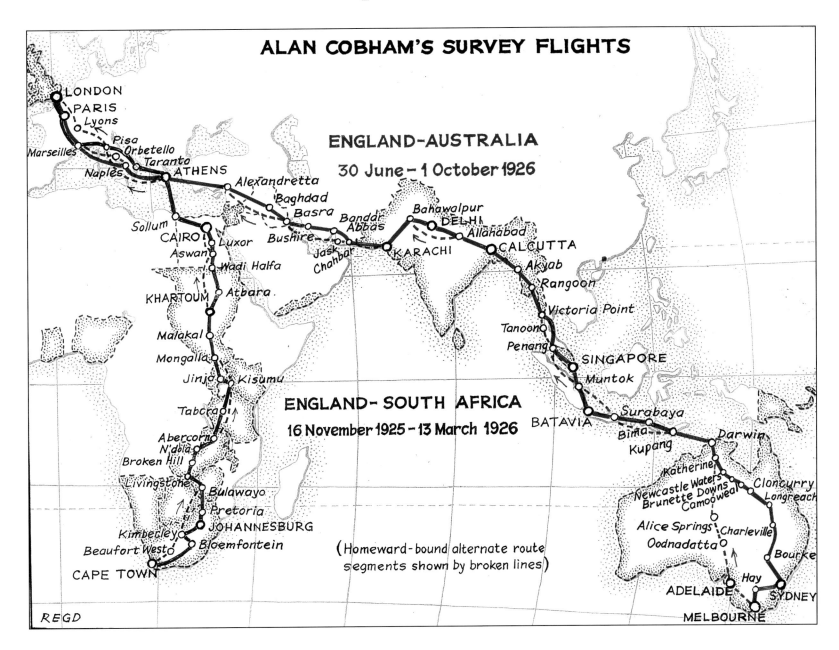

ALAN COBHAM'S SURVEY FLIGHTS

ENGLAND-AUSTRALIA
30 June – 1 October 1926

ENGLAND-SOUTH AFRICA
16 November 1925 – 13 March 1926

(Homeward-bound alternate route segments shown by broken lines)

LONDON
PARIS
Lyons
Pisa
Marseilles
Orbetello
Taranto
Naples
ATHENS
Alexandretta
Baghdad
Basra
Bandar Abbas
Bahawalpur
DELHI
Allahabad
Sollum
CAIRO
Luxor
Bushire
Jask
KARACHI
CALCUTTA
Aswan
Chahbar
Akyab
Wadi Halfa
Rangoon
KHARTOUM
Atbara
Victoria Point
Tanoon
Malakal
Penang
Mongalla
SINGAPORE
Jinja
Kisumu
Muntok
Tabcra
Surabaya
Abercorn
BATAVIA
Bima
N'dola
Kupang
Darwin
Broken Hill
Katherine
Livingstone
Newcastle Waters
Cloncurry
Bulawayo
Brunette Downs
Longreach
Pretoria
Camooweal
Kimberley
JOHANNESBURG
Alice Springs
Charleville
Beaufort West
Bloemfontein
Oodnadatta
Bourke
CAPE TOWN
Hay
ADELAIDE
SYDNEY
MELBOURNE

REGD

First Routes to the East

The de Havilland D.H. 50 G-EBFO had carried Alan Cobham to most of the Empire "upon which the sun never sets." But while it could carry two people and extra fuel for survey purposes (see drawing on this page), this fine single-engined aircraft was clearly not suited to carry a reasonable passenger load; and in any case Imperial Airways demanded multi-engined aircraft for safety purposes, and a lot more comfort too.

The aircraft also had to be versatile in its performance and adaptability to all climates and conditions. Imperial's major objective was to serve the Empire, and this meant an aircraft specification that included more range with payload than the small de Havillands', and the new breed of transport aeroplanes would have to cope with very high desert temperatures, airfields at high altitudes, and maintenance service thousands of miles away from skilled labour and spare parts.

The first destination on the master plan was India, Britain's "Jewel in the Crown" and this involved crossing Europe, the Mediterranean, and the Arabian Desert. Each of these major segments of the route posed special problems, including diplomatic negotiations for traffic rights, trans-Mediterranean range, and navigation installations.

Not a cubic inch of space was wasted in Cobham's D.H.50. In addition to space for spare parts underneath the pilot's seat, a spare propeller was fastened to the fuselage. One of the engineer's tasks was to pump fuel from the lower fuel tanks up to the gravity-feed tank above the wing. He was also equipped with a rifle, in case of special emergencies.

This single D.H.50 was Alan Cobham's survey aeroplane for all of his three flights to India, South Africa, and Australia.

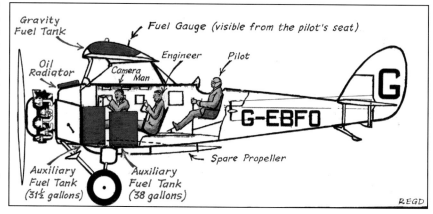

Alan Cobham's D.H.50—carrying an early example of commercial sponsorship advertising—was specially equipped for the demanding journeys and for its survey mission. One of its extra fuel tanks was aerodynamically shaped, and the fuel gauge was visible to the pilot. For the survey work, the photographer could make use of a small hatch, with a sliding panel when not in use.

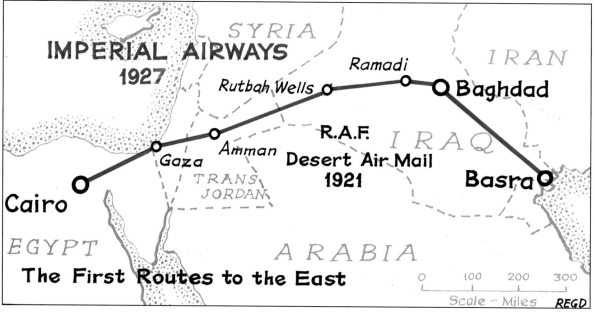

In the case of the desert crossing, Imperial was able to take over an operation pioneered by the Royal Air Force, which had bases in Cairo and near Baghdad, and as early as 1921 had established the Desert Air Mail. For navigation— as radio aids were non-existent at that time—landing grounds were marked out every score of miles or so and an oil-based furrow marked out across the featureless terrain between them. Fuel supplies were made available at some of the landing grounds. The R.A.F. operated D.H.9As, Vickers Vimys, Vernons, and Victorias from 23 June 1921 until Imperial's D.H.66s took over on 7 January 1927. Air mail service was opened to the public on 8 October 1921, and using surface transport as far as Cairo, the mails could reach Baghdad in two weeks.

De Havilland D.H.66 Hercules

7 seats • 100 mph

Conscious of the stringent conditions of flying in the tropics, and which were emphasized by the reported results from Alan Cobham's survey flights, Imperial Airways specified its airliners with tougher standards than had hitherto been accepted. For the Bristol Jupiter-engined **de Havilland Hercules**, designer Arthur Hagg replaced the spruce structural members with welded steel tubing, although the fuselage continued to be plywood covered. Yet this passenger aircraft's pilot was still in an open cockpit, as the skippers still preferred to feel the wind in their hair. Even the windows in the passenger cabin could be opened. The age of airliners that could fly too fast to permit this habit was still almost a decade away, and they would not see service with Imperial Airways until the late 1930s.

The first of these de Havilland tri-motors made its first flight on 30 September 1926. The second one met the airline's specifications satisfactorily, and made a flight to Cairo on 20 December of that year, so as to be in position for Imperial Airways to take over the Desert Air Mail from the Royal Air Force two weeks later. The Hercules fleet had a mixed career. Some lasted only a few years, but one, G-ABMT, which was acquired from the only other Hercules customer, West Australian Airlines, flew on until it was scrapped in 1943, and one was even destroyed by enemy action, flying for the South African Air Force during the Second World War.

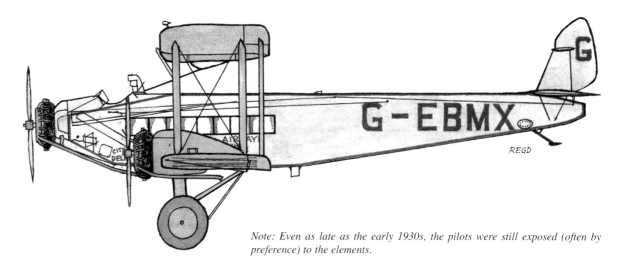

Note: Even as late as the early 1930s, the pilots were still exposed (often by preference) to the elements.

Engine	Bristol Jupiter
	420 hp x 3
MGTOW	15,600 lb.
Max. Range	450 miles
Length	55 feet
Span	79 feet

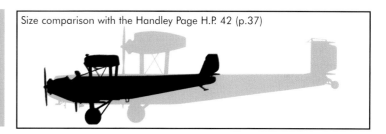

Size comparison with the Handley Page H.P. 42 (p.37)

DE HAVILLAND D.H.66 HERCULES FLEET

Regn.	MSN	Date of C of A	Name	Remarks and Disposal
G-EBMW	236	18 Dec 26	City of Cairo	Crashed in Timor, 19 Apr 31
G-EBMX	237	22 Dec 26	City of Delhi	To South African Air Force, Nov 34
G-EBMY	238	17 Dec 26	City of Baghdad	Withdrawn from use in 1933
G-EBMZ	239	21 Feb 27	City of Jerusalem	Destroyed by fire at Jask, 6 Sep 29
G-EBNA	240	7 Mar 27	City of Teheran	Damaged beyond repair at Gaza, 14 Feb 30
G-AAJH	393	26 Nov 29	City of Basra	To South African Air Force, Apr 34
G-AARY	303	25 Jan 30	City of Karachi	Withdrawn from use in Dec 35
G-ABCP	347	N/A	City of Jodhpur	ex-G-AUJR of West Australian Airways; crashed in Uganda, 23 Nov 35
G-ABMT	346	N/A	City of Cape Town	ex-G-AUJQ of West Australian Airways; to South African Air Force, July 34. Eventually scrapped in 1943

The names given to the aircraft reflected the ports of call en route or were a courtesy to the countries served.

This picture was taken after the pilots conceded that the winds of the desert could not be tolerated — but a passenger could still lean out of the window. Note the additional tailplane (horizontal stabilizer) that, together with the triple fin (vertical stabilizer) were needed to assure complete control.

The Silver Wing

The main task facing Imperial Airways at its formation in 1924 was to improve its fleet from a selection of types that had been modified bomber designs to aircraft that were specifically designed to carry passengers. By 1926 it had two types (having rejected some others), the de Havilland D.H.66 Hercules (see previous pages) and a fine aircraft from **Armstrong Whitworth**. Much stronger than the Handley Page bomber conversions, the **Argosy**, with tubular-steel fuselage and metal wing centre sections, made quite a name for itself, even though the traditional open cockpit for the pilots died hard. It was originally intended for the Middle East service, but the D.H.66 was preferred, and the first 18-seat Argosy (G-EBLO, *City of Birmingham*) went into service on the London-Paris route on 16 July 1926.

Its size — almost three times as many seats as in the D.H.66 — was better suited for the then busiest air route in the world; and also the cabin was spacious enough to challenge the interior designers. The outcome was a new departure in air transport, arguably the first luxury air service in the world. On 1 May 1927, Imperial Airways introduced its *Silver Wing* service on the London-Paris route, with G-EBLF, *City of Glasgow*. The fuselage was a silver-like polish, and the passengers paid a pound extra for the privilege of a first-class meal and bar, served by a steward.

Imperial may also have stimulated the world's first airline competition in terms of passenger amenities, as within two months, in July, the French airline, Air Union, introduced its *Golden Ray* service with Lioré et Olivier Le O 21s. Not to be outdone, Imperial answered in October with a choice of first- or second-class service. The former was the Argosy, which made the trip in 2 hr. 30m, at a fare of £9.0.0., while the latter was offered with the old Handley Pages, in 2 hr. 50m, but at a fare of £7.10.0.

For all its apparent superiority in comfort, the Argosy was no pace-setter in journey times. On 15 June 1928, an unusual air race was carried out, with an Argosy flying from London to Edinburgh in competition with the *Flying Scotsman* of the London and North Eastern Railway (L.N.E.R.). The Argosy won, but only by about 15 minutes

Until the big Handley Page H.P.42s entered the European fray in 1931, the Argosies started the first segment of Imperial's first service to India on 30 March 1929. They flew as far as Basle, Switzerland, whence the passengers had to continue by train, because of unsuccessful negotiations with Italy concerning landing and transit rights over its territory.

Except for the prices, the Silver Wing tariff of 1927 would not be out of place today (except for the Bovril), when airlines are beginning to charge for refreshments. Presumably, the passengers did not have to pay for a cup of tea. Another card distributed to them was FACTS ABOUT THE SILVER WING. This described the aircraft and also its engines, which, it emphasized, were the same that had powered Sir Alan Cobham's aircraft to Australia and South Africa and back. All three, it stated, were started by starting handles. The amenities included ventilation, electric light for night flying, and "wireless apparatus." The passengers were assured that "there is a fire-proof bulkhead behind the middle engine and petrol is stored in two tanks carried under the top plane."

This was Imperial's first insignia before adopting the famous Speedbird in 1931.

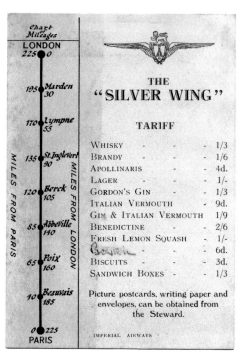

THE "SILVER WING"

TARIFF

Whisky	1/3
Brandy	1/6
Apollinaris	4d.
Lager	1/-
Gordon's Gin	1/3
Italian Vermouth	9d.
Gin & Italian Vermouth	1/9
Benedictine	2/6
Fresh Lemon Squash	1/-
Bovril	6d.
Biscuits	3d.
Sandwich Boxes	1/3

Picture postcards, writing paper and envelopes, can be obtained from the Steward.

IMPERIAL AIRWAYS

The Argosies must have made quite an impression when they ventured beyond the countries of western Europe. This picture was taken in the early 1930s, at Khartoum, when it was re-named the City of Arundel, *from the original* City of Wellington. *It was one of the earliest of its type to be delivered, in 1927, and was finally written off in 1934—at a ripe old age for commercial aeroplanes of that period.*

Armstrong Whitworth Argosy

18 seats • 90 mph

THE ARMSTRONG WHITWORTH ARGOSIES

Regn.	MSN	Date of C/A	Remarks
Armstrong Whitworth Argosy			
G-EBLF	154	29 Sep 26	*City of Glasgow*; withdrawn from use Sep. 34
G-EBLO	155	30 Jun 26	*City of Birmingham*; crashed at Aswan, 16 June 31
G-EBOZ	156	23 Apr 27	*City of Wellington*; renamed *City of Arundel*; written off, October 1934
Armstrong Whitworth Argosy Mark II			
G-AACH	362	19 May 29	*City of Edinburgh*; crashed and burned at Croydon, 22 Apr 36
G-AACI	363	3 June 29	*City of Liverpool*; crashed at Dixmude, Belgium, 28 March 33
G-AACJ	364	6 July 29	*City of Manchester*; to United Airways, July 35
G-AAEJ	400	21 Aug 29	*City of Coventry*; dismantled 1935

Note: the first three Argosies were designated as Mark I only after the Mark II variant was produced. These had geared Jaguar engines, more powerful than the direct-drive ones of the earlier model.

Armstrong Whitworth Argosy	Mark I	Mark II
Engines: Armstrong Siddeley Jaguar x 3	385 hp	410 hp
MGTOW	18,000 lb.	19,200 lb.
Max. Range	330 miles	520 miles
Length	66 feet	67 feet
Span (lower wing)	90 feet	90 feet

Size comparison with the Handley Page H.P. 42 (p.37)

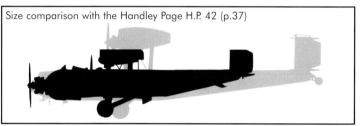

This picture shows the well-travelled City of Arundel, *G-EBOZ, one of the earlier Argosies, along with* City of Coventry, *G-AAEJ, one of the Mark IIs, at Khartoum, in the early 1930s. While famous for their use to launch Imperial's famous* Silver Wing *service to Paris, they were used for the first segment of the first service to India in 1929, and started the first service to Africa in 1931. They were replaced by the Handley Page H.P.42s.*

Imperial Reviews its Options

The years from 1926, when the Argosy went into service, and 1931, when the big Handley Page 42s made their debut, covered a period when Britain's national airline was breaking new ground in every aspect of airline organization and operation, involving technical evaluation, diplomatic negotiation, and business standards. It was not alone. France, Germany, Italy, the Netherlands, the United States, and the Soviet Union all had aircraft manufacturers which could supply the aeroplanes, and Imperial was expected to "Buy British." But with the construction of efficient commercial airliners still being largely a case of "trial and error," Imperial's role in the development of an ideal specification for its use on both the European and the Empire routes was essential. While it was thus in a position to influence the manufacturers in their products, it also had to share in the development process.

While the Argosy and the Hercules (see pages 23 and 25) were machines that could meet Imperial's varied operational and commercial requirements, other aircraft missed selection past the prototype stage, or were not ordered for front-line service. These types are listed in the accompanying tabulation.

Imperial's home base at Croydon was also enlarged, as it needed to be to accommodate the larger aircraft. It became operational on 30 January 1928, and was officially opened on 2 May by the Air Minister's wife, Lady Maud Hoare.

Two of the aircraft that served Imperial Airways in a supporting role were the Westland Wessex, two of which are in the foreground of this picture taken at Croydon in the early 1930s. The third aircraft is the Avro Ten Apollo, which crashed in Belgium in 1933. It was the British-built Fokker F.VIIb, and it sister ship, the Achilles, survived into the B.O.A.C. register in 1939. Just off the picture to the left was the little Desoutter, used by Imperial for air taxi work.

THOSE THAT MISSED THE CUT

Regn.	MSN	Date of C/A	Remarks
De Havilland D.H.54 Highclere			
G-FBKI	151	1926	Owned by the Air Council. Lent to Imperial Airways for evaluation, 7 Nov 26. Destroyed at Croydon when hangar roof collapsed under weight of snow, 1 Feb 27
Vickers Vanguard			
G-EBCP	1	11 Mar 26	Lent by Air Ministry for route trials; crashed at Shepperton, 16 May 29
Supermarine Swan			
G-EBJY	1173	30 Jun 26	Lent by Air Ministry; scrapped 1927
Supermarine Southampton II			
G-AASH	S1235	12 Nov 29	Lent by Air Ministry to replace the Short Calcutta G-AADN that had been forced down near Spezia on 26 Oct 29
Westland Wessex			
G-AAGW	1867	21 Oct 29	Converted from Westland IV; to Air Pilots Training, March 36
G-ABEG	1901	2 Oct 30	Damaged beyond repair in Northern Rhodesia, 1936
G-ACHI	2151	23 Jun 33	To Air Pilots Training, March 36
Avro Ten (Avro 618)			
G-AASP	384	23 Apr 31	Named *Achilles*; passed to B.O.A.C., 1939
G-ABLU	528	18 Jun 31	Named *Apollo*; crashed at Ruysselede, Belgium, 30 Dec 33
Desoutter I			
G-ABMW	D.28	6 Jan 31	Used for air taxi work until 1935

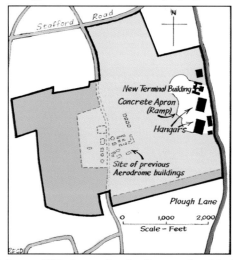

On 30 January 1928, the new Croydon Airport replaced the former Croydon Aerodrome on Plough Lane. Still a grass field, it was an enlargement of the former site, The buildings, offices, and hangars on Plough Lane were replaced by a handsome administrative and passenger reception building on Purley Way. Larger hangars could accommodate the largest Imperial Airways airliners of the 1930s.

This view shows the new buildings at Croydon Airport after it had been enlarged from the old Plough Lane site. Imperial Airways's hangars, large enough to admit its flagship aircraft, are behind the handsome terminal building that survives today as a museum that is well-stocked with models, maps, memorabilia, and exhibits of the communications equipment of a by-gone era.

This picture epitomises the transition of the British national flag-carrier, as it girded its loins in the late 1920s, discarding the inadequate aircraft that had done the pioneering in the post-war years of pre-1924. Put into a storage hangar, the remnants of an old fleet were left to corrode or rust away. From left to right are the Vickers Vulcan, the de Havilland D.H.54 Highclere, two ex-Daimler de Havilland D.H.34s, Instone's Vickers Vimy, and another D.H.34. Their demise was accelerated by Imperial's decision to operate only multi-engined types.

First Flight to India

The main Empire-linking destination for Imperial Airways was India, which was still the "Jewel in the Crown" of Britain's overseas territories and dominions, with about three quarters of its population. But the planning, surveying, international negotiation, and selection of equipment had all presented problems and difficulties. Planning and surveying had been carried out, notably by Alan Cobham, but Imperial ran into difficulties with operating rights through Italy, and crossing the Mediterranean was considered too risky for the landplanes whose range was short. Except for Malta, there was no place for an emergency landing. Also, there was considerable support at high levels for a lighter-than-air solution, i.e., airships, for long-range routes. The early dirigibles, all based on the Zeppelin basic design, had already proved their ability to fly thousands, rather than hundreds of miles, and in the 1920s, a route to India, with only one stop, in Egypt, seemed practicable (see pages 32–33).

On 26 December 1926, in a demonstration to confirm the survey flights and the selection of aircraft, the D.H.Hercules G-EBMX left Croydon, crewed by Imperial pilots, and carrying no less than Sir Samuel Hoare, the Secretary of State for Air, and his wife, with other prominent officials, including the Director of Civil Aviation, Sir Sefton Brancker, and Imperial's General Manager, George Woods Humphery. The route followed was similar to Cobham's route (see page 21) except that it was routed via Malta and north Africa. They reached Karachi on 6 January 1927, and Delhi two days later. To honour the occasion, the aircraft was named *City of Delhi*, and it returned on 1 February, reaching Cairo on 7 February, where it joined two other D.H.66s to inaugurate the first segment of what was to become the trunk route to India (see page 22–23).

The controversy concerning the choice of aircraft continued. The R.A.F. attempted a non-stop flight to India on 20 May 1927, using a Hawker Horsley bomber, but it reached only as far as the Persian Gulf, after flying 3,420 miles. Then the Air Force made a strong case for the flying boat, leaving its Felixtowe base on 17 October. Four Supermarine Southampton flying boats flew to Singapore, then to Australia and Hong Kong, before completing a 27,000-mile cruise at Singapore on 11 December.

The case for the necessity of the flying boat for the Mediterranean crossing was made, and Imperial's choice was the three-engined Short Calcutta (see page 31), which had made its first flight on 14 February 1928. Experimental services with these were made from Southampton to Guernsey

in the summer, and from Liverpool to Belfast from 24 September to 4 October. On 28 February 1929, the Calcuttas were transferred to the Mediterranean, and at last, five years after its foundation, Imperial Airways was ready to launch its first seven-day service from London to India.

At this time, the main payloads for the flights were sacks of mail, and the passenger loads were not only small, but

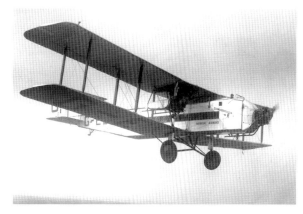

This flying view of the Armstrong Whitworth Argosy tri-motor is illustrative of the level of commercial airliner design in Britain in the late 1920s. The pilot is still in his cockpit, open to all weathers, and this was to include the heat of the Arabian Desert and India.

were confined mainly to diplomats, politicians, and company directors. The single fare was £130—half a year's wages for the average working man, who in any case, did not have the luxury of having even the time to travel. The idea of travelling to India for leisure or personal reasons was still half a century away. Nevertheless, the objective of linking Britain's "Jewel in the Crown" with the home country by air was a desirable objective in the 1930s.

This historic photograph recorded the arrival of the Minister of State for Air, Sir Samual Hoare, and his official party, when he arrived at Delhi on 8 January 1928. It set the seal on the imminent inauguration of Imperial's air service to India on 30 March 1929.

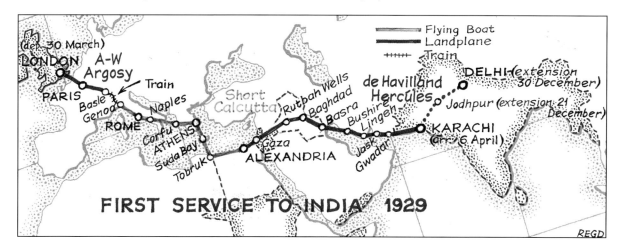

FIRST SERVICE TO INDIA 1929

Around Africa by Flying Boat

After establishing service to India, Imperial's next objective was to reach South Africa, and once again much preliminary work had to be done by survey flights. Much of the territory to be covered was inimical to aviation, whether by land or water. In the late 1920s, much of the African continent had only recently been introduced to aeroplanes by individual pilots flying to Cape Town; and in many countries aeroplanes had never been seen at all.

The first landplane survey by **Alan Cobham** in 1925/26 (page 21) had been a start, but was regarded as much as an adventure as a survey flight. Much more was needed, especially to address the controversy between the advocates of landplanes versus seaplanes or flying boats. The obvious advantage of waterborne craft was that, as with ocean liners, there was no limit to the size or weight. On the other hand, commercial operations needed to be close to the cities they served, a prime example being the need for air passengers leaving London to have to take a train to Southampton. Flying boats needed ocean, sea, lake, or river alighting areas.

In the case of a route to South Africa, a choice had to be made between east and west of the continent. The western route had some operational advantages, but the "all-red" "Cape-to-Cairo" route, already visualized as a complete railway line, was commercially more desirable. The geographical and operational convenience of the River Nile, and a series of large lakes that seemed to be designed for a flying boat route, were fully recognized; and also the segment from London to Egypt could be shared with the route to India.

Accordingly, backed by the oil industrialist Sir Charles Wakefield, Alan (now Sir Alan) Cobham, flying a **Short Singapore** flying boat, set off from the manufacturer's base at Rochester, Kent, on a 20,000-mile journey around Africa. This was to demonstrate that to establish regular airline service along the whole length of Africa would not be easy. Cobham managed to return to Plymouth only after more than six months of strenuous, sometimes hazardous flying. He was delayed in Malta for six weeks because of repairs to a damaged wing; and spent a month in the Ivory Coast while awaiting spare parts for an engine. This strongly emphasized the need for adequate maintenance support along the line, and he was able to report on the hazards of mooring the flying boat against currents and swells, and problems of floating obstructions, including curious boating crews.

On the other hand, the Short Singapore did complete this formidable mission, in spite of the fragility of the hull, whose metal was less than one sixteenth of an inch (or about a millimetre) thick and vulnerable to the slightest knock by another vessel. Interestingly, much was made of the fact that he was accompanied by no less than a *woman*—his wife, Lady Maud. In the 1920s, the female sex was not yet thought to be ready for flying. Another passenger that completed the journey was a canary, donated by the Governor of Malta.

Sir Alan Cobham and his co-pilot, Capt. Worrall.

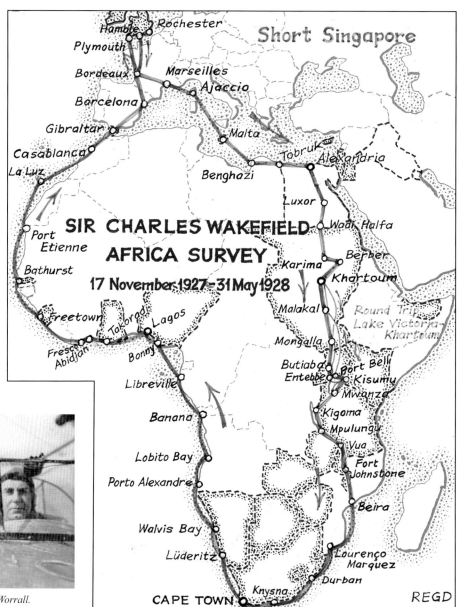

Imperial to East Africa

Enormous problems faced the British authorities in planning a commercial air route to South Africa. The Cape-to-Cairo route was selected because much was known from previous surveys in connection with the projected railway (which was never completed) and much pioneering trailblazing had been accomplished by Alan Cobham (see previous pages). The River Nile segment as far south as Khartoum and Kisumu had also been the subject of flights by both the North Sea Aerial and General Transport (see page 14) and the Royal Air Force, early in 1927, but these were experimental and the aircraft were damaged on take-off.

Sir Alan's achievement in flying around Africa was impressive, but it emphasized the need for a sturdier flying boat than the Singapore, and the need for good mooring and anchorage installations at every point along the route, together with adequate stores of spare parts and maintenance equipment. Many lessons were learned from the experience at Malta, illustrated in the photographs below. The solution was sought with the Short Calcutta, which made its first flight at Rochester on 20 February 1928 (see page 31).

Not until 1931 was Imperial Airways able to venture south of the Mediterranean, to penetrate what was then still referred to as "Darkest Africa." It had had to contend with diplomatic difficulties with Italy (see page 30), necessitating a circuitous route through central Europe, and the need to use a combination of landplanes and flying boats. As shown on the map, the passengers (who initially were carried only as far as Khartoum) and the all-important mail had to make four changes of vehicle, including a train from Alexandria to Cairo, during the ten-day journey.

Home at last: disembarking at Plymouth

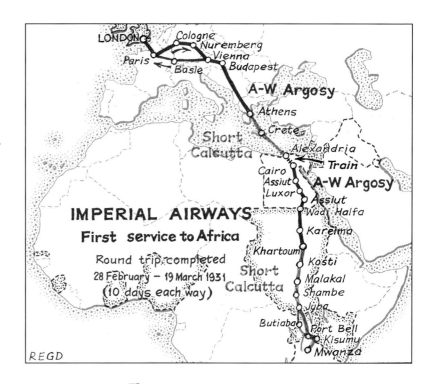

The difficulties of flying boat operations are vividly illustrated in these photographs taken during Sir Alan Cobham's circumnavigation of Africa (see opposite page). Early in the journey, at Malta, the Singapore was caught in a heavy swell and gale-force winds. The lower wing was damaged (left picture) and had to be repaired by a team sent out from England. The damaged aircraft was first anchored to prevent further damage and eventually towed to the shore. Even the weight of six men was not enough to restore its balance and a hundred men could not tow it on to the slipway (centre). By an amazing stroke of good fortune, a mighty wave lifted the Singapore on to the slipway, and the men held fast (right).

Italian Intransigence

The territories of Great Britain's empire during the inter-war years had gaps in it, not only trans-ocean, but also much closer to home, across continental Europe. The Five Freedoms of the Air, to be thrashed out at the 1944 Chicago Conference that established the International Civil Aviation Organization (ICAO), were not yet agreed between the nations. Over-flying and transit rights were jealously guarded. Imperial's route development in that case were not seriously impeded, but its aspirations towards the mission to link the Empire were compromised in its efforts to reach across the eastern Mediterranean.

The obvious route was across France and along the length of Italy. Unfortunately, the distance from Genoa in the north to any point in the south was about four hundred miles, which was beyond the range of any transport aero-plane of the time to fly non-stop with both enough fuel and enough payload. As early as 1926, Mussolini tried to trade for landing rights at Gibraltar. In 1928, the Italians bargained the rights of passage on behalf of its own air-line, Societa Anonima di Navigazione Aerea (SANA), which was charged with serving Libya, then an Italian col-ony, and on as far as Alexandria. Imperial paid £5,000 per year. In the event SANA's traffic was almost negligible, so in due course the case became moot. But Imperial was able to start its service to India on 30 March 1929.

Italy's terms were considered to be unacceptable, and an alternative route was decided: to fly across central and southeastern Europe. This meant stopping at only one point in each country, except Yugoslavia, before reaching Athens, the terminus for the trans-Mediterranean flying boats. This itinerary began of 2 November 1929.

Even so, the ingenious solution was short-lived, as the terrain, the weather, and the short hours of daylight in the Balkans, were not condusive to regular flying to a commercially-accepted schedule. After only two services, from 16 November 1929, the journey from Cologne to Athens was taken by train, and even with the approach of spring, when flying resumed on 12 April 1930, the seg-ment from Skopje to Salonika was still covered by train.

This rather ponderous improvisation was modified on 20 September 1930, as shown on the map, but because of the several inconvenient changes between rail and air, pas-sengers were advised to take the train from Paris to Athens by the famous Simplon-Orient Express. A semblance of order was finally restored on 16 May 1931, when the east-ern route was abandoned, and the previous system of 1929 was re-introduced, with the trans-Alpine Basle-Genoa seg-ment by train. But the Calcutta flying boats were replaced by the larger four-engined Short S.17 Scipios.

Imperial's first Short Calcutta flying boat.

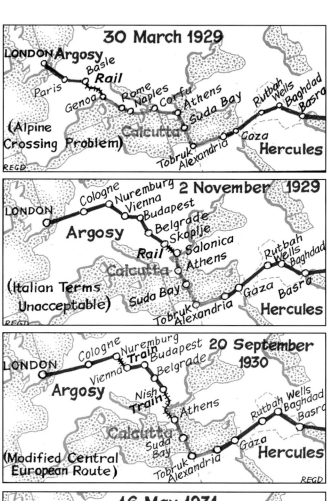

Short S.8 Calcutta
12 seats • 97 mph

For several years, the specification for an ideal transport aeroplane had ranged back and forth in aviation circles; biplane versus monoplane, landplane versus seaplane, and in the latter case, floatplane or flying boat. In previous pages, some of the arguments have been discussed. Sir Alan Cobham had flown all the types extensively, and as the most famous aviator in Britain, his opinion was respected. In his book, he had remarked on the effect of tropical storms on landing fields, and on the question of safety—still an issue in the late 1920s and early 1930s—he had "always maintained that I would far sooner be in a flying boat flying over the land than I would be in an aeroplane flying over the sea."

Imperial Airways apparently played it safe. It had introduced the three-engined Argosy landplane in 1926, and it had proved its worth by being deployed on the prestige London-Paris route, on other European routes, and in India and Africa. But Cobham's views on the preference for flying boats seemed to make sense for over-water routes such as the Mediterranean and on routes such as along the River Nile, where currents and waves were of little consequence, and where anchorages could be established and equipped relatively easily. And so Imperial decided to combine both landplanes and flying boats on its Empire routes, using each type where it was most adaptable to the local conditions.

Its flying boat choice was the three-engined biplane, the **Short Calcutta**. It made its first flight on 20 February 1928, was commissioned on 26 July 1928, The aircraft created quite an impression by alighting on the River Thames in London in August 1928, then made some proving flights from Liverpool to Belfast in September 1928, and served briefly from Southampton to Guernsey until 28 February 1929, when Imperial closed the route. By demonstrating that it could maintain height with only two engines, the Calcutta won its spurs, and on 16 April 1929 it was flown to Genoa to operate on Imperial's trans-Mediterranean services.

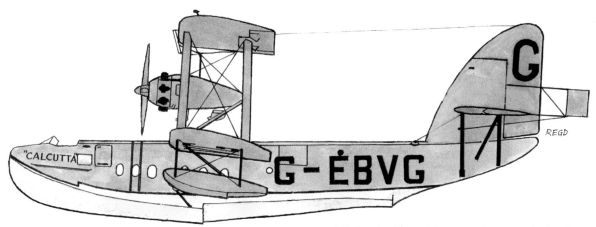

Artist's note: The red lines were to warn attendant boat crews not to risk being in line with the propellers. The underside of the hull was painted in white enamel.

Engine	Bristol Jupiter
	840 hp x 3
MGTOW	22,500 lb.
Max. Range	650 miles
Length	67 feet
Span	93 feet

Size comparison with the Short S.23 (p.93)

SHORT S.8 CALCUTTA FLEET

Regn.	MSN	Date of C of A	Name	Remarks and Disposal
G-EBVG	S.712	25 Jul 28	City of Alexandria	Capsized at Crete, 28 Dec 36
G-EBVH	S.713	13 Sep 28	City of Athens	Renamed City of Stonehaven, dismantled, 1937
G-AADN	S.748	11 Apr 29	City of Rome	Forced down off Spezia, 26 Oct 29
G-AASJ	S.752	13 Jan 30	City of Khartoum	Crashed off Alexandria, 31 Dec 35
G-AATZ	S.754	3 Jun 30	City of Salonika	Renamed City of Swanage, scrapped, 1939

During the late 1920s, the airfields in the eastern Mediterranean were inadequate for larger landplanes such as those used by Imperial Airways; and so the Calcuttas maintained the services. These were succeeded by the larger Short S.17 Kent class aircraft in 1931 (see page 36).

Airship Digression

Since 1937, when the German *Hindenburg* disaster put an end to all aspirations for the future of giant dirigible airships as the solution for long-distance air travel, the shattered dreams of the 1920s and even the early 1930s have almost been erased from memory. But often forgotten is that, in those days, heavier-than-air aircraft were thought to be capable of carrying passengers or mail over distances of only a few hundred miles, and airships were very much in the public and political eyes, not only because their very size was spectacular, but because they could remain in the air without refuelling for thousands, not hundreds of miles. This invited the prospect of trans-oceanic flight.

In the mid-1920s, the record of the large airships did seem promising, and the only major disaster, of the American *Shenandoah*, was put down to a severe storm "comparable to those which bring disaster to ships at sea." This was the statement In the special Air Ministry report, a Memorandum by the Secretary of State for Air, Sir Samuel Hoare, titled *The Approach towards a System of Imperial Communications*, and tabled at the Imperial Conference in 1926. It went on to state that "airships have a record of practical achievement over a period of years. They have definitely proved their capacity on occasion to fly fast and continuously by day and night through great distances over sea and land while carrying relatively heavy loads."

These were fine words, but even then the term "fast" was questionable, as an airship's average speed of about 70 mph was slower than the aeroplane's 100 mph; and the terms "on occasion" and "relatively heavy loads" were vague. Nevertheless, the emphasis of the report was clearly in favour of determined airship development. Sir Samuel's statement of policy concluded "I wish to see a commercial airship line started at the earliest possible moment between Great Britain and the various Dominions." In the main part of the whole document, thirteen pages were devoted to Imperial Airship Services against only three pages to Imperial Aeroplane Services.

The construction of two large airships was started immediately, under direction by the Air Ministry. The R-101, was built at Cardington , near Bedford, by the Royal Airship Works, with engineering by Boulton & Paul, of Norwich. The R-100 was built at Howden, Yorkshire, by the Airship Guarantee Company, with engineering by Vickers. Both airships were larger than the famous *Graf Zeppelin* that was already operating successfully, and both made their first flights late in 1929, the R-101 on 14 October and the R-100 on 16 December.

For ground handling and service, the British approach was different from the German. At Friedrichshafen, the *Graf Zeppelin* was moored close to the ground, and the crew and passengers entered the gondola cabin up a short flight of built-in stairs. At Cardington, Ismailia, Karachi, and Montreal, high mooring masts were erected, to permit better flexibility in changing wind directions, and entry to the airships was through the nose of the hull. In both cases, the enormous machines were ponderous to manage when they were not in their equally enormous sheds. Every time the *Graf Zeppelin* (and later, the Hindenburg) arrived or departed, every able-bodied man in the vicinity was mobilized to keep them under control.

The R.100 and the R.101 were intended to form the foundation of Britain's long-distance air services, with visions of routes to Australia, with only three or four stops; to South Africa with two or three; and non-stop across the Atlantic. In the Memorandum, the general areas of intended operation are shown as on the upper map on this page, and the confidence for the future of the airship was reflected in the wording of the caption — "probably," not "possibly." Extensive preparations were made, as illustrated on page 33.

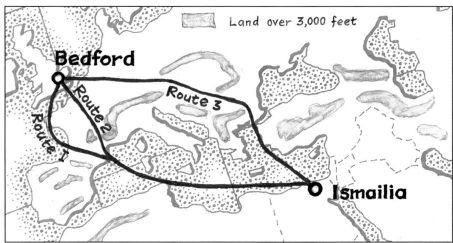

The great airships could not fly at high altitudes, and 1,000–2,000 feet was their customary operating height. For the initial survey flight to Egypt, they had to avoid mountains that were higher. Thus the recommended routes across Europe kept over the sea or followed river valleys. Thus, the preferred route was one that involved the minimum of overland flying, across southern France, north of the Pyrenees. Second choice (the one taken by the ill-fated R.101) followed the Seine and Rhone, avoiding the Alps; and the longest overland course followed the Danube, avoiding the Carpathians and the mountains of the Balkans.

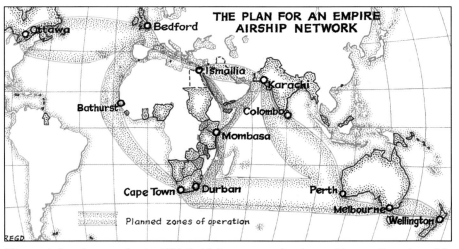

This map is from the comprehensive 1926 Air Ministry report, referred to on this page. Once clear of the European mainland, the high ground to which airships were vulnerable could be avoided, so that lighter-than-air routes seemed possible to almost every corner of the British Empire, and especially to all the dominions.

Airships to India—the Preparations

The R.100 Length: 709 feet. Max. diameter 133 feet. Engines: Rolls-Royce Condor (660 hp) x 6. Gas capacity: 5 million cubic feet. Estimated lift: 156 tons. Max. range: 3,000 miles.

The R.101 Length 732 feet (lengthened to 777 feet). Max. diameter 132 feet. Engines: Beardmore Tornado (diesel) (585 hp) x 5. Gas capacity: 5 million cubic feet. Estimated lift: 150 tons. Max. range: 3,000 miles.

The two airship sheds at Cardington, near Bedford. Length: 812 feet. Height: 157 feet. Width: 180 feet.

The mooring tower at Ismailia, Egypt. The R.101 crash occurred before work was under way on the airship shed.

The airship shed at Karachi, India (now Pakistan). Length: 850 feet. Height: 170 feet. Width: 180 feet.

In 1929, the American airline promoter, Clement Keys, declared that "90 percent of aviation is on the ground." Nowhere was this more true, or necessary, than in the operations of dirigible airships. Everywhere one of these giant machines went, it demanded a large shed to protect it from winds of even moderate strength, and certainly from inclement weather. When moored at its mast, it needed clear ground over a radius exceeding its own length — desert or near-desert territory was fine. Ground crews numbering a hundred or moe were needed to secure its landing and mooring. Had airship operations ever increased beyond the infrequent services operated by Germany and only visualized by Great Britain, the infrastructure needed to support multiple services would have needed several square miles at each station, many huge sheds, and the ready availability of substantial manpower.

End of an Era — the R.101 Disaster

The Trials

In 1930, the Conservative Air Minister Sir Samual Hoare had been replaced by Labour's Lord Thompson, who was no less enthusiastic in his support for the airship policy for Imperial air communications. He was looking forward to attending the Imperial Conference in New Delhi in October of that year, and planned to arrive, along with the Director of Civil Aviation, Sir Sefton Brancker, in great style, in Britain's new giant airship, the R.101.

There were warning signs. The initial 732-foot hull design had, during the summer of 1930, been lengthened by 45 feet, with an extra section inserted, so as to improve the useful load from 39 to 54 tons. The airship had made some useful trial flights, some of them of long duration, but the flight to Delhi was undertaken after only one test flight had been made with the extra bay in the hull, and that only on 1–2 October. Also, in the first week of October, the weather was not promising, and airships were especially vulnerable to high winds. Further, the loading seemed to have been irresponsible, with unnecessary surplus items, including excess luggage for Lord Thompson. Curiously, although the preferred route to the Mediterranean, according to all the intensive studies and researches by the meteorological specialists, was along the west coast of France (see page 32), the R.101 took the shorter route, via Paris.

The Flight

It left Cardington late in the afternoon of 4 October, and to the horror of the entire world, it crashed into a low hill north of Paris later that night. Almost all on board were killed, including Thompson and Brancker, and the tragedy reverberated throughout the aviation community. The British airship program was abandoned, and the wisdom of this decision seemed to be confirmed a year later when the American Akron was lost at sea during a storm in April 1933 and the *Macon* suffered a similar fate in February 1935. Germany continued its scheduled trans-Atlantic airship services, but it too had to call a halt when the *Hindenburg* was destroyed in flames at Lakehurst, New Jersey, on 6 May 1937. The continued series of disasters and the consequent severe loss of lives ensured that airships were no longer a factor in the development of air transport.

The framework of the airship shed at Karachi. Some idea of the size can be gleaned from the small bus on the right of the picture.

Another view of the Karachi airship shed, showing the railway line that was built to transport the structural materials, and would no doubt have been utilized to take the passengers into the city, had services ever been started.

This is the mast at Cardington, Bedfordshire, an impressive structure. The photographer had some intrepid assistants to stand on top to emphasize the height and size. Though not in evidence in this picture, the lift provided was not always reliable. The climb up to the loading platform was arduous indeed, and demanding of much stamina.

A New Era Begins

Until the R.101 tragedy, and as described in the foregoing pages, the great airships had received the maximum attention from the politicians and the public alike. Imperial Airways, representing Britain's heavier-then-air commercial aspirations, seemed to be playing second fiddle to the dirigibles. Delays because of disabled machines, or bad weather, were all too frequent and the political problems of flying across Europe, where both the French and Italian authorities were uncooperative (see page 30) did not help. Nevertheless, on 30 March 1929, the first scheduled service to India left Croydon Airport, bound for Karachi (see page 27).

Compared to the spectacular airships, this was a case of the tortoise and the hare; for the prospects of a British airship service to India died in on 5 October 1930, in the early morning at Beauvais, near Paris; and Imperial Airways was able to get into gear and re-double its efforts to modernize its fleet. For, as shown in the previous map, and in the fleet list on this page, the need was urgent.

For the few travellers who availed themselves of the service to India, it must have been quite an adventure, as in addition to the trans-Alpine train journey, three different types of aircraft were used, and Karachi was reached, if punctual, just over a week after leaving London. But undeterred, Imperial had extended the route to Jodhpur on 20 December and ten days later to Delhi. Once again, the political path had been strewn with obstacles, as the Indian Government claimed territorial rights, and the domestic segments were flown by Imperial under charter to the Indian Government.

But at last, the British flag carrier was getting into its stride, and help was on the way in the shape of new four-engined aircraft, first of all, four-engined flying boats for the Mediteranean and four-engined landplanes for the overland routes. These aircraft were no faster than the older aeroplanes; but they were bigger; and far more important, and though still vulnerable to turbulence — the "air-pockets," as they were then called — were far more comfortable, as illustrated in the following pages.

Indeed, although the British public was shocked to witness the demise of the great airships in 1930, it was, only a few months after the R.101 disaster, able to welcome in a new era. With new equipment, as described in the following pages, Imperial Airways began to establish itself with luxury aloft, with transport aeroplanes that could be described as airliners.

IMPERIAL AIRWAYS FLEET, 31 DECEMBER 1929

Aircraft Type	Seats	Number in Fleet	Remarks
Armstrong Whitworth Argosy	20	7	European services
De Havilland D.H.66 Hercules	8	5	Middle East to India service
Short Calcutta (flying boat)	12	3	Mediterranean service
Supermarine Southampton (flying boat)	(mail)	1	Mediterranean service
Handley Page W.8b	14	1	
Handley Page W.8f	12	2	
Handley Page W.10	16	2	Obsolescent types, used in reserve and for private charter
De Havilland D.H.50	2	1	
Westland Wessex IV	4	1	

As this list indicates, Imperial Airways did not enjoy, in its formative years, the luxury of a large fleet. The 20-seat Argosies, which operated the Silver Wing services to Paris, were the flagships, but most of the other aircraft were either obsolescent or were short-lived.

Two of Imperial's Short flying boats photographed at anchor at Mirabella, Crete. This was an essential refuelling base, and as the hinterland suggests, not a traffic stop.

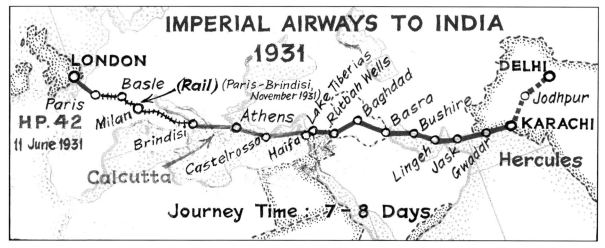

The route to India was still the victim of protracted political obstructions beyond Imperial Airways's control. Although it was able to introduce the handsome Handley Page H.P.42s in the summer of 1931, it was obliged to carry its passengers by rail all the way from Paris to the southern tip of Italy in November. And on reaching India, the charter agreement with the Delhi government was terminated in December, to be replaced by an arrangement with the Delhi Aero Club.

Short S.17 Kent

16 seats • 105 mph

During the early 1930s, Imperial Airways realized that larger aircraft were needed to meet the demands of passenger and mail service, and at the same time could cross the Mediterranean with safety. The landplanes and flying boat designs on offer still did not have the guaranteed range to fly from mainland Europe to Egypt or the Levant, but at least the boats were built to be water-borne, and so the choice was made in their favour for that mission, in case of a forced landing.

Work started on the **Short S-17 Kent** series at Rochester in October 1930, the same month when the R.101 airship dashed the hopes of all the supporters of a lighter-than-air solution for the service to India. It was much bigger than any of Imperial's previous types — 60% heavier than the Argosy and Hercules landplanes and 50% heavier than the Calcutta flying boat. It could carry more passengers than the Argosy or the Calcutta, and in better comfort, but its range was no greater. Flying boats did not need special airfields, and there was no limit to their all-up weight. However they had to have good weather for anchorage and a cleared surface for take-off and landing. Also they were often difficult for mooring with strong winds and currents.

First flown on 24 February 1931 by Short's chief pilot, John Lankester Parker, the *Scipio* was able to take off in 21 seconds and climb to 7,000 feet in seven minutes. Even though lightly-loaded, this was impressive. It could carry 16 passengers in a comfortable cabin, with a meal service and a bar. However, as summarized in the tabulation on this page, it was unlucky in its career. Nevertheless it proved itself well enough for Short to build a landplane version — see page 44.

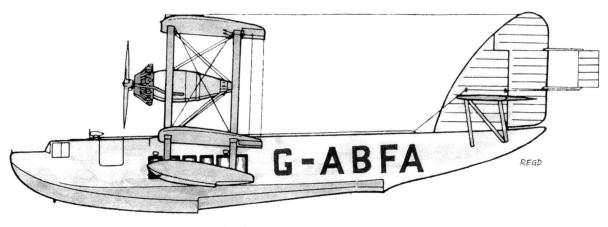

Artist's note: The four engines were exactly in line abreast, whereas those for the Handley Page H.P. 42/45 were paired — two on each wing (see pages 37–39)

Engine	Bristol Jupiter
	455 hp x 4
MGTOW	32,000 lb.
Max. Range	450 miles
Length	78 feet
Span	113 feet

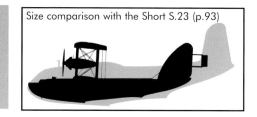

Size comparison with the Short S.23 (p.93)

The Satyrus was the third of the Short S.17 Kent class flying boats and provided service on the Mediterranean route until 1938.

IMPERIAL'S SHORT S-17 KENT FLEET

Regn.	MSN	Date of C of A	Name	Remarks and Disposal
G-ABFA	S.758	24 Feb 31	*Scipio*	Entered service early May 1931; Sank at Mirabella, Crete, after heavy landing, 22 Aug 36
G-ABFB	S.759	31 March 31	*Sylvanus*	Damaged in collision with Dornier Wal at Genoa, June 31; set on fire (arson) at Brindisi, 9 Nov 35
G-ABFC	S.760	2 May 31	*Satyrus*	Damaged on first flight, 2 May 31 (Sir Samuel Instone on board); Scrapped at Hythe, June 38

Handley Page H.P.42/45

38 seats (Western); 18 seats (Eastern) • 105 mph

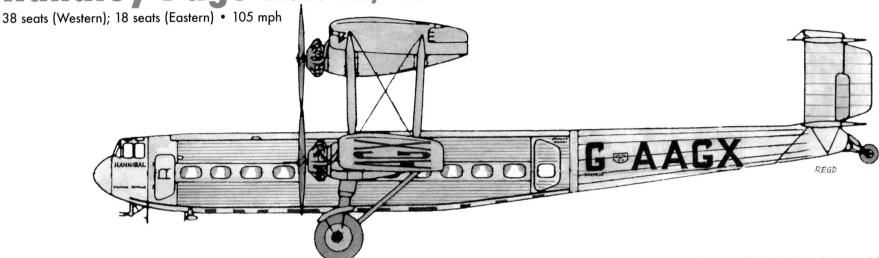

This large four-engined biplane was slow and almost ponderous to fly, but it offered the kind of luxury that matched first-class train travel. The first order for what was then regarded as a giant aeroplane was placed with Handley Page on 15 April 1929, and significantly the order came straight from the customer and not by the former procedure of ordering through the Air Ministry. The first of these 14-ton machines, which were justly graced with the term airliner, made its first flight on 14 November 1930, piloted by Thomas England, Handley Page's chief pilot. Only six weeks after the R.101 airship's tragic crash, the event seemed to symbolize "out with the old, bring in the new."

This first **Handley Page H.P.42** went into London-Paris service on 11 June 1931, and was widely acclaimed as the epitome of aerial comfort and elegance — as indeed it was, for seldom have the standards been equalled since, except possibly in the Concorde. As illustrated on the next pages, the wooden decor and rich upholstery was accompanied by a five course luncheon, an amenity made possible by the two-and-a-half journey time for the 225 miles from Croydon to Le Bourget.

In later years, the 105 mph alleged cruising speed was not always achieved, and after a few years, the Handley Pages were subjected to certain criticisms because French, German, Italian, and especially American airliners flew faster. But none matched the comfort standards of the big biplane. The facts were that the air journey saved about four hours or more over the fastest surface travel, which involved a train ferry across the English Channel, and saving half an hour on the air journey

mattered little to the business travellers or the rich and famous who travelled by Imperial Airways during the 1930s.

By the end of 1931, only six months after the inaugural service, Handley Page had delivered eight of these big aeroplanes, an impressive manufacturing achievement for that time. The first four, designated H.P. 42W (for Western) were fitted with 38 seats, in two cabins, fore and aft, with the space between for luggage, two toilets, and a bar. This center section was in line with the engines and was a safety measure in the event that a propeller flew off and penetrated the fuselage. The second four, the H.P. 42E (for Eastern) had smaller cabins for only 18–24 seats but a much larger space for mail. The H.P.42Ws were later distinguished as H.P.45s, although both types are generally referred to as H.P.42s.

Throughout its eight years of intensive service, and in spite of a few near misses, the big Handley Pages never killed a fare-paying passenger.

Artist's note: Because of the limitations of the size of the drawing, the corrugations on the fuselage are not drawn exactly to scale. The word **IMPERIAL** *was painted on the underside of the fuselage.*

	Hannibal	Heracles
Engine	Bristol Jupiter	Bristol Jupiter
	490 hp x 4	555 hp x 4
MGTOW	28,000 lb.	29,500 lb.
Max. Range	300 miles	300 miles
Length	90 feet	90 feet
Span	130 feet	130 feet

THE HANDLEY PAGE H.P.42/H.P.45 FLEET

Regn.	MSN	Date of C of A	Name	Remarks and Disposal
H.P.42 (Hannibal Class) (or H.P.42W)				
G-AAGX	42/1	5 June 31	Hannibal	Tail torn off on emergency landing in Kent, 8 Aug 31. Wings torn off at Tiberias, 17 Nov 32. Lost between Jask and Sharjah, 1 March 1940.
G-AAUC	42/4	19 Sep 31	Horsa	Taken over by B.O.A.C. 1940
G-AAUD	42/3	30 Jul 31	Hanno	Coverted to H.P.45 standard. Wrecked in gale at Bristol, 19 Mar 40
G-AAUE	42/2	10 Jul 31	Hadrian	Taken over by B.O.A.C. 1940

Regn.	MSN	Date of C of A	Name	Remarks and Disposal
H.P.45 (Hercales Class) (or H.P.42E)				
G-AAXC	42/5	31 Aug 31	Heracles	Damaged on landing at Hanworth on 19 June 32. Wrecked in gale at Bristol, 19 Mar 40
G-AAXD	42/6	13 Nov 31	Horatius	Wrecked in forced landing at Tiverton, Devon, 7 Nov 39
G-AAXE	42/7	10 Dec 31	Hengist	Converted to H.P.42 standard. Destroyed by fire at Karachi, 31 May 37
G-AAXF	42/8	31 Dec 31	Helena	Converted to H.P.42. Impressed into military service as AS983

Luxury Aloft

Good-natured humorists would talk about the H.P.42s "built-in headwinds" — a reference to the drag caused by the big wings and the anything-but-stream-lined structure. But in clear air it was as steady as the Rock of Gibraltar, even though cynics said that the latter was just as fast. The air-travelling public loved the sheer luxury of the cabins, the like of which had never been seen before in an aeroplane. Never mind the headwinds or the leisurely pace, they loved the comfort, the meals, and to be waited on with style.

The Forward Saloon of the H.P.42

The After Saloon of the H.P.42

The crew had never had such comfort

Though slow and ungainly by later, more modern, standards, Imperial's eight H.P. 42s had a perfect safety record during eight years of regular service in Europe and the Middle East. Its design allowed passengers to board without the aid of elaborate steps.

The wheels of the H.P.42 were big enough for a man to get inside the tyre — although there is no record of anyone doing so.

Behold: a True Air Liner

Imperial Airways excelled in its publicity and promotion during the 1930s, with detailed artistic drawings such as these, available for travel agents and many a picture to be framed as a souvenir of an eventful journey. The Head of Publicity was C.F. Snowden Gamble and on the staff was John Stroud, who was to become the doyen of British air transport writers and authors. The splendid coloured cutaway drawings, of which the H.P.42 on this page is a prime example, also featured the "Speedbird" insignia, designed by Thèyre Lee-Elliott.

Early in 1931, Imperial Airways introduced what was to become a famous insignia of the British national flag carrier overseas. At first simply used for luggage labels, the "Speedbird" was adopted as a widely-used symbol, but was not painted on Imperial's Aircraft until 1939, on the de Havilland D.H.91 Albatross.

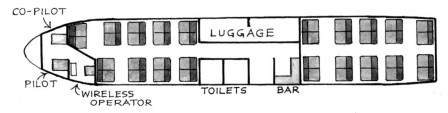

Layout of H.P.42 (Western Type)

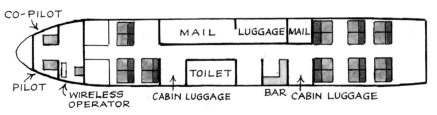

Layout of H.P.42 (Eastern Type)

Cape to Cairo (mostly) by

AFRICAN SERVICE

ENGLAND—EGYPT, EAST AFRICA, SOUTH AFRICA
Service in force from 1 Mar. 1933 until further notice

	Departure and Arrival Times (Local Standard)			Miles Port to Port	Miles from London
Airway Terminus, Victoria, London, S.W.1	dep.	Wed.	11.45		
Air Port of London, Croydon, England	dep.	,,	12.30		
Paris, Gare de Lyon, France 🚂🚌	dep.	,,	*21.30	225	225
Paris to Brindisi 🚂🚌		Thurs.			
Brindisi, Italy	arr.	Fri.	Morn.	1147	1372
,,	dep.	,,	11.30		
Athens, Greece 🛥	arr.	,,	Aftn.	380	1752
,,	dep.	Sat.	07.00		
Alexandria, Egypt 🚌	arr.	,,	Aftn.	580	2332
Cairo ,,	arr.	,,	Even.	125	2457
,,	dep.	Sun.	07.30		
Assiut ,,	dep.	,,	10.30	205	2662
Assuan ,,	dep.	,,	14.15	265	2927
Wadi Halfa, Anglo-Egypt-Sudan 🛥	arr.	,,	Even.	190	3117
,,	dep.	Mon.	05.00		
Atbara ,,	dep.	,,	10.20	344	3461
Khartoum ,, 🛥	arr.	,,	Aftn.	177	3638
,,	dep.	Tues.	05.00		
Kosti ,,	dep.	,,	07.45	180	3818
Malakal ,, 🛥	dep.	,,	11.45	270	4088
Juba ,,	arr.	,,	Aftn.	375	4463
,,	dep.	Wed.	05.00		
Entebbe, Uganda ‡	dep.	,,	10.40	370	4833
Kisumu, Kenya Colony	dep.	,,	14.30	150	4983
Nairobi ,, 🛥	arr.	,,	Even.	185	5168
,,	dep.	Thurs.	07.30		
Moshi, Tanganyika Territory†	dep.	,,	10.05	160	5328
Dodoma ,,	dep.	,,	13.35	230	5558
Mbeya ,, 🛥	arr.	,,	Even.	250	5808
,,	dep.	Fri.	07.10		
Mpika, N. Rhodesia	dep.	,,	09.30	255	6063
Broken Hill ,,	dep.	,,	13.15	270	6333
Salisbury, S. Rhodesia 🛥	arr.	,,	Even.	300	6633
,,	dep.	Sat.	07.00		
Bulawayo ,,	dep.	,,	10.25	240	6873
Pietersburg, Transvaal	dep.	,,	14.25	270	7143
Johannesburg ,, 🛥	arr.	,,	Even.	180	7323
,,	dep.	Sun.	06.00		
Kimberley, Cape Province	dep.	,,	09.40	270	7593
Victoria West ,,	dep.	,,	12.40	215	7808
Cape Town ,,	arr.	,,	Even.	340	8148

SOUTH AFRICA, EAST AFRICA, EGYPT—ENGLAND
Service in force from 1 Mar. 1933 until further notice

	Departure and Arrival Times (Local Standard)			Miles Port to Port	Miles from C.Town
Cape Town, Cape Province	dep.	Wed.	06.30		
Victoria West ,,	dep.	,,	11.20	340	340
Kimberley ,,	dep.	,,	14.35	215	555
Johannesburg, T'svaal 🛥	arr.	,,	Even.	270	825
,,	dep.	Thurs.	07.00		
Pietersburg ,,	dep.	,,	09.55	180	1005
Bulawayo, S. Rhodesia	dep.	,,	13.55	270	1275
Salisbury ,,	arr.	,,	Even.	240	1515
,,	dep.	Fri.	05.45		
Broken Hill, N. Rhodesia	dep.	,,	09.55	300	1815
Mpika ,,	dep.	,,	13.40	270	2085
Mbeya, Tanganyika T. 🛥	arr.	,,	Even.	255	2340
,,	dep.	Sat.	07.30		
Dodoma ,,	dep.	,,	11.25	250	2590
Moshi ,, †	dep.	,,	14.45	230	2820
Nairobi, Kenya Colony 🛥	arr.	,,	Even.	160	2980
,,	dep.	Sun.	06.45		
Kisumu ,,	dep.	,,	10.30	185	3165
Entebbe, Uganda ‡	dep.	,,	12.45	150	3315
Juba, A.-E.-Sudan 🛥	arr.	,,	Even.	370	3685
,,	dep.	Mon.	05.00		
Malakal ,,	dep.	,,	11.10	375	4060
Kosti ,,	dep.	,,	15.45	270	4330
Khartoum ,, 🛥	arr.	,,	Even.	180	4510
,,	dep.	Tues.	07.30		
Atbara ,,	dep.	,,	11.00	177	4687
Wadi Halfa ,, 🛥	arr.	,,	Even.	344	5031
,,	dep.	Wed.	06.00		
Assuan, Egypt	dep.	,,	09.15	190	5221
Assiut ,,	dep.	,,	13.15	265	5486
Cairo ,, 🛥	arr.	,,	Aftn.	205	5691
,,	dep.	Thurs.	06.30		
Alexandria ,, 🚌	dep.	,,	08.30	125	5816
Athens, Greece 🛥	arr.	,,	Even.	580	6396
,,	dep.	Fri.	07.30		
Brindisi, Italy 🛥	arr.	,,	Morn.	380	6776
,,	dep.	,,	Even.		
,, to Paris 🚂🚌		Sat.			
Paris, Gare de Lyon, France	arr.	Sun.	Morn.	1147	7923
Air Port of Paris, Le Bourget	dep.	,,	09.00		
Air Port of London, Croydon	arr.	,,	Morn.	225	8148
Airway Terminus, Victoria, London, S.W.1	arr.	,,	,,		

🛥 = A passenger spends the night in bed at this port or in the train
🚌 = by rail
† = This call may be made alternatively at Arusha, according to the prevailing circumstances
* = On and after 29 March this train will leave at 22.25 hours
‡ = This call may be made alternatively at Kampala according to the prevailing circumstances

N.B. Passengers for destinations on the Empire routes may travel by any of the Company's services to Paris, leaving the Air Port of London, Croydon, before 16.30 hours on the day for which their ticket is valid. Passengers should not travel by the evening service as connexion with the train leaving Paris cannot be guaranteed

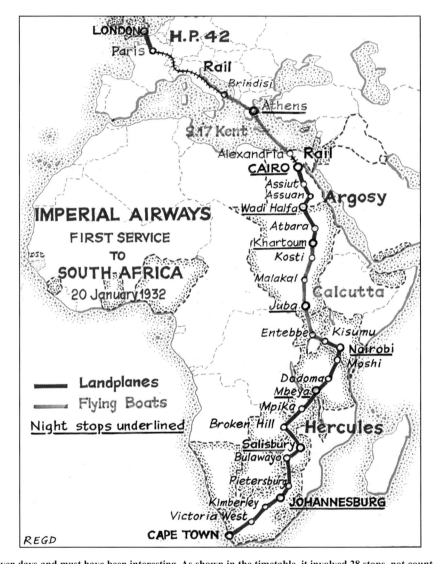

IMPERIAL AIRWAYS FIRST SERVICE TO SOUTH-AFRICA 20 January 1932

— Landplanes
— Flying Boats
Night stops underlined

Finally, on 20 June 1932, the Imperial Airways service was extended to South Africa. The journey took eleven days and must have been interesting. As shown in the timetable, it involved 28 stops, not counting the non-scheduled ones, and two railway connections. Five types of aircraft were used: H.P.42s to Paris, Short Kents across the Mediterranean, Argosies from Cairo to Khartoum, onwards by Calcuttas to Kisumu, and (at first) D.H.66 Hercules to Cape Town, replaced by Atalantas early in 1933. With scenic views of the Nile, Kilimanjaro, and the Victoria Falls, this would constitute an attractive inclusive package tour today.

Armstrong Whitworth A.W.XV Atalanta Class

9–11 seats • 130 mph

Imperial Airways needed a sturdy aircraft that could bear the brunt of the high temperatures, high altitudes, and unprepared airfield strips of eastern and central Africa, en route to South Africa. With "four-engined safety" clearly in mind, the airline ordered its first monoplane, the Armstrong Whitworth A.W. XV, which soon became known as the Atalanta Class. Designed by John Lloyd, it made its first scheduled flight, to Brussels and Cologne, on 26 September 1932.

With its monoplane design, and with spats, enclosing the wheels, it was the fastest in the fleet, cruising at 120–130 mph. It supported and then replaced the H.P.42 and the D.H.66 Hercules on the African route. During the summer of 1932, it also made three special flights from Croydon to Cherbourg, to connect with the *Empress of Britain* trans-Atlantic ocean liner. The African climate required leather and wood rather than the upholstery on the London-Paris route.

The big Handley Pages received most of the popular attention, but the Atalantas deserved more credit than was granted to them as they performed sterling work along the air arteries of the Empire. On 29 May 1933, Major Brackley left Croydon in *Astraea* on a proving flight to Australia. When Indian Trans-Continental Airways was formed on 21 June 1933, its fleet consisted of two Atalantas (see fleet list). The prototype, renamed *Arethusa*, inaugurated the first Indian route extension to Calcutta, and when the air mail route to Australia was opened on 8 December 1934, an Atalanta made the vital non-stop crossing of the Timor Sea (then considered to be a formidable challenge to heavier-than-air range capabilities).

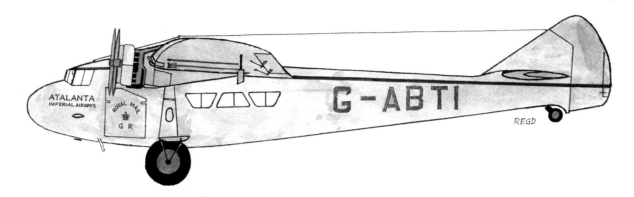

Engine	Armstrong Siddeley Double Mongoose/Serval
	340 hp x 4
MGTOW	21,000 lb.
Max. Range	400 miles
Length	72 feet
Span	90 feet

Size comparison with the Handley Page H.P. 42 (p.37)

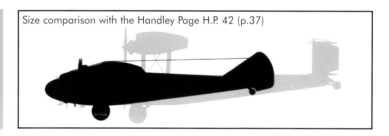

Last of the line, Aurora, *pictured at Croydon Airport, possibly just before being flown to India for service in the sub-continent.*

The Andromeda *pictured at Moshi, Tanganyika, with Africa's highest mountain, Kilimanjaro in the background.*

THE ARMSTRONG WHITWORTH XV ATALANTA FLEET

Regn.	MSN	Date of C of A	Name	Remarks and Disposal
G-ABPI	A.W.740	15 Aug 32	Atalanta	Damaged, October 1932 at Coventry; rebuilt as VT-AEF *Arethusa* for Indian Trans-Continental Airways
G-ABTG	A.W.785	12 Sep 32	Amalthea	Crashed at Kisumu, 27 Jul 38
G-ABTH	A.W.741	27 Sep 32	Andromeda	Retired, June 39
G-ABTI	A.W.742	2 Jan 33	Atalanta	To B.O.A.C., 1940
G-ABTJ	A.W.743	18 Jan 33	Artemus	To B.O.A.C., 1940
G-ABTK	A.W.744	18 Mar 33	Athena	Destroyed by fire at Delhi, 29 Sep 36
G-ABTL	A.W.784	4 Apr 33	Astraea	To B.O.A.C.,1940
G-ABTM	A.W.786	20 Apr 33	Aurora	To Indian Trans-Continental Airways as VT-AEG

Trailblazer to Australia

As related on page 41, the Atalanta class fleet was soon busy as it came into service. Historian John Stroud has recalled that while the inaugural service to South Africa was achieved — somewhat laboriously, as indicated in the timetable and map on page 40, the return journey, starting from Cape Town on 27 January 1932, was plagued with misfortune. Most of the problems were with the D.H.66 Hercules. After G-AAJH *City of Basra* took over from G-AARY *City of Karachi* at Johannesburg, it crashed at Salisbury on 29 January. G-EBMX *City of Delhi* took over, but also crashed at Broken Hill on the same day. The mail eventually arrived at Nairobi in G-EBMY City of Baghdad on 3 February.

The Atalantas thus seem to have arrived just in time; and it was fortunate for Imperial Airways that they became available just as the Hercules were badly in need of reinforcement. On 5 January 1933, G-ABTI Atalanta left Croydon and flew all the way to Cape Town, arriving on 14 February, and soon afterwards the type replaced the Hercules entirely on the South African route south of Kisumu.

On 29 May G-ABTL *Astraea*, as already mentioned, flew to Australia, reaching Brisbane on 23 June. It then flew to Sydney, Canberra, and Melbourne, and returned to Calcutta on 16 July. Two days later, it went into scheduled service on the trans-Indian route to Karachi. This route had already been inaugurated (see page 41) and on 23 September it was extended to Rangoon, with the first return flight leaving on 2 October. By the end of the year, a further extension reached Singapore on 9 December, returning on the last day of 1933.

A year later, the Armstrong Whitworth four-engined airliner was in the news once again. On 8 December 1934, Imperial Airways opened a regular air mail service to Australia, the necessary formalities of territorial rights having been satisfied there by the formation of Qantas Empire Airways (Q.E.A.) to operate east of Singapore. But until February 1935, when the Australians obtained their own four-engined type, the D.H. 86 Express, to cross the Timor Sea, the route depended on the Atalantas.

Travelling in comfort, air travelers to South Africa were able to see things from the air that no-one had ever seen before, for example (left) wild elephants, (centre) the Murchison Falls in Uganda, and (right) the destination city, Cape Town, at the foot of Table Mountain.

An Empire Network

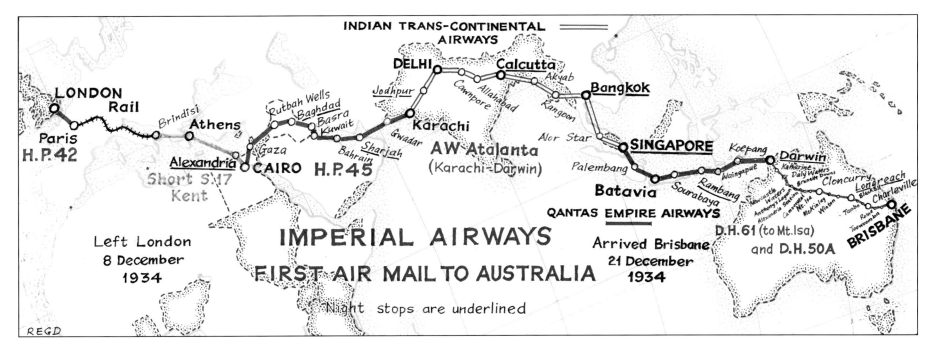

By the mid-1930s, Imperial Airways could at last point to the foundations of a route network that could link all the dominions and most of the colonies, protectorates and mandated territories in the eastern hemisphere. This had been fashioned by a conservative approach in aircraft technology, as the air travelling public was essentially affluent and more interested in comfort and cabin amenities than speed. To reach India, South Africa, or Australia, any air service was far quicker than the fastest ocean liners.

The British flag carrier also had to contend with a realistic recognition of the "self-governing" aspects of the defined dominion status, and a continuous through route to Australia was completed only after negotiations with India and Australia that led to the establishment of indigenous airlines, jointly owned or technically assisted by Imperial. South Africa also took over the final domestic stages of the Cape Town route.

Several years also were to pass before Imperial's airliners were able to fly without hindrance across Europe, but an all-air route was finally inaugurated in December 1934. This was achieved only by overcoming technical problems as well as the diplomatic hurdles. As vividly illustrated by the map on this page, in its determination to fly the mails to Australia before Christmas, Imperial's inauguration was almost a triumph over adversity. On 8 December, Captain Walters flew the H.P.42 *G-AAXE Hengist* all the way to Karachi; but this was an exceptional delivery flight for the Middle East service; subsequently the regular service was as shown on the map. Attempts were made to eliminate the trans-European rail segment; but this was not satisfactorily accomplished until the introduction of the Empire boats in 1937.

The dependence on the Atalanta landplanes has already been observed on page 42. Two of these sturdy aircraft, *G-ABTL Astraea* and *VT-AEF Arethusa* (of Indian Trans-

Continental Airways) carried the mail onwards as far as Singapore. The newly-formed Qantas Empire Airways took over from there with the D.H. 61 Giant Moth *VH-UJC Diana* and the *D.H.50J Hippomenes*; but *Diana* was damaged at Camooweal and the Hippomenes handed over to D.H.50A *VH-UJS* for the final leg of the mail delivery to Darwin on 21 December.

This was acclaimed as a great step forward in Britain's air mail and passenger service ambitions for the Empire (the mail sacks contained letters from the Royal Family) but the event ended incongruously. The D.H.50A was only marginally different from the same aeroplane that had carried Sir Alan Cobham to Australia in 1926 (see page 21). In spite of much defensive posturing in official circles in London, the writing was clearly on the wall. Fortunately for the future progress of British commercial aviation, the officials could read the writing, and something was done about it (see page 76).

Short L.17 (Scylla/Syrinx)

39 seats • 105 mph

The first landplane version of the **Short S.17 Kent** Class flying boats (see page 36), the *Scylla*, G-ACJJ, made its first flight on 26 March 1934. The choice seemed unusual, as the size, performance, and comfort standards were almost identical with those of the well-tried Handley Page H.P.45, which were well-established on the London-Paris route. Certainly the Kents had given a good account of themselves by crossing the Mediterranean with fewer stops than the Calcuttas or the Singapores. And there may have been some advantage in maintenance and spares provisioning, as the S.17 and the L.17 had much in construction commonality.

The *Scylla* went into service on 16 May 1934, and did not enjoy an incident-free record. In August, on landing at Le Bourget, the pilot forgot to unlock the wheel brakes (which were applied during flight, to prevent vibration-generating rotation) and the aircraft stood on its nose. All the passengers — seat-belts were not in vogue during the 100-mph 1930s — ended up in a heap at the nose-end of the cabin, together with the contents of the bar. The *Syrinx*, which made its first flight on 17 May of the same year, met a worse fate at Brussels, in November 1935, fortunately when parked outside with nobody inside. It was turned upside-down in a gale, with predictable results. The pieces were returned to Rochester by barge and rebuilt. After retirement in 1940, the *Syclla* had the same experience, at Drem, in Scotland, with Nature helping the process of scrapping the aircraft.

Aircraft with such large wing areas, especially biplanes (which the Germans and Americans had consigned to museums and history by this time) were dangerously vulnerable to high winds. Even in flight, except in calm weather, they used to wallow "like a fish out of water." The pilots, somewhat ungenerously, said that it was like "flying a block of flats."

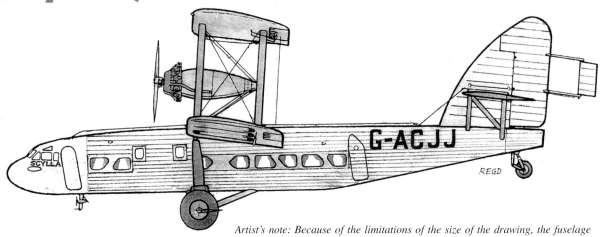

Artist's note: Because of the limitations of the size of the drawing, the fuselage corrugations are not drawn exactly to scale.

Engine	Bristol Juniper
	555 hp x 4
MGTOW	33,500 lb.
Max. Range	450 miles
Length	84 feet
Span	113 feet

Size comparison with the Handley Page H.P. 42 (p.37)

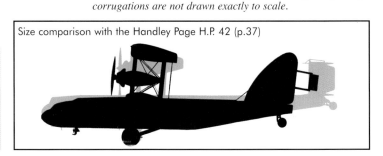

THE SHORT L.17 SCYLLA CLASS FLEET

Regn.	MSN	Date of C of A	Name	Remarks and Disposal
G-ACJJ	S.768	1 May 34	*Scylla*	To Royal Air Force, March 1940 crashed at Drem, Scotland, 14 April 1940
G-ACJK	S.769	8 Jun 34	*Syrinx*	To Royal Air Force, March 1940 broken up at Exeter 1940

The *Scylla* in flight.

The engineer inspecting the third engine shows the size of the *Syrinx*.

Comfort before Speed

This publicity picture of the Short *Scylla*, like the one of the Handley Page big biplane (page 39), illustrates why Imperial Airways dominated the cross-Channel route to Paris during the 1930s. Air France had introduced the 150-mph Wibault 282 in 1933 and the Potez 62 monoplanes soon afterwards; but these were smaller aircraft, seating 10 and 14 passengers respectively.

The discriminating clientèle who patronized the air route willingly exchanged the twenty minutes saving in flying time for the five-course meals offered in Imperial's luxurious cabins in the larger aircraft. For the airline, however, a certain pride was involved, and the years of the biplane were numbered. But even with their "built-in headwinds," the 100-mph giants of their time more than held their own against the competition until only a few months before the outbreak of the Second World War in 1939. Only two of the Scylla class were built but they had much commonality with the Short Kent class (page 36).

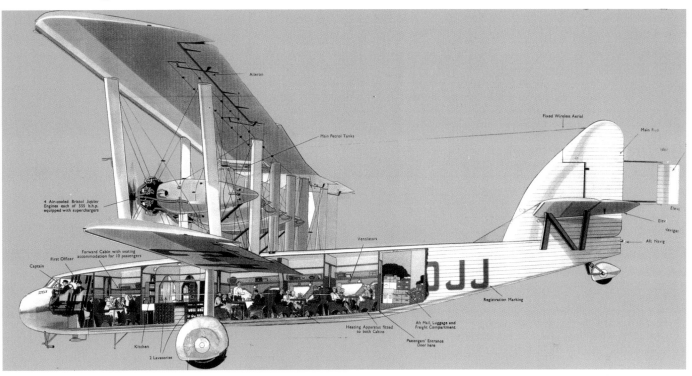

During the early days of regular commercial flying, to view places from the air was quite a novelty. On the left is La Cité in Paris, normally seen only from the river level; on the right is the Arch of Ctesiphon, near Baghdad rarely seen at all until Imperial Airways opened up the route to India.

Taking to the Air

During the early 1930s, when Imperial Airways was feeling its way into the basic elements of operating an airline network, the records are clear concerning the aeroplanes operated, the routes developed, the people involved, and the techniques of flying improved. But the statistics and the photographs do not show another important feature of the state of commercial aviation at that time. This was the almost negligible part that it played in lives of ordinary people. The cost of operating the relatively primitive transport aeroplanes was such that high fares had to be paid by the passengers; and by definition, the only people who could afford to fly at all were in the higher income strata; and even they were not too enamoured at the idea of taking to the air, which was regarded as only marginally safe.

Thus, although the pictures and the maps looked impressive, the output did not reflect the true picture. In 1931–2, for example, Imperial Airways carried a total of only 34,000 passengers in the whole year — an average of less than 100 per day, or the capacity of a large commuter aeroplane today. The luxury of the Handley Page upholstered cabins matched those of the cabins of the *Queen Mary*, and the volume of potential business was limited to the same percentage of the privileged few who enjoyed such levels of travel comfort.

Imperial Airways took steps to try to popularize the idea of taking to the air; and although the effect on its operations was negligible, it was not for the want of trying; and some of its efforts were to take their place as some of the most advanced examples of promotion in airline history.

The fares for the special flights described on this page appear to be cheap by today's standards. But the cost of an afternoon tea flight over London was about the same as an average working man's weekly wage. The day trip to le Touquet was twice that amount. While attractive to those who could afford such special luxuries, the pleasures of air transport had not yet reached the pockets of the vast majority of the public, even those for whom travel was necessary in their work, for emergencies, or even celebratory occasions.

Imperial Airways put the new Handley Pages to good use. Realising that there were periods when the demand for flights to Paris was slight, it offered afternoon joy-rides over London, with a traditional tea service, and the ability to "move about in the cabins — an amenity that only the big biplanes could offer. Passengers were invited to view the Houses of Parliament, Buckingham Palace, Trafalgar Square, St. Paul's Cathedral, and the Tower of London. The fare was £1.10.0, including tea. This route is no longer operated.

Imperial Airways, with considerable initiative, had started flights to le Touquet (via the nearby airfield at Berck-sur-Mer) during summer weekends as early as 15 July 1927. By the early 1930s, these were popular enough to justify the use of the big Handley Page H.P.45s. The cheerful cover drawing of this leaflet invites the traveller to Gaiety, Casino, Tennis, Fun, Bathing, Sunshine, Golf, Polo, Dancing, and Roulette. The Sunday day return fare was £3.15.0, and included dinner on the return flight. Passports were not required.

The Second Line

In its efforts to expand its activities on all fronts of aviation, Imperial Airways tried to introduce smaller aircraft, partly to operate over routes with low traffic demand, partly for special charters, and partly for air taxi work. Two aircraft seemed to meet the specification requirements, which in essence were: fewer than ten seats but up to 50 percent faster than the 38-seat 100-mph Handley Page and Short biplanes used on the routes to the Continent.

First of these was the seven-seat **Boulton & Paul P.71A**, or Imperial's **Boadicea** Class, named after the first aircraft, *Boadicea*, which was delivered in January 1935. *Britomart* was delivered shortly thereafter (see overleaf). Although speedier than Imperial's other aircraft, and used almost entirely for air taxi work, the total fleet of two did not, as the tabulation shows, have a happy career, even though it was featured on the airline's handsome poster-sized publicity folders.

The other "second-line" airliner, also well-publicized, was the four-seat **Avro 652**, or Imperial's **Avalon** Class. The basic design was distantly derived from the Fokker monoplane tradition, but the wing was through the lower section of the fuselage, not on the top. Designer Roy Chadwick's main innovation was the inclusion of a retractable undercarriage. This was Imperial's first, indeed, Britain's first, and even though the pilots sometimes forgot to lower it (this took two minutes of hard work) the 652 was resilient and versatile. It had a good turn of speed, more than 160 mph, and it was even looped — though not with paying passengers.

Avalon was delivered on 11 March 1935 and was also used for air taxi flights. The sister ship, *Ava*, opened, on 28 April, the air mail link from Paris to Brindisi, via Marseilles and Rome. This service, operated only intermittently in parallel with the train, was taken over by the de Havilland D.H. 89 Diana Class and became redundant when the Empire boats were introduced in January 1937.

THE AVRO 652 AVALON CLASS FLEET

Regn.	MSN	Date of C of A	Name	Remarks and Disposal
G-ACRM	698	1 Mar 35	*Avalon*	To Air Service Training July 38
G-ACRN	699	8 Mar 35	*Avatar*	Renamed *Avra*; to Air Service Training, July 38

4 seats • 165 mph

Avro 652

Note: The Avro 652 Avalon was the first British twin-engined aircraft to have a retractable undercarriage/landing gear.

Engine	Armstrong Siddeley Cheetah (290 hp x 2)
MGTOW	7,500 lb.
Max. Range	750 miles
Length	42 feet
Span	56 feet

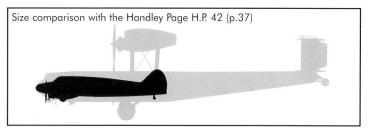

Size comparison with the Handley Page H.P. 42 (p.37)

Although it did not follow the stressed-skin construction of the pioneering American Boeing 247, the Avro 652 did have its engines faired into the wing; and with its retractable undercarriage, its 165 mph cruising speed was Imperial Airways's fastest until the advent of the Empire flying boats.

Last of the Biplanes

Boulton & Paul P. 71A Boadicea

The early 1930s witnessed the dying years of adherence to the biplane design principle. Until the outbreak of the Second World War in 1939, the big Handley Page H.P.45s and the Short L.17s were successful on short-haul routes to the Continent because they were luxuriously appointed and the 100-mph speed was not a serious disadvantage against the train and ferry-boat competition across the English Channel. For the second-line market — for charter work or for services with low traffic demand, Imperial tried one more biplane type. Interestingly, there was no provision for seat-belts. The **Boulton & Paul P.71A**, however, was not a success, even though its 150-mph speed at first showed promise. Delivered to Imperial at the beginning of 1935, both aircraft were lost within two years.

The Boadicea's cabin was practical, if somewhat austere.

Engine	Armstrong Siddeley Jaguar (490 hp x 2)
MGTOW	9,500 lb.
Max. Range	600 miles
Length	44 feet
Span	54 feet

Size comparison with the Handley Page H.P. 42 (p.37)

THE BOULTON & PAUL P. 71A BOADICEA CLASS FLEET

Regn.	MSN	Date of C of A	Name	Remarks and Disposal
G-ACOX	P.71A-1	19 Sep 34	Boadicea	Lost in the English Channel, 25 Sep 36
G-ACOY	P.71A-2	14 Oct 34	Britomart	Crash Landing at Brussels, 25 Oct 35

Testing the Waters

At the beginning of the 1930s, the prospects for internal British airlines to risk being formed, much less get under way, were bleak. Imperial Airways was able to keep going only because it was subsidized by government appropriations, and was assisted in many other ways in the provision of the necessary infrastructure, both at home and abroad. Within the British Isles there was little encouragement. The politicians were not interested; investors correctly regarded air transport, in 1930, as a sure way to lose its collective shirt; and the public had little or no interest, partly because aeroplanes did not appear to be better than trains, and partly because the aviation environment, with its daredevil air displays and the urge for breaking records, suggested a certain risk.

Whilte this public scepticism did not translate into a wide-spread fear of flying, the suggestion of danger was not misplaced, as aeroplane crashes and other losses were not uncommon. If not of "stick-and-string," i.e., wood-and-fabric, construction, the machines of the day, even with tubular steel frames, not exactly robust. More important, they were small, so that they could not carry enough fuel to fly more than a few hundred miles at best, or they could not carry more than two or three people in addition to the pilot. And most of them, invariably single-engined, could, even then, only manage either one or the other, but not both. One advantage, however, was that, in good weather, they could land at and take off from almost any level field which had about 500 yards of clear space without any obstructions.

The aspirant airline promoters were thus faced with a fundamental problem: while the small aircraft were not outrageously expensive, their revenue-earning potential was small. They could not fly enough people over a distance for which high enough fares could be charged to recoup the costs of operations. And the basic laws of demographics meant that, almost by definition, the only places with enough people who could afford the necessary high fares were the big cities such as Birmingham, Manchester, and Liverpool in England, and Glasgow and Edinburgh in Scotland. The trouble was that these cities were served very well by the main line railways; and the airlines could not offer

effective competition to the trains, at least not until better aeroplanes came along.

The first courageous individuals who took fare-paying passengers into the air from one place to another were therefore restricted by geography in the available opportunities to try their luck. These were localities where the railways could serve only by circuitous routes, notably the river esturaries; and the offshore islands where the sea routes were slow and required intermodal transfers. These are shown on the map. Other opportunities were where the railways' service was handicapped by difficult terrain, and unavoidably slow — in short, the Highlands of Scotland.

Curiously, of all the estuarial opportunities, the first experiment was across a stretch of water that seemed not to have an adequate population base to justify the risk. Unlike more obvious connections such as across the Thames Estuary, the Severn, or the Humber, where sizable separated populations, the first demonstration of what an aeroplane could do was across the Wash. Skegness had a resident population of barely 10,000 and Hunstanton less than 5,000; but the summer visitors at the two seaside resorts multiplied these figures several times over. In the aerial context, this was the equivalent of the biblical cloud no bigger than a man's hand, and it would lead to much more.

THE ENGLISH ESTUARIES

Estuary	City Pairs (and population)	Remarks
Humber	Hull (300,000) Grimsby (80,000)	Lincolnshire resorts (Cleethorpes, Mablethorpes, etc.)
The Wash	Skegness (10,000) Hunstanton (5,000)	Summer Holiday resorts only
Thames Estuary	Southend-on-Sea (150,000) Medway towns (150,000)	Kent resorts (Margate, Ramsgate, etc.)
Severn Estuary	Cardiff (and nearby South Wales, Newport) (350,000) Bristol (450,000)	Someset resort (Weston-super-Mare)
Mersey	Liverpool (800,000) Birkenhead, etc. (200,000)	Mersey Road Tunnel opened 1934

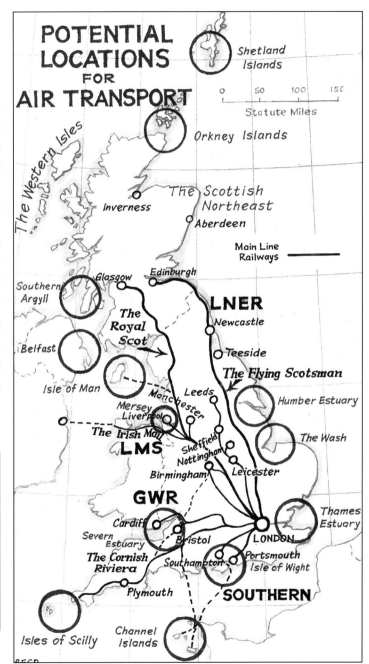

POTENTIAL LOCATIONS FOR AIR TRANSPORT

The First British Domestic Routes

Any incentive to start airline routes in the British Isles during the 1920s was not in evidence. Excellent express train services, connected London with all the main English cities within three or four hours. Even Scotland's Edinburgh and Glasgow, 400 miles distant, were only five or six hours away by the *Flying Scotsman* or the *Royal Scot*. Dublin was reached by the *Irish Mail* and a rapid overnight ship from Holyhead, and during the summer, the *Cornish Riviera* took Londoners to the southwestern sunshine. But towards the end of the decade, the railways began to show signs of interest in the possibility of taking to the air.

In January 1929 the Great Western Railways General Manager, Sir Felix Pole, met Imperial's General Manager, George Woods Humphery, to discuss cooperation, as yet undefined. At the same time, the Southern Railway had, through nominees, been quietly buying shares in Imperial. Air powers to the railways were given the royal assent on 10 May 1929. Imperial and the Southern Railway reached agreement to ensure that the railway would not act in any way to each other's disadvantage. During the next three years, railway interest in air transport lay dormant, but in 1932, a new element appeared on the scene: the first domestic air services of substance in Great Britain by independent entrepreneurs.

This had been generated by developments in road transport. Long-distance motor-coach services had proliferated and during the summer seasons could take vacationers to the seaside resorts more cheaply than could the railways. But in 1931, the government curbed the unrestricted profusion of coach companies, and directed the road transport industry to organize itself into regional groups. Several motor coach pio-

neers then moved into air transport. They were the pioneers of a British domestic airline industry.

The proverbial cloud no bigger than a man's hand appeared during the summer of 1931, when **Michael Scott** operated a short route across the Wash. This was between two holiday resorts and was a popular local novelty (see page 51).

Then during 1932, other pioneer airlines emerged from companies that had been engaged in offering joy-rides at seaside resorts, or from others operating air surveys or special charters with small aeroplanes across short stretches of water, within the limited range of the flying equipment, and where the only competition was by boats. (see page 53)

The one notable exception was **Hillman Saloon Coaches and Airways**, founded by **Edward Hillman**, a colourful ex-taxi-driver, who, only three years previously, had started

a highly successful bus company to take Londoners to the Essex beaches. On 1 April 1932, he opened service from a small rented field near Romford, on the northeastern fringe of London to Clacton, Essex (see pages 56–57).

Two other pioneering airlines deserve special mention. **Portsmouth, Southsea and Isle of Wight Aviation** offered cheap flights across Spithead, and carried almost 2,500 passengers in 1932 — more than all the other companies combined (see page 68). **Norman Edgar** successfully launched a service, also with the little Puss Moths, across the Severn Estuary, linking Cardiff with Bristol.

These little airlines were all unsubsidized, and they were metaphorically testing the waters — almost literally, as most routes were over water. During the following year, they took the plunge, and in 1933, Imperial Airways itself, though charged with developing only Empire routes, became involved.

The railways also had an interest in Scottish Motor Transport. *(see page 52)*

Britain's first rail-air line, organised by the Great Western Railway, was opened by the inauguration of a regular combined service from Cardiff to Torquay/and Teignmouth (Haldon Aerodrome). The journey took 45 minutes against the train time of four hours. The fares were £3 single, and £5 return.

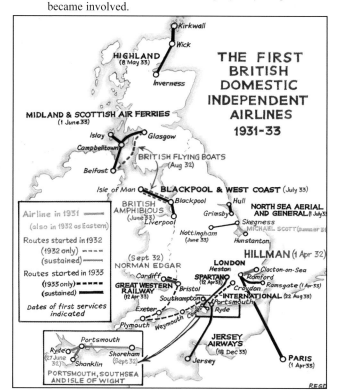

THE FIRST BRITISH DOMESTIC INDEPENDENT AIRLINES 1931-33

A Modest Beginning

Long forgotten in the annals of British domestic air transport history (except by John Stroud), **Michael Scott** must be remembered as the first entrepreneur to carry out what was then regarded as a bold experiment: to use aeroplanes to carry passengers on a regular route within the British Isles without any form of support or subsidy from the Government or from any other source. During the summer of 1931, when nobody else had dared to try, he began an air ferry service across the Wash, a distance of 17 miles, between Skegness and Hunstanton.

Scott's flights took about ten minutes compared to the two-hour circuitous surface route which was 60 miles by road. To go by rail involved involving several changes of train, and took all day. Even so, the natural market was not large, as there was little community of interest between the two places. His clientèle consisted mostly of holiday-makers who, like many others to follow at other seaside resorts, would have flown for the novelty of flying rather than to make a journey. The round-trip fare was £1.00.

De Havilland D.H.80 Puss Moth

Engine	De Havilland Gypsy Major (130 hp)
MGTOW	2,050 lb.
Max. Range	400 miles
Length	25 feet
Span	37 feet

Size comparison with the Handley Page H.P. 42 (p.37)

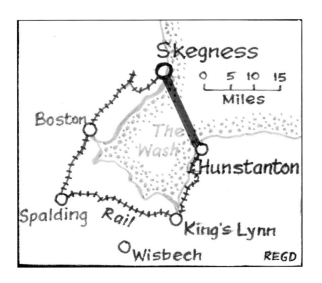

Michael Scott's de Havilland Puss Moth was built to carry two passengers, or, by adjusting the seats, three at the most. This family must have been a tight fit, and the fuel load probably only two or three cans of petrol. G-AAXL (MSN 2010) was certificated on 16 June 1930, and served for two summers until it was destroyed by fire on a sandbank, 5 miles off Hunstanton, on 26 May 1932.

The Pioneer

The tabulation of people and companies on this page lists the early aspirants to enter the risky business of air transport in the early 1930s. They are listed in chronological order of the first recorded services, not the dates of foundation — for several were thought of, some even formed, but never operated. Some tested the market and decided not to enter it. Some lasted a couple of seasons. Some stayed the course and expanded their operations. As mentioned on page 50, almost all the routes were over water, even short distances; some were for the sheer novelty of flying, as in those early days, very few people had even dared to take an aeroplane trip at all.

Because of the vague definitions of what then constituted a regular airline service, and the fact that the promoters were all quite independent and unsubsidized from any government or official source, the qualifications for inclusion in the roll of honour as to "who was first" have to be subjective. In this book, the credit is given to **Michael Scott** (see previous page), who, during the summer of 1931, when no other British internal activity in the air transport category was recorded, made a series of flights across the Wash, a distance of only 17 miles. With no commercial incentive to make such a journey, the passengers must have paid their pound fare just for the fun of it.

A big problem was that, except for contracts from Imperial Airways, very few aeroplanes were built specifically to carry passengers. The two-seater de Havilland D.H. Puss Moth and the four-seater Fox Moth, designed by Arthur Hagg, were the most popular. The pioneers could not survive financially unless a better aeroplane became available, with more seats, and at a reasonable price. A larger, twin engined, D.H. Moth series was just what the embryo British domestic airline industry needed. And this is just what happened.

On 24 November 1932, inspired by one of the bus operators, the D.H. 84 Dragon made its first flight. The full story of this important development is told on page 55. At last the pioneers could move ahead with some degree of confidence.

THE PIONEER INDEPENDENTS, 1931–32
(IN CHRONOLOGICAL ORDER OF DATE OF FIRST SERVICES)

Date	Operator	Routes (and aircraft)	Remarks
Summer 1931	Michael Scott	Skegness-Hunstanton (Puss-Moth G-AAXL)	Fare: £1 return. On 27 February 32, became **Eastern Air Transport**, with daily service, 22 May 1932, Re-opened summer 1933.
March 1932	British Amphibious Airlines	Blackpool-Isle of Man (Saunders-Roe Cutty Sark G-ABBC, *Progress*)	Founded by Messrs Kirston and Mace on 22 February 32. Regular service started in June. Joint bookings with W. Armitage and Sons (Progress buses) for connections to Yorkshire cities. 348 passengers carried by September. Re-opened summer 1933.
1 April 1932	**Hillman Saloon Coaches and Airways**	Romford-Clacton (Puss Moths and Fox Moth)	Founded by Edward (Ted) Hillman, as an extension of his busy bus and coach services from London to East Anglian resorts. Fare £1 return. See pages 54-55.
27 June 1932	**Portsmouth, Southsea and Isle of Wight Aviation** ("The Spithead Express")	Portsmouth-Ryde, Shanklin, Shoreham (Westland Wessex, Fox Moth, Spartan, Monospar)	Four return flights each day to Isle of Wight until 30 September; service to Shoreham, September-November 2,455 passengers during 1932. Services maintained until 1939.
11 July 1932	British Air Navigation Company	Bristol-Cardiff (Fokker F.VIIa G-EBTS, *The Spider*)	Four flights per day, 15 shillings single. Operated one week only, 199 passengers (*The Bristol Evening Times* had operated an experimental service for one week with an Avro Ten chartered from Imperial Airways)
14 Aug 1932	British Flying Boats	Greenock-Belfast (Saunders-Roe Cloud G-ABXW *Cloud of Iona*)	Company registered on 23 June. Chairman was Duke of Montrose; general manager Lord Malcolm Douglas Hamilton. Also Greenock-Belfast 15 August but once-daily service lasted only one week.
26 Sep 1932	**Norman Edgar**	Bristol-Cardiff (Fox Moth G-ABYO)	Twice daily return 12 shillings 6 pence single (See also British Air Navigation, above) 258 passengers carried
Oct 1932	National Flying Services	Hull-Grimsby (Desoutter)	Operated for about one month. Fare: seven shillings single journey.

Note: From 18 July until 31 October 1932, the Scottish Motor Traction Company carried 4,000 passengers, in an extensive program of experimental, survey, and pleasure flights, over various routes in Scotland. Thus by the time Highland Airways started the first scheduled air service in Scotland in May 1933 (see page 51), the S.M.T. had already given the Scots a preview of commercial flying.

Among various aircraft used by the Scottish Motor Traction Company (S.M.T.) was this small Avro Cadet. In its efforts to popularize air travel in Scotland, the company offered what were then called joy-rides. In many parts of the country north of Glasgow and Edinburgh, few aeroplanes had ever been seen, and so quite often the joy was also a thrilling experience. Any person who had taken such a flight was the talk of the town and a news item in the local newspaper.

Cooperation with surface public transport was started in March 1932 by British Amphibious Airlines, using a four-seater Saro Cutty Sark amphibian to cross the Irish Sea to the Isle of Man.

The Curtain Rises

During the year 1932, the aspirant operators were feeling their way into the business of air transport. They were—as most of the initial experimental routes were over water—almost literally testing the waters. The following year, having liked the experience, some of them dived in again, with investment into what would soon become a group of companies that would establish a British domestic airline industry.

A comparison of the tabulation on this page with the one on the page opposite well illustrates the progress made. Much credit must go to Edward "Ted" Hillman, who persuaded Sir Geoffrey de Havilland to build a larger, twin-engined development of the four-seater Fox Moth. The Hillman story is told on pages 54–55. Sufficient to state in this context is that the resultant D.H.84 Dragon changed the course of British domestic airline development. It carried six passengers in a more comfortable cabin, and could carry them further.

Taking advantage of greater faith in the equipment, the airlines started in Scotland and in Lancashire were able to consolidate genuine social services, the former providing a faster link than the ships for mail and goods, as well as for passengers, to the offshore islands; the latter to cater for the holiday-makers of the industrial north of England to the Isle of Man.

The entry of one new operator was significant. The railway companies (the "Big Four"—the Southern, L.M.S., L.N.E.R., and the Great Western) had kept an eye on the potential competition from the aerial developments. In April 1933, borrowing a Westland Wessex from Imperial Airways, the G.W.R. experimented with a cross-country service to take holiday-makers from south Wales and the Midlands to the vacation resorts in Devon. It heralded a major decision by the railways in a case of "if you can't beat 'em, join 'em," the full story of which is told on page 76.

This Blackburn Segrave operated across the Humber estuary during the summer of 1933 for North Sea Aerial and General Transport. It was painted bright red.

THE INDEPENDENT SURVIVORS AND NEWCOMERS, 1933
(IN CHRONOLOGICAL ORDER OF DATE OF FIRST SERVICES)

Date	Operator	Routes (and aircraft)	Remarks
(from 1932)	Hillman (see 1932 tabulation). Became **Edward Henry Hillman** on 8 November 1933.	Romford-Clacton (continued) Romford-Paris (1 April) Romford-Manston (1 April) (see pages 56–57 for details)	"Ted" Hillman opened the first British independent international air service. He sponsored the widely-used D.H.84 Dragon, which set new standards for the British domestic airlines as they became established.
(from 1932)	**Portsmouth, Southsea and Isle of Wight Aviation**	Shoreham-Portsmouth-Ryde-Shanklin (continued) Portsmouth-Bournemouth (17 May) (1 each Westland Wessex, Monospar, Klemm, Puss Moth, 2 Fox Moths)	During the summer, the 5-mile Portsmouth-Ryde segment frequency was 18 round trips per day. 9,640 passengers carried on scheduled flights, 6,283 on other pleasure trips, and 427 on special charters—more than 16,000 in total.
(from 1932)	**Norman Edgar** (Western Airways)	Bristol-Cardiff (continued) (1 DH Dragon, 1 Fox Moth, 3 Puss Moths)	**Norman Edgar** registered as listed on 7 September. Five years later, on 18 Oct 38, renamed **Western Airways**. Services had continued during the 1932-33 winter irregularly. 1,671 passengers carried in 1933.
12, April 1933	Great Western Railway	Cardiff-Teignmouth (serving Torbay)-Plymouth (Westland Wessex, G-AAGW)	Aircraft chartered from Imperial Airways. Route extended to Birmingham, 22 May, but services terminated on 30 September, 714 passengers carried in 1933.
12 April 1933	**Spartan Air Lines**	London-Ryde-Cowes (Spartan Cruiser)	Operated from the new Heston aerodrome, founded by Airwork, in west London. Service ended 2 October, 1,459 passengers carried in 1933.
8 May 1933	**Highland Airways**	Inverness-Wick-Kirkwall (Monospar ST.4 G-ACEW *Inverness*, D.H.84 Dragon)	Founded by Capt. E.E. Fresson. Connected at Inverness with trains from the south. Also Thurso-Wick service but short-lived because of unsafe landing ground. Inverness-Kirkwall fare: £3 single, 1,502 passengers and 6 tons of mail and freight, in 1933.
1 June 1933	**Midland and Scottish Air Ferries**	Glasgow-Campbeltown, Islay, Belfast. Liverpool-Dublin (1 Sept) (2 D.H.84, 4 Fox Moths, 2 Airspeed Ferry, 1 Avro 10, 1 Spartan Arrow, 1 Avro Cadet)	Founded by bus operator **John Sword**. First air service to the Inner Hebrides, and from Great Britain to Ireland. 3,658 passengers and 8 tons of mail and freight in 1933.
June 1933	British Amphibious Air Lines	Blackpool-Isle of Man (Saunders-Roe Cutty Sark)	Re-opened summer service until October. 130 passengers on scheduled service, plus 4,200 on pleasure flights.
June 1933	**Blackpool and West Coast Air Services**	Liverpool-Blackpool-Isle of Man (1 D.H.84, 2 Fox Moths, 1 Avro Avian)	Company formed in March 1933, in association with Olley Air Service. 1,863 passengers in 1933 on scheduled service, plus 19,271 on pleasure flights, and 205 on special charters.
June 1933	Eastern Air Transport	Nottingham-Skegness (D.H. Fox Moth)	**Michael Scott** re-opened his local operation to serve the east Midlands, until September.
1 July 1933	North Sea Aerial and General Transport	Hull-Grimsby (1 Blackburn Segrave and 1 D.H. Fox Moth)	Took over the 1932 service by National Flying Services. Company associated with the Blackburn Aeroplane and Motor Company. Services ended 4 November. 1,300 passengers carried in 1933.
22 Aug 1933	International Airlines	London-Portsmouth-Southampton-Plymouth (Monospars)	Operation ceased after a few weeks. (Route operated in 1934 by Provincial Airways—q.v.)
18 Dec 1933	**Jersey Airways**	Portsmouth-Jersey (D.H. Dragon)	Founded by **W.L. Thurgood**, operator of People's Motor Coach Services, of Ware, Herts. Early services were operated from the beach at St Helier, Jersey, but only at low tide.

The airlines that survived, independently or by merger, to become part of the evolving British domestic airline industry, are shown in bold type.

De Havilland D.H.83 Fox Moth

If the years 1932 and 1933 were the years in which the stage was set for the British domestic airline theatre performance, the year 1934 was to witness the launching of the production, and the stage was set. The aviation aspirant actors had tentatively explored the possibilities of short local airline services. The development of small passenger-carrying aereoplanes combined with the initiatives of the entrepreneur busmen to expand these fragments into a whole cloth to establish a national network.

The properties of the leading actors—the mini-airline promoters—were mainly from Hatfield, Hertfordshire, where the de Havilland company had gained a reputation for reliability when Sir Alan Cobham had, in 1925 and 1926, made his long-distance surveys to the Empire (see pages 20-21). His aircraft then was the **D.H.50** which, though not used extensively in Britain, did find success in Australia, where de Havilland set up an overseas subsidiary. Subsequently, the **D.H.51**, described by Ord-Hume as "too big for a light aircraft and too small for a commercial airline," was, however, the forerunner of the famous series of de Havilland Moths. Hundreds of D.H.82 Tiger Moths were built for private flying, and solved the first of Ord-Hume's descriptive deficiencies..

The first one that tried to solve the latter was the D.H.61 Giant Moth which was also operated in Australia but not in Britain. Then came the D.H.75 Hawk Moth, a two-seater light aeroplane, but this was not a success. But the D.H.80 Puss Moth was a better aeroplane, and partly because two passengers could sit behind the pilot. First flown on 9 September 1929, it made several notable long-distance flights, and was used by some of the early British airline pioneers (see page 50). 260 Puss Moths were built in the U.K., but it was too small to be a complete commercial success.

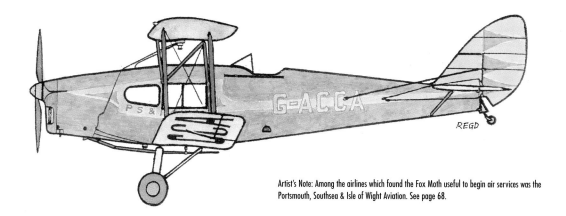

Artist's Note: Among the airlines which found the Fox Moth useful to begin air services was the Portsmouth, Southsea & Isle of Wight Aviation. See page 68.

The de Havilland D.H.83 Fox Moth paved the way for the successful series of de Havilland passenger aircraft which provided most of the aircraft for the independent British airliner fleets of the 1930s. The fuselage was wide enough to take two passengers abreast and thus to be able to carry four altogether. This improvement over the two-seater D.H.80 Puss Moth held out the possibility of a financially viable operation.

Engine	D.H. Gipsy Major (130 hp)
MGTOW	2,050 lb.
Max. Range	300 miles
Length	25 feet
Span	31 feet

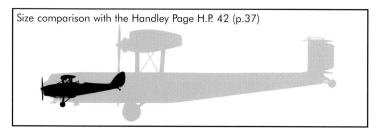

Size comparison with the Handley Page H.P. 42 (p.37)

The D.H. 50 (pages 20–22) was good only for survey or charter work, but de Havilland eased its way back into the design of passenger transport aeroplanes. At the end of 1928 the D.H.75 Hawk Moth, a monoplane, (left) was not a success; but the D.H. 80 Puss Moth (centre) attracted attention as "an occasional 3-seater." 260 were built in the U.K., and among the customers was Edward Hillman, who started his first airline service on Christmas Day, 1931, from his field, east of London, to Clacton-on-Sea. Even better was the 4-seat D.H. 83 Fox Moth. Again, Hillman was the first customer in 1932 (see pages 56–57), while (right) the P.S. & I.O.W. ferry service also used them.

De Havilland D.H.84 Dragon

This aircraft symbolized the turning point in the rapidly-maturing British domestic airline industry. The D.H. 89 Rapide which followed two years later became more famous (see page 77) but it owed its development to the **D.H.84 Dragon**, just as, in the United States, the icon of the 1930s era, the Douglas DC-3, owed its origins to the DC-2.

First called the Dragon Moth, Geoffrey de Havilland himself credited Edward Hillman with the development of this twin-engined variant. Towards the end of 1932, that audacious newcomer to the airline scene approached the Hatfield company, and the manufacturer said later that the design "was largely due to Hillman's far-sighted and courageous action in ordering a small fleet of them 'off the drawing board'." The Iraqi Air Force had also asked for a similar design, but this was Ted Hillman's aeroplane. His instincts had been exactly right, and designer Arthur Hagg added spats on the wheels and Bendix brakes. The performance was better than expected—a feature of aircraft production that was unusual for its time.

Hubert Broad took the Dragon on its first flight on 24 November 1932. It climbed well to 12,000 feet, and carried its six passengers, with their baggage, at what was then the brisk speed of 109 mph, thanks to Frank Halford's two 130 hp Gipsy Major engines. This was a little faster than Imperial Airways's well-upholstered and well-catered for big Handley Pages. Hillman's on-board service and comfort were more austere, but the Dragon did at least have a toilet. The public would cheerfully exchange a five-course meal for the lower fare that Hillman's Airways could offer.

Including those built in Australia by a newly-formed de Havilland subsidiary, more than 200 Dragons were built, and it was the pride of the British domestic airline fleets until its successor, the D.H.89 Dragon Rapide, came along in 1934.

6 seats • 109 mph

De Havilland D.H.84 Dragon

This drawing is, in the British context, as significant as one would be of T.W.A.'s Douglas DC-1 in the United States. It was the prototype of a whole series of successful airliners that would still be flying commercially after the Second World War.

Engine	D.H. Gipsy Major (130 hp x 2)
MGTOW	4,200 lb.
Max. Range	460 miles
Length	34 feet
Span	47 feet

Size comparison with the Handley Page H.P. 42 (p.37)

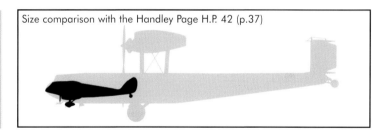

In 1935, Captain Eric Starling flew Ted Hillman's first D.H. 84 Dragon to Aberdeen, where it served Eric Gandar Dower for many years to link the Orkneys and Shetlands with mainland Scotland. It is seen here at Glasgow's Renfrew Airport.

One of John Sword's Midland & Scottish Air Ferries D.H. 84s in flight, Like Edmund Fresson's Highland Airways (page 57) he brought swift air travel to the Island of Islay.

Edward "Ted" Hillman

Edward "Ted" Hillman was the quintessential self-made man. Born in 1890, in Essex, he had grown up in the countryside and had joined the cavalry during the 1914–18 Great War. By the end of that conflict, he had advanced from horses to driving a Rolls-Royce for diplomats. The war over, he continued his driving in taxis, began his own car-hire service, and bought his first motor-coach in 1928. This was a period during which motor-coach travel flourished, as effecient operators could offer lower fares than could the railways. Three years later, he owned at least 200 coaches. He did not believe in paying high wages to his drivers — this was a period of high unemployment — and so his operating costs were low and he could thus offer cheap fares to his clientèle — mainly London's East Enders who sought a day or so at the Essex seaside resorts.

In 1931, the government reorganized the bus and coach industry, creating, among other sweeping changes, the London Passenger Transport Board (L.P.T.B.). Hillman received £145,000 in compensation for the compulsory purchase of his bus service. In November of that year, he added the word Airways to the name of his coach company and on 1 April 1932 he started his first scheduled air service, still in his home county, from Romford to Clacton-on-Sea. His fleet consisted of two two-seat Puss Moths and two four-seat Fox Moths. He regarded his pilots as equivalent to aerial bus-drivers, and paid them accordingly; yet there is no record of any dissent.

His success in filling his aeroplanes encouraged him to ask de Havilland to design a larger replacement for the Fox Moth. Designer Arthur Hagg obliged. The resultant **D.H.84 Dragon Moth** (as it was first called) had six seats and could manage eight without baggage — adequate for a small bag for a weekend in Paris, which the Dragon could reach comfortably. With this appropriate equipment, Hillman started a twice-daily serviced from Romford to Paris on 1 April 1933. This was no April Fool's joke. He charged £5.10.0 return (£5.50 in today's currency). This was less than a pound more than Imperial's and Air Frances's single fare, and he did it without subsidy. Special weekend fares were even less. He brought the pleasures and privileges of air travel down to a lower stratum of income level, where a trip to Paris and back could cost little more than a fortnight's wages for a working man.

Edward "Ted" Hillman did more to bring the privileges of air travel, to a wider public than businessmen and other affluent passengers, than any other British airline pioneer.

Ted Hillman is seen here with some of his team of crew and ground staff. They were overworked and underpaid but loved their work and made airline history with the de Havilland D.H. 84 Dragon.

The term intermodality is now used to denote the need for coordination between different forms of transport. Edward Hillman introduced it in 1932, by providing bus services from the pick-up points in east London direct to the aeroplane — an even more direct connection than is safely possible today. The top picture shows a coach at Brentwood, while the lower one shows one at its transfer point to a D.H.86.

Not long before he died, Ted Hillman treated himself to a Rolls-Royce, of which only three of this model were made. Interestingly, as today he was able to make operating profits by offering cheap fares to the public.

Hillman's

With the opening of the service to Paris on 1 April 1933, **Ted Hillman** abandoned the short route from Romford to Clacton and a week later started instead to Manston serving the resorts of Margate and Ramsgate. Then from 30 June to 4 September he extended the Paris route to Vichy, the spa in the French Auvergne.

In spite of his lowly origins, his enthusiastic initiatives were paying off. On 24 September, he was honoured at a grand civic reception in Romford, where he wished everyone their "Good 'Ealth." On 24 November, when he took delivery of the first D.H.84 Dragon, the famous pilot **Amy Johnson** named G-ACAN as *Maylands* with the traditional bottle of champagne. She flew several flights on the Paris route from late August until mid-September. Whether or not Hillman paid her his non-union rate is unrecorded.

On 10 January 1934, Ted transferred his fleet of almost 100 Gilford coaches to the London Passenger Transport Board, and by the end of March he had sold the whole of his coach business for £168,000. On 1 June 1934, he moved from Maylands to nearby Stapleford, where the airstrip was comfortably longer, in anticipation of bigger aircraft to come, and he had already linked up with John Sword's Midland and Scottish Air Ferries service to the North but which had had to close down on 14 July (see page 62). Hillman's re-opened the route two days later, but under competitive pressure from the new Railway Air Services (R.A.S.) (see page 76) which had the advantage of a post office mail contract, had to close this route down on 30 July. Undaunted, and with the new D.H. 89 Dragon Rapide (see page 77), he augmented his Paris service and on 1 December reinstated the domestic route to Belfast and Glasgow, this time with his own post office contract.

Sadly, Edward Hillman died, from a heart attack, on the last day of 1934. His airline had become a public company on 19 December, and control shifted to the financial group, **Whitehall Securities**, in which the d'Erlanger banking house had a considerable interest (see pages 74 and 75). It opened services to Hull, on 6 June 1935, and more ambitiously, from Stapleford to Belgium (see map) on 19 June. Whitehall established **British Airways** on 1 October 1935, by merging Spartan Air Lines and United Airways. Hillman's published its last timetable in that month, and on 11 December it too became the third element of the triumvirate that was, within a few short years, to challenge the nation's chosen instrument, Imperial Airways.

HILLMAN'S AIRWAYS FLEET LIST

Regn.	MSN	Hillman's Unit No.	Date of C of A	Name	Remarks and Disposal
D.H. 60G Moth					
G-ABCW	1552	3	16 Jul 30	—	To Hillman's 18 Jan 32. Sold to India April 1933 as VT-AEC (Madras Flying Club). Written off 15 Mar 35.
D.H. 60 Moth Major					
G-ACGX	5029	—	30 May 33	—	To Hillman's, Dec 34. To Cinema Press, Ltd., Croydon, June 1936. Still flying until 1941.
D.H. 80A Puss Moth					
G-ABSB	2213	1	24 Nov 31	Sonny	Withdrawn from use, after accident at Clacton, 7 May 33.
G-ABSO	2217	2	30 Dec 31	Babs	Sold 2 June 33, to Brian Lewis Co.
G-ABVX	2228	4	22 Apr 32	Gilford	To British Airways, Oct 35, but not used.
D.H. 83 Fox Moth					
G-ABVI	4004	5	17 Jun 32	Chris	Cost $993. To Essex Aero Ltd, July 36.
G-ABVK	4005	6	23 Jun 32	Doreen	To British Airways, 11 Dec 35.
G-ABWB	4007	—	5 Jul 32	—	Sold as new to **Scottish Motor Traction**, 7 Jul 32, then to **North Sea General** (Hull Grimsby) 9 Jul 33. To India Dec 38 as VT-AKV. Retired 30 Jul 41.
G-ABWF	4008	—	8 Jul 32	—	Sold as new to **Scottish Motor Traction**. Crashed at Haslingden, Lancs, 31 Jan 33 but repaired. Damaged at Limerick, Ireland, 7 Jul 33. To India, Oct 34. Crashed at Belgaum, 28 Mar 35.
D.H. 84 Dragon					
G-ACAN	6000	7	16 Dec 32	Maylands	Delivered to Hillman's by Amy Johnson. Sold to **Aberdeen Airways**, 16 Aug 34.
G-ACAO	6001	8	3 Feb 33	Goodmayes	Sold to **Norman Edgar**, 15 Oct 35.
G-ACAP	6002	9	9 Feb 33	Romford	Accident at Stapleford, 23 Jun 35. To British Airways, Dec 35.
G-ACBW	6009	10	13 Apr 33	Gidea Park	Sold July 34 to **Provincial Airways**. Intended for Spanish Republicans but detained. Retired 22 Oct 41.
G-ACEU	6022	11	10 May 33	Brentwood	To British Airways, Dec 35.
G-ACEV	6023	12	12 Jun 33	Ilford	(Two sisters, Elizabeth and Jane DuBois, committed suicide, jumping from aircraft 21 Feb 35) To Airwork, Dec 35.
D.H. 89 Dragon Rapide					
G-ACPM	6251	—	5 Jul 34	—	Crashed near Folkestone, 2 Oct 34
G-ACPN	6252	—	2 Aug 34	—	To British Airways, Dec 35 and sold to Highland Airways, Sep 36.
G-ACPO	6253	—	4 Sep 34	—	Damaged in Isle of Man, 26 Jan 35. To British Airways and sold.
G-ADAG	6266	—	6 Feb 35	—	To British Airways, Dec 35, then to Northern & Scottish Airways, 30 Jul 36.
G-ADAH	6278	—	19 Feb 35	—	To British Airways, 11 Dec 35, then to Northern & Scottish Airways, 10 Aug 36.
G-ADAI	6287	—	14 May 35	—	To British Continental Airways, then to British Airways 1 Aug 36.
G-ADAJ	6276	—	5 Jun 35	—	To British Airways, Jan 36.
G-ADAK	6281	—	14 May 35	—	To British Continental Airways, then to British Airways 1 Aug 36 but not used.
G-ADAL	6263	—	2 Mar 35	—	To British Airways, 11 Dec 35, but not used.
G-ADDF	6284	—	8 Aug 35	—	(Ordered by Aberdeen Airways, but not delivered) To Hillman 27 Aug 35, then **British Airways**, 11 Dec 35. To Northern & Scottish Airways, 29 Aug 36.

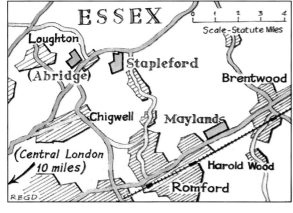

D.H. 86A Express					
G-ADEA	2323	—	5 Jun 35	Drake	To British Airways, 11 Dec 35
G-ADEB	2324	—	20 Jun 35	—	To British Airways, 11 Dec 35
G-ADEC	2325	—	1 Jul 35	—	To British Airways, 11 Dec 35

Edmund Fresson

Unlike Ted Hillman, who was a sharp-witted business-man but had not been especially air-minded, and certainly not a pilot, **Captain Edmund Freeson** had been a pilot first, and had also realized the potential for air travel where surface modes were slow and often unreliable. Although others could claim to have been just as devoted to the cause of bringing airline service to Scotland, Fresson was the first, and certainly the one who saw where it was needed most: to bring the Orkney and the Shetland Islands to within a few hours of the mainland instead of at least a whole day, and often more by sea.

He had spent his early years in China, after leaving his English school in 1911. He learned to fly with the Royal Flying Corps during the Great War, and went back to China in 1919, doing some local flying with an Armstrong Whitworth biplane. With government support, he tried to establish an aeroplane factory at Taiyuan, but was frustrated by the warlord in-fighting that was rampant during the early 1920s. Returning to England in 1929, he founded the North British Aviation Company at Hooton, near Liverpool. Then, on 22 August 1931, during a joy-riding tour of Scotland, he flew across the Pentland Firth, and realized that there was a natural demand for air service. The boat trip from Caithness to Orkney took only a few hours, but the weather was often too rough The discomfort of air sickness during a short flight was no worse than sea-sickness for several hours.

Fresson surveyed the route during 1932, with a Gipsy Moth, and sought some financial support from local transport interests. On 3 April 1933, he registered **Highland Airways**. He was the managing director, doubling as chief pilot. He started with a small twin-engined three-passenger-seat Monospar ST-4, and he named it *Inverness*, when he began scheduled service from Inverness to Kirkwall, via Wick, on 8 May 1933 (and from Thurso to Kirkwall three days later). The 1 hr. 20 m. flight saved nine hours by surface transport.

The service was heartily welcomed. In the summer, Fresson added an 8-seat D.H.84 Dragon to his fleet, and hired a 4-seat Fox Moth from Scottish Motor Traction which had apparently abandoned its idea of starting air service itself. Highland Airways carried more than 1,500 passengers and five tons of freight during its first short season. Not only that, Orcadians received their mail and the *Scotsman*, Scotland's national newspaper, a day earlier than before.

The next year, on 7 May, Ted Fresson opened direct service from the much larger city, Aberdeen, which was also clos-

er by rail to Glasgow and Edinburgh than Inverness. The D.H. Dragon, G-ACIT *Aberdeen*, had to use a field at Seaton, close to the city, because rival airline pioneer, Eric Gandar Dower, would not allow him to use the airfield at Dyce. This was not an example of intemperate obstructionism; as related on page 58, Eric had had to build Dyce with his own bare hands.

Highland Airways made substantial progress during 1934, as chronicled on page 57. But the population he served was not enough to support its airline, by flying, by writing letters, or by buying enough newspapers. Also, Fresson had to find another airfield at Aberdeen, because the local council needed Seaton for the Highland Show. He had to move to a field at Kintore, ten miles from Aberdeen (and away from low-flying cabers).

In June 1935, in financial difficulty, he merged his interests with **United Airways**, which had been founded in April

by Whitehall Securities. Together with Spartan Air Lines, Allied British Airways, as the merged company was called, changed its name to British Airways; but like John Sword's Midland and Scottish Air Ferries, Highland continued to operate under its own name in 1936.

Flying in northern Scotland was no easy ride. Shetland is on the same latitude as Anchorage, Alaska. But there were inevitable losses. One pilot crashed two D.H.84s and was known as St. George the Second, because he slew two Dragons.

Captain Edmund Fresson died on 25 September 1963, after having led Scotland into the airline age thirty years previously. He is remembered north of the Border not only as an airline promoter but as a public benefactor; and a memorial to his memory bears witness to such recognition in Kirkwall today. He came to be regarded as an honorary Orcadian.

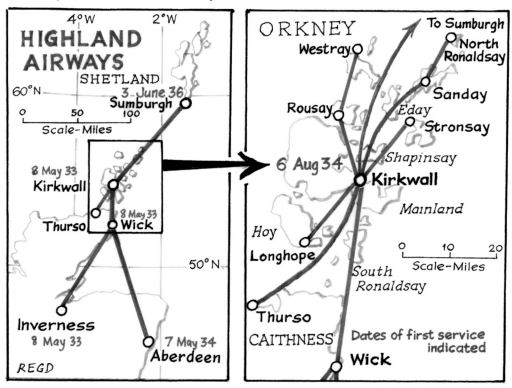

Highland Airways

HIGHLAND AIRWAYS FLEET

Regn.	MSN	Name	Date into Service	Remarks and Disposal
D.H. 60M Moth				
G-AAWO	1235	"Ah-Wo"	9 Feb 32	Leased from Miss Heloise Pauer. Used only for survey flights; purchased mid-1934. Sold 13 Nov. 48, and after various owners, returned to Inverness for commemoration ceremonies of Highland Airways foundation on 1 Aug 86.
Monospar ST-4				
G-ACEW	11	Inverness	8 May 33	Purchased new. Crash-landed at Kirkwall, 3 July 33; Sold 30 June 37, damaged beyond repair on rough landing, Croydon, 13 Dec 37.
De Havilland D.H.84 Dragon				
G-ACCE	6010	Caithness	29 May 34	Hired from Brian Lewis. Inaugurated Britain's first domestic air mail service without surcharge, Inverness-Wick-Kirkwall. Written off after bad take-off at Kirkwall, 29 Aug 34.
G-ACET	6021	Kirkwall	Sep 34	Purchased from S.M.T., 26 Sep. 34. Exchanged for D.H. 89 Dragon Rapide, G-AEWL, 24 June 37
G-ACGK	6033	Loch Ness	23 July 34	Purchased from E.C.G. England. Crashed into sea near Inverness and written off, 8 Jan 35.
G-ACIT	6039	Aberdeen	7 Aug 33	Purchased new. Inaugurated Aberdeen service. Renamed *Orcadian*, 1939. Passed to B.E.A. April 1948. Preserved by National Science Museum.
G-ADCT	6095	Orcadian	2 June 35	Purchased new. Crash-landed at Inverness and written off, Feb 1940
De Havilland D.H.89 Dragon Rapide				
G-ADAJ	6276	Inverness	28 Dec 36	Transferred from British Airways (originally Hillman's Airways). Operated throughout Scotland during Second World War; passed to B.E.A., then to French colonies and eventually struck off register in Hanoi (F-BEDY), 22 May 53
G-AEWL	6367	Zetland	24 Jun 37	Acquired in exchange for Dragon, G-ACET, 24 June 37. Operated throughout Second World War; passed to B.E.A., and eventually went to French Ivory Coast (F-OATT) 24 Jan 56. Fate unknown.

(During July 1933, a D.H.83 Fox Moth was hired from Scottish Motor Traction)

Captain Fresson is seen here, plus-foured, with the aircraft with which he inaugurated scheduled airline service to the Orkney Islands on 8 May 1933. With engines running, he was ready for take-off.

4 seats • 115 mph

General Aircraft Monospar ST-4

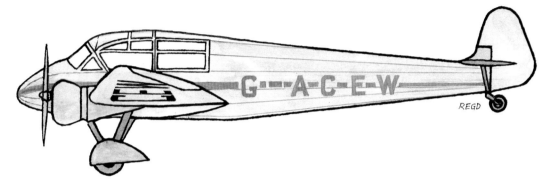

Engine	Pobjoy "R" (85 hp x 2)
MGTOW	2,500 lb.
Max. Range	540 miles
Length	26 feet
Span	40 feet

Size comparison with the Handley Page H.P. 42 (p.37)

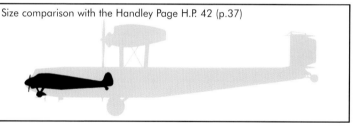

Two examples of Scotland's first airline promotional luggage stickers. The oval one was probably issued when service started, but the one on the left was ahead of its time, as Highland Airways did not operate between Glasgow and Perth.

This picture of the D.H. 84 Dragon, G-ADCT Orcadian, was taken at Wideford Airport, Kirkwall, in 1935, and well illustrates the rural conditions in which the early independent airlines operated, with little help from official quarters, in the air or on the ground.

Eric Gandar Dower

Most of the airline entrepreneurs of the early 1930s were bus operators, or involved with transport of some kind. Born in 1895, **Eric Gandar Dower** was an exception. He had inherited wealth, in the form of property ownership, had been to a good public school, was a good sportsman, had joined the Royal Naval Air Service in 1915, and after the Great War, having attended the Royal Academy of Dramatic Art (RADA), went back to his adopted vocation, the theatre. But when his father learned about this (because the Royal Humane Society had recognized, at a theatre performance, his act of diving off Ryde Pier to rescue a boy from drowning) his father stopped "all this acting" and put the inheritance in trust until 1923. He then earned a master's degree at Cambridge, drove a bus during the 1926 General Strike, and happened to meet Robert Cowell Smith, a Scottish aviation enthusiast, who suggested to Eric that Aberdeen needed a flying school.

His suggestion fell on receptive ears. Aviation was among Eric's many interests. In 1909, the year after he had read about the Rheims aviation meet in France, and aged only 14, he had motorcycled to Dover to see Blériot's aircraft after its historic cross-Channel flight. In 1913 he had made his first flight from Shoreham as a passenger. The sequel to the meeting with Smith was that, in 1931, Eric Gandar Dower flew to Aberdeen — the Blackburn Bluebird was a rare sight in that northern city in those days — and bought 200 acres of land at Dyce, a village near Aberdeen. After three years of toil, which involved the removal of thousands of tons of rock, diverting streams, and building a culvert, Eric opened Dyce Airport on 28 July 1934.

He never did things by half. He had already formed **Aberdeen Airways** on 2 January of the same year. He opened service to Glasgow on 11 September, using his own Short Scion, and hired Eric Starling as his chief pilot. This other Eric had distinguished himself in 1933 during his night-flying pilot training by losing his way to Folkestone, and landing in the dark in a street in Calais. Gandar Dower hired him on the grounds that "you're as mad as I am."

Even with the larger D.H.84, leased from Hillman's, and providing a door-to-door bus service, he could not compete with the excellent L.N.E.R. rail service, and so he turned his attention to a route where the trains could not go: to the Orkney Islands. Starting service on 27 May 1935, he was forced to fly via Thurso, Caithness, and Stromness, Orkney, because Edmund Fresson commanded the rights at Kirkwall,

and was not about to offer favours to the man who — with some reason — denied him access to Dyce.

You cannot keep a good man down. On 11 June 1935, Aberdeen Airways started service to Edinburgh, instead of Glasgow, connecting with North Eastern Airways, which had opened a service to London. But this enterprising code-share met with opposition from the L.N.E.R., which ordered all travel agents not to book air journeys, at the peril of losing their bread-and-butter train travel business. The next year, on 2 June 1936, Eric Starling took the first D.H.89 flight (G-ADDE, and temporarily named *The Starling*) to Sumburgh, in the Shetlands, to parallel Fresson's Highland Airways service.

The two Scottish pioneer airlines subsequently provided excellent service to Britain's northern island outposts. Aberdeen Airways changed its name in March 1937 to **Allied Airways (Gandar Dower)** and continued its pioneering ways, still rigidly independent, as will be narrated later in this book.

This photograph was taken on 2 June 1936, when Aberdeen Airways made its first flight to the Shetland Islands. In front of the de Havilland D.H. 84 The Aberdonian, are (left to right) Eric Gandar Dower, Captain Eric Starling, Viscount Arbuthnott, and Caroline Brunning, Eric's long-time secretary who subsequently became his wife. The object in the foreground appears to be an improvised filter, with chamois leather, to ensure the purity of the petrol when refuelling.

Vigorously independent to the last, Eric Gandar Dower was eventually recognized, though not as handsomely as was his due, for his pioneering work in helping to bring air service to Scotland. He is seen here receiving a commendation for his lifetime's work from Princess Alexandra.

By what would now be called a code-share operation, Eric Gander Dower pioneered an air route from London to Norway, by a cooperative arrangement with North Eastern Airways. Stavanger was connected by rail to Oslo.

Aberdeen/Allied Airways

ABERDEEN AIRWAYS/ALLIED AIRWAYS FLEET

Regn.	MSN	Name	Date into Service(S) or Delivery	Remarks and Disposal
Short Scion				
G-ACUV	S.774	Scion	10 Sept 34	Purchased by Gander Dower because the D.H.84 G-ACRH, had crashed on take-off from Aberdeen on 13 July 34.
De Havilland D.H.84 Dragon				
G-ACRH	6078	Aberdonian	—	(See above)
G-ACAN	6000	The Starling	11 Sept 34 (S)	Prototype Dragon, named Maylands by Amy Johnson for Hillman (q.v.). Crashed at Dunbeath, Caithness, 21 May 41.
G-ADFI	6100	The Silver Ghost	14 Oct 34	Crashed at Thurso on 3 July 37
G-ACLE	6044	Old Bill	30 Sept 37	Purchased from Airwork (YI-AAC). Crashed South Ronaldsay, in 1939, but rebuilt and sold to Western Airways in 1939. Served with R.A.F. but struck off, 12 May 41.
G-ACNJ	6072	Sir Rowland	23 Nov 37 (S)	Purchased from Jersey Airways. Carried first air mail direct from Aberdeen to the Shetlands, and named after the founder of the Post Office. Broken up, 1946.
De Havilland D.H.89 Dragon Rapide				
G-ADDE	6282	The Aberdonian	July 35	Impressed into R.A.F. service, 23 March 40. Survived minor accidents. Sold back to Allied Airways in 1945 for spares.
G ADAH	6278	Pioneer	26 May 38	Purchased from Northern & Scottish Airways. First named The Thurso Venturer. Crashed Kirkwall 1940, but repaired. Re-purchased in 1945, after wartime service. Preserved at Royal Scottish Museum at East Fortune as only surviving D.H.84.
G-ACZF	6268	Carina	16 May 39	Purchased from Anglo-Persian Oil Company; damaged at Kirkwall in 1941. Repaired. Crashed in Orkney, 27 Dec 45.
G-ACZE	6264	The Don	21 Sept 41	Originally sold to Anglo Persian Oil Company, then wartime service before purchase by Allied. Crashed at Grimsetter, Orkney, 27 Dec 45. Stored at Dyce until 1966, and restored.
G-AGDM	6584	Eldorado	11 Nov 41	Purchased new. Damaged at Sumburgh in collision with two Spitfires, but repaired on site. To B.E.A. 15 Jan 47, then to private owners. Sold to France (F-OAXX) in 1957.
G-AGHI	6455	The Shetlander	13 Jan 43	First operated by R.A.F. from 1939 as P9588. Withdrawn from use at Croydon, Sept. 50. **(D.H.89B)**
G-AIDL	6968	The Wanderer	23 Aug 43	First operated by R.A.F. in 1946. To B.E.A. 1 Feb 47, then to private operators. **(D.H.89B)**
De Havilland D.H.86B Express				
G-AETM	2353	The Norseman	29 Jun 37	Purchased new. Sold to Western Airways, April 39, then to Finland as OH-SLA. Destroyed on ground, Malmi, 2 May 40.

The aircraft are listed in order of entry into service of each type.

Aberdeen's chief pilot, Eric Starling, with the airline's first aircraft.

6 seats • 114 mph

De Havilland D.H.84 Dragon

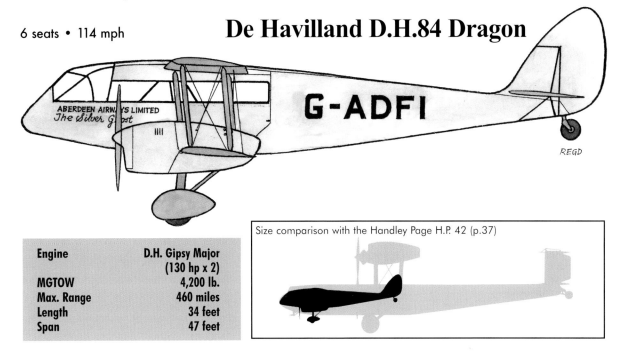

ABERDEEN AIRWAYS LIMITED
The Silver Ghost

G-ADFI

REGD

Engine	D.H. Gipsy Major (130 hp x 2)
MGTOW	4,200 lb.
Max. Range	460 miles
Length	34 feet
Span	47 feet

Size comparison with the Handley Page H.P. 42 (p.37)

One of Allied Airways (Gander Dower's) D.H.89 Rapides, photographed in 1937, is seen here at Shetland's Sumburgh Airport. The modest terminal building advertised rival Highland Airways, with the slogan "Safety, Speed, Comfort."

John Sword: First to the Hebrides . . .

On 1 June 1933, **Midland & Scottish Air Ferries** began air services from Glasgow's Renfrew Airport to Campbeltown, on the southern tip of the Kintyre peninsula, and the Inner Hebridean island of Islay. The airline also connected Scotland with Ireland by air, with a service to Belfast, via Campbeltown. The distances were not great, and the crossing of the North Channel was an obvious leap over the water. Although Campbeltown was on Scotland's mainland, the long indentations of the sea lochs meant that the road journey from Glasgow was as long as that to Inverness. There was no railway, and the boat journeys were slow and not always regular when the sea was rough.

The effort to provide air service to the nearest and most accessible of the Inner Hebridean islands was not spectacular in establishing an aerial "Road to the Isles" but it was a good start. Much credit must go to **John Sword**, a bus operator from Ayr, who had sold his operation to the larger Scottish Motor Traction (S.M.T.); had become general manager of its Western Division; and simultaneously founded M.& S.A.F. with a capital of £20,000.

Sword's enterprise was highly commendable; but he must have known that his action involved a conflict of interest, especially as S.M.T. had itself conducted extensive survey flights on its own behalf. Had he confined his activities to reaching the western islands, where neither rail nor road could serve, he might have survived and flourished; but instead of flying to the other Hebridean islands, he turned his attentions to the south.

On 1 September 1933, John Sword went south, and started a service from Liverpool to Dublin, at first from Hooton, across the Mersey, then from Liverpool's new airport. Having built up a fleet of close to a dozen aircraft, he then began to flex his muscles, and introduced an Avro 642, a much larger aircraft.

Three days later, Sword opened a service from London to Glasgow, via Birmingham and Liverpool, with connections to Dublin and, via the Isle of Man, to Belfast. His London

(Left) John Sword's fares were quite reasonable, and the journey time from Glasgow's city centre to Islay's main town of less than two hours would be difficult to emulate today.

(Right) As with so many of the pioneer independent airlines, the de Havilland D.H. 84 Dragon was the mainliner of the small fleet.

This Midland and Scottish Dragon, at Liverpool's Speke Airport, was on a special charter for Leyland Motors, three of whose senior staff are seen here, along with a Mrs Williamson (far left), and A.B.Chadwick (next left) . John Sword is second from the right, and his son is held up by one of the clients. Note also, as shown in the exhibit, that surface-to-air intermodality was not a problem in 1933.

. . . and across the Irish Sea

terminus was Ted Hillman's Romford airfield, and the two worked closely together. This was apparently too much for the S.M.T., which by now had a substantial railway shareholding. Josiah Stamp, chairman of the L.M.S. main-line railway network from London to Glasgow and the north of Scotland, and which operated the Irish Mail to Dublin, may have feared that Sword was about to rename his airline the London, Midland, and Scottish. S.M.T. delivered Sword an ultimaturm: either continue as a well-paid manager of S.M.T. or leave the company to run your airline. Sword capitulated and all services were discontinued on 14 July 1934, except the route to Islay, which ceased on 30 September.

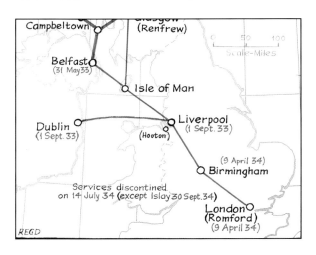

Like most of the independent British pioneer domestic airlines, Midland & Scottish Air Ferries turned to the reliable de Havilland biplanes, first the D.H.83 Fox Moth, then the twin-engined D.H.84 Dragon, pictured here, which started a minor airliner dynasty.

Avro 642 Eighteen

16 seats • 150 mph

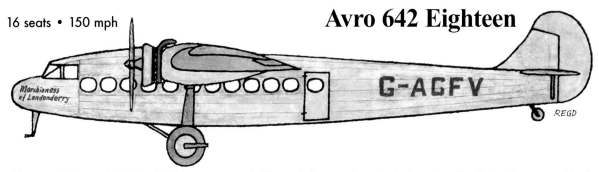

Pride comes before a Fall. On 6 April 1934, at a ceremony in Liverpool, the new twin-engined 18-seat Avro 642 (G-ACFV) was named by the Marchioness of Londonderry (after whom it was named) in the presence of her husband, the Secretary of State for Air, and also Lt-Col F.C. Shelmerdine, the Director of Civil Aviation, and Prime Minister Ramsey MacDonald. Some months later, the airline ceased operations. The exterior appearance of the aircraft belied its interior comfort, with the main spar and structural members obstructing easy movement along the cabin.

Engine	Armstrong Siddeley Jaguar (450 hp x 2)
MGTOW	11,800 lb.
Max. Range	450 miles
Length	54 feet
Span	71 feet

Size comparison with the Handley Page H.P. 42 (p.37)

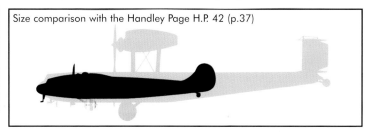

MIDLAND & SCOTTISH AIR FERRIES FLEET

Regn.	MSN	Date of C of A	Remarks and Disposal
Airspeed A.S.4 Ferry			
G-ACBT	6	7 Feb 33	Dismantled at Renfrew.
G-ACFB	9	2 Jun 33	To Air Publicity, Nov. 36
De Havilland D.H. 83 Fox Moth			
G-ACBZ	4040	2 Feb 33	To Australia as VH-UZD
G-ACCB	4042	10 Feb 33	To Giro Aviation. Ditched 25 Sep. 56
G-ACCT	4047	7 Mar 33	To West of Scotland Air Serivces, Aug. 35
G-ACCU	4048	3 Mar 33	To Australia as VH-UZC
De Havilland D.H.84 Dragon			
G-ACCZ	6015	11 May 33	To Crilly Airways, May 35
G-ACDL	6016	12 May 33	To Provincial Airways, Sep. 34
G-ACJS	6042	4 Aug 33	To Northern & Scottish Airways, Jan. 35
Avro 618 Ten			
G-ACGF	527	3 May 33	Reg'n cancelled Dec. 46
Avro 640 Cadet			
G-ACFX	647	23 Jun 33	To Perck Flying Club as VR-RAJ, Nov 36
G-ACIH	657	9 Mar 34	To North of Ireland Aircraft, Nov 38
Avro 642 Eighteen			
G-ACFV	642	29 Jan 34	Marchioness of Londonderry. Commercial Air Hire May 35. To Australia, as VH-UXD, Mandated Airlines, New Guinea. Destroyed by Japanese 1942.

John Sword's first aircraft was an Airspeed A.S.4 Ferry. a tri-motored biplane that, in spite of its ungainly appearance, performed well, could carry ten passengers, and although slow, could take off and land smartly from small fields — all too common in the early 1930s.

Highland Scrapbook

A Flying Start to the Day

Capt. Fresson's pioneering Highland Airways was based at Inverness, not far from the railway station. Longman Aerodrome is now an industrial estate.

Air Road to the Isles

This was Wideford Airfield in the 1930s, where Capt. Fresson carried the first air mail to the Orkney Islands on 8 May 1933.

Rivals in the North

This painting is of Sumburgh Links, Shetland's aerodrome, during the 1930s. The de Havilland aircraft are of Fresson's Highland Airways and Gandar Dower's Aberdeen Airways.

Flying Against the Elements

Aberdeen Aerodrome in the late 1930s. Most of the aircraft are of Allied Airways (Gandar Dower) Ltd. The airfield was built by Eric Gandar Dower himself.

Nowhere in the British Isles were the benefits of airline service realized so emphatically as in northern Scotland. These paintings, by Edmund Miller, G.Av.A. are reproduced through the courtesy of the artist and the Fresson Trust. For those readers who may like to identify all the aircraft, and personalities so well portrayed, can obtain prints of the paintings from Peter Clegg at 9, Park Chase, Godalming, Surrey GU7 1TL.

Wings Across the Minch

In the early days of flying, golf courses offered convenient landing grounds. This one at Stornoway, Lewis, brought the convenience of air travel to the furthest corner of the British Isles.

Sword in the Sky

This was a typical scene during the early years of Renfrew Aerodrome in 1934. The aircraft are all of John Sword's Midland and Scottish Air Ferries (except the Bristol Fighter).

Wings Over the Glens

Glen Brittle aerodrome, almost in the shadow of Skye's Cuillin Hills, in 1937. The aircraft, a Spartan Cruiser II and several de Havillands, are part of the fleet of Northern & Scottish Airways.

Busy Day at the Beehive

Not exactly in the Highlands, this was Gatwick Airport in the late 1930s. In the foreground is a D.H.86 in the early colours of British Airways (the pre-war one) which had direct connections to Scotland.

Independence Eroded . . .

The hiatus created by the demise of Midland & Scottish did not last long. Already **George Nicholson** had, on 1 August 1934, conducted an experimental service to the Isle of Man from Newcastle, via Carlisle, and on 21 November he established **Northern & Scottish Airways** as a private company. On 1 December he began service on the Glasgow-Campbeltown-Islay route, with a de Havilland Dragon. This was not the best time to start an air service in Scotland, and by the end of the month only 31 passengers had been carried, an average of one per day. But by the summer of 1935, the traffic demand justified two flights per day, and on 17 May Glaswegians could fly once again to the Isle of Man.

In October of that year, an important change in owner-ship occurred, one which was far-reaching in the part it played in the development of British internal air services during the latter half of the 1930s. The Whitehall Securities Corporation, headed by the Hon. Clive Pearson, had taken over the non-contracting activities of S.Pearson, which had been highly successful in big engineering projects overseas, including the building of the East River Tunnel in New York. Pearson, who was the third Lord Cowdray's uncle, would exert a considerable influence on the course of commercial aviation in Britain throughout the ensuing period, as Whitehall was a major shareholder in Spartan Air Lines, which was part of the merger that formed British Airways — see page 75.

In July 1936, Northern & Scottish took over all the internal routes of the newly-formed British Airways, but its routes were restricted from flying south of Liverpool; and on 12 August 1937, resulting from recommendations of the Maybury Committee (see page 72) it amalgamated with Highland Airways to form Scottish Airways.

In company with most of the 1930s independent British internal airlines, Northern & Scottish first relied on de Havilland biplanes. This D.H.89 is pictured at Newtownards airfield, Belfast, as it was being refuelled. Passengers used the steps seen on the right of the picture.

NORTHERN & SCOTTISH AIRWAYS FLEET

Reg'n	MSN	Date of C of A	Remarks and Disposal
D.H.83 Fox Moth			
G-ACED	4064	6 May 33	To Australia as VH-UZL, March 1937
D.H.84 Dragon			
G-ACFG	6027	24 Jun 33	Sold overseas, Feb 37
G-ACJS	6042	4 Aug 33	Registration cancelled, Nov 36
G-ACMO	6062	31 Jan 34	To Australia as VH-ABK, March 38
G-ACNG	6069	23 Mar 34	To Scottish Airways, crashed Kirkwall, 19 Apr 40
G-ACNH	6070	26 Mar 34	Registration cancelled, Jan 37
G-ACOR	6073	19 Mar 34	To British Airways, Mar 37
D.H.89 Dragon Rapide			
G-ADAG	6266	6 Feb 35	To Airwork, Sep 37
G-ADAH	6278	19 Feb 35	To Airwork, Aug 37
G-ADBU	6280	29 Apr 35	Damaged beyond repair, Nov 36
G-ADDF	6284	8 Aug 35	To Airwork, Aug 37
Spartan Cruiser II			
G-ACSM	10	13 Jun 34	To Scottish Airways, then to R.A.F. (as X9433) Apr 40
G-ACVT	11	2 Aug 34	To Scottish Airways
G-ACYL	12	24 Oct 34	Crashed, Isle of Man, 23 Mar 36
G-ACZM	14	13 Dec 34	To Scottish Airways, withdrawn from service, Jan 40
Spartan Cruiser III			
G-ACYK	101	16 Apr 35	Crash-landed at Largs, 14 Jan 38
G-ADEL	102	18 Apr 35	To Scottish Airways, then to R.A.F. (as X9432) Apr 40
G-ADEM	103	3 Jun 35	To Scottish Airways, Crashed, Blackpool, 20 Nov 36

For Index See Page 10

On 5 December 1935, Northern & Scottish opened the first service to the Outer Hebrides, with a circular route, taking in all the main islands, and a stop was made at Tiree later, as an extension of the route to Islay. Connections to Harris and Benbecula were made on demand only, and during the short stop at Glenbrittle Airport on Skye, "tea and sandwiches could be obtained at the usual prices."

Control of the airline passed to Whitehall Securities in the autumn of 1935, and Northern & Scottish added six-seat Spartan Cruiser tri-motors to its fleet. This one is photographed on the sands at Barra, where the beach served as the airstrip and the pilots claimed that if the seagulls were paddling, not swimming, it was safe to land.

. . . but Independence Retained

In association with Olley Air Service, **Blackpool & West Coast Air Services** was formed in April 1933, with the main objective of providing air service to the Isle of Man for holiday-makers in the industrial north of England. Blackpool had long been the main seaside destination for the "Wakes Week" annual respite from the satanic mills, and by the mid-1930s, some ventured farther afield across the Irish Sea. Regular services starting from Liverpool began on 22 June and in addition, almost 20,000 people were carried on local joy-rides, using the ubiquitous de Havilland D.H. Dragon.

The summer flights resumed on 1 May 1934, and extended into the winter months at a reduced frequency, and on 3 February 1935 the airline received an official blessing with the award of a mail contract. Flights to the Isle were also added direct from Liverpool. The airline maintained its independence from the Railway interests, partly because of the connections with the Olley organization. **Captain Gordon Olley**, a former Imperial Airways pilot, had become a successful commercial aviation entrepreneur, but had wisely hedged his bets by specializing in lucrative special air charters, as well as airline interests.

As the map and exhibit show, the airline expanded in 1935 from its Liverpool base. Additionally it offered train connections to London, the South, and to Scotland and good bus services at the city airfields. It was, after its own amalgamation with another airline in 1937 (see page 87) to survive during the years when the railways' own airline dominated the airways of Great Britain.

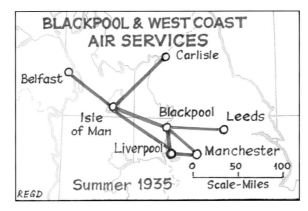

By 1935, the word Blackpool was relegated to small print.

THE FLEET OF BLACKPOOL & WEST COAST AIR SERVICE

Regn.	MSN	Date of C of A	Remarks and Disposal
D.H.83 Fox Moth			
G-ACFC	4053	24 Mar 33	To Olley Air Service, Jan 36
G-ACFF	4060	22 Apr 33	To Great Western & Southern Air Lines, July 39
D.H.84 Dragon			
G-ACGU	6034	28 Jun 33	Crashed on take-off at Heston, 16 July 35
G-ACPY	6076	10 May 34	To Aer Lingus, May 36, as EI-ABI
G-ADCP	6092	30 Mar 35	To Royal Air Force, Apr 40, as X9440
G-ADCR	6094	6 Apr 35	Crashed, 25 June 38
D.H.86B Express			
G-AENR	2352	8 Feb 37	To Royal Navy, July 1940 (as AX 842)

In the 1930s, the de Havilland aircraft, such as this Dragon, refuelled at the pump almost in the same way that a bus or car would fill up at a roadside garage.

By 1937, the Blackpool name was dropped altogether. The traditional link with the bus services was still remembered on the Fox Moth.

The Spithead Express

There has never been an airline quite like the **Portsmouth, Southsea & Isle of Wight Aviation** company. When it started operations on 27 June 1932, over the four miles of water between Portsmouth and Ryde, the nearest of the several Isle of Wight seaside resorts, it could claim to be the shortest air route in Britain, and beaten into that claim worldwide only by Walter Varney's air ferry service across San Francisco Bay, which lasted until the Bay Bridge was opened. Subsequently, Edmund Fresson could point to some of the short connections in the Orkney Islands.

The name of the stretch of water was Spithead, which was adopted by the airline, and there must have been an amused feeling of "dignity and impudence" among the pilots and staff, as only a few miles away, on Southampton Water, Imperial Airways would establish its impressive base for the large flying boats to serve the longest routes in the British Empire.

Founded by a group of businessmen headed by **Lionel Balfour**, P.S.& I.O.W Aviation could, curiously, because of its almost instant popularity, have been the first airline to have had its initials, in friendly fashion, misinterpreted. The locals called it Pip, Squeak, and Wilfred, after a children's comic strip in one of the national daily newspapers.

The **Spithead Express** carried almost two and a half thousand passengers during that first summer of 1932, mostly in its Westland Wessex trimotor, but during the following winter, the flights were made, as was customary with all the British airlines at the time, on request only, and the Portsmouth-Ryde-Shanklin route was augmented by a link to Shoreham, which served the several resorts along the south coast of Sussex. Such was the airline's popular success that ridership trebled in 1933 to almost 10,000, plus almost 7,000 more on pleasure trips and charters. On 1 May 1934, a daily service opened from London's new Heston Airport, and frequent connections to Bournemouth were added on 17 May. But in that year the local air ferry service reached new heights, 2,338 passengers being carried in the third week of August alone.

For Britons who were recovering from the depression years of the late 1920s and early 1930s, taking a ride on the Spithead Express must have been a welcome little extravagance. In 1936, the Portsmouth-Ryde air ferry flew every half-hour from 9.10 a.m. until sunset. The trip took ten minutes, and two minutes only were allowed for the turnaround at Ryde. The adult single fare was 4/6 (one U.S. dollar at the then rate of exchange); 3/- for children under 12, and 1/6 for

The Westland Wessex en route across Spithead, flying over the pier at Soutsea, the seaside suburb of Portsmouth.

dogs. Lap-dogs went for free. Following railway practice, a day return ticket cost 7/-.

Special fares for dogs reflected the popularity of the canine pets throughout the country, and, if not unique, this was certainly unusual, and no doubt permitted only because of the shortness of the journey. But it must have caused a minor problem occasionally, as by 1937, some passengers seemed to have adopted a broad definition of a lap-dog, not to mention that of a lap. The airline changed its regulations to include a charge of 2/6 per dog applied to all types, and "larger dogs will in no circumstances be carried, and it is at the company's discretion to decide on what constitutes a lap dog, and to refuse any animal likely to be objectionable to other passengers." Thereby, no doubt, had hung a tail or two.

This remarkable airline maintained its independence until the outbreak of the Second World War in September 1939, and although it experimented with a service to Paris in 1935, it concentrated on what its name proclaimed. By the time the Spithead Express ceased operations, it had carried a quarter of a million people, and had made a substantial contribution to the creation of airmindedness in Great Britain.

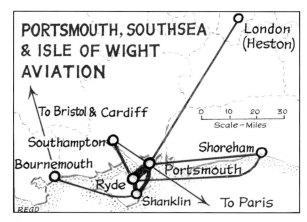

Dignity and Impudence: almost next door to Imperial Airways's base in Southampton Water, from which the flying boats flew to Australia during the latter 1930s, P.S.I.O.W.A claimed to operate the shortest airline flights in the world.

Westland Wessex

8 seats • 108 mph

The West Country aircraft manufacturer at Yeovil, Somerset had built its first commercial aircraft, the single-engined Westland Limousine, in 1919, and the six-seater Mark III version of 1920 had won the Air Ministry Commercial Aeroplane competition first prize in the small aircraft category. But this was before the government recognized the need to subsidize fledgling airlines, and Westland built only nine Limousines, none of which went into regular service.

In 1928, it tried again, with the **Westland IV/Wessex**, a three-engined four-seat monoplane, a promising design that was aimed to meet the requirement by the nascent small British airlines. This standard aircraft was up against strong competition from de Havilland, and although used sporadically by Imperial Airways, it did not see sustained regular service. The developed **Wessex**, however, deserved a better fate. Only one of this variant, with its forward fuselage of metal, was built, but it was a real workhorse for its customer, Portsmouth, Southsea, and Isle of Wight Aviation, flying across Spithead at least four times a day during the summer months from 1932 until 1936.

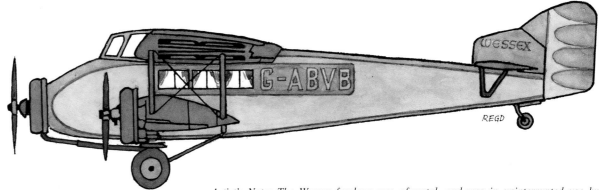

Artist's Note: The Wessex fuselage was of metal, and was in uninterrupted use by P.S.I.O.W.A. from 1932 until its accident on take-off at Ryde in 1936.

Engine	Armstrong Siddeley Genet Major (140 hp x 3)
MGTOW	6,300 lb.
Max. Range	340 miles
Length	38 feet
Span	57 feet

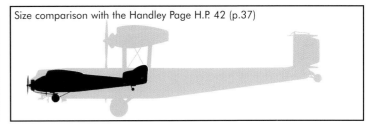

Size comparison with the Handley Page H.P. 42 (p.37)

THE FLEET OF PORTSMOUTH, SOUTHSEA & ISLE OF WIGHT AVIATION

Regn.	MSN	Date of C of A	Remarks and Disposal
Westland Wessex			
G-ABVB	W.A. 2156	6 Sep 32	Damaged beyond repair at Ryde, 30 May 36
De Havilland D.H. 83 Fox Moth			
G-ACCA	4041	2 Feb 33	To Australia, as VH-UTY, Feb 36
G-ACIG	4072	12 Jul 33	To Royal Air Force, March 40, as X9299
Airspeed A.S.5 Courier			
G-ACLR	11	21 Nov 33	To PS10WA Apr 39; to R.A.F; March 40, as X9344
G-ACLF	12	13 Dec 33	To PS10WA Apr 39; to R.A.F; March 40, as X9342
G-ACNZ	20	22 Jun 34	To PS10WA Nov 39; to R.A.F; March 40, as X9346
G-ACZL	25	35	Leased by Airspeed to PS10WA
G-ADAX	26	15 Apr 35	Leased by Airspeed by PSIOWA, March 40 as X9347
G-ADAY	27	17 May 35	Leased by Airspeed to PSIOWA, March 40 as X9343
De Havilland D.H.85 Leopard Moth			
G-ADBH	7030	21 Feb 34	Believed hired from Birkett Air Services
De Havilland D.H.84 Dragon			
G-ACRF	6077	18 May 34	To Australia as VH-UXG, Feb 36
Airspeed A.S.6A Envoy			
G-ADCA	36	2 May 35	To Spain, August 36

The Airspeed AS.5 Courier was built at Portsmouth, and intended to compete with the popular de Havilland commercial aircraft. It was faster (140 mph) and was the first British aircraft to have a retractable landing gear.

Western Enterprise

Comparatively isolated from the early activities in London, the North, and in Scotland, another tempting area for an airline venture was across the Severn Estuary to link the two important cities of Cardiff and Bristol, a straight-line distance of 20 miles. In the 1930s, the circuitous train journey via the Severn Tunnel took about two hours, and the road journey via Gloucester (there was no road bridge in the 1930s) was not far short of 100 miles. To meet this apparent demand, on 26 September 1932, **Norman Edgar** expanded his modest joy-riding business into a regular Bristol-Cardiff air service, using a de Havilland D.H.83 Fox Moth.

A year later, on 7 September 1933, he registered his company as **Norman Edgar (Western Airways)**, and soon placed a D.H.84 Dragon into service, carrying 1,600 passengers on regular flights, and 2,000 more on pleasure and on charters. On 1 May 1934, he added flights from Cardiff to the seaside resort Weston-super-Mare, and two weeks later, extended the Bristol service to Bournemouth, advertising it as the "Sunshine Air Express."

By the following year, the cross-Severn service was almost a shuttle, with six flights each way every day during the summer, and ambitiously — possibly as a reflection of Britain's recovery from the depression years — was, as indicated by the publicity leaflets, able to take Bristolians for a little gambling at leTouquet or even a weekend in Paris. Not only did Western Airways offer comfort, safety and speed (to visit Paris by train via London would have taken all day) the charter service customers did not need passports.

During the winter months, the network was always curtailed to the Bristol-Cardiff shuttle, but by 1937 this was operated almost hourly in the summer, and in August 1937, flights were made to Weston from Birmingham, by which time the Cardiff-Weston summer frequency was also every hour.

In later years, control of the company passed to the **Straight Corporation** in January 1938, which transferred the operational base to Weston-super-Mare, and on 18 October of that year, reduced the company name simply to **Western Airways**, which continued to thrive until the outbreak of the Second World War.

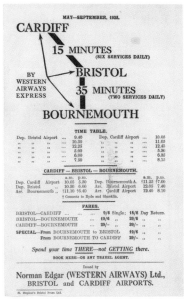

This photograph, taken in 1938, shows a Western Airways D.H. 89 Dragon Rapide on the east-bound shuttle service between Cardiff and Weston-super-Mare. The island in the foreground is Flat Holme, with its lighthouse to warn the once-frequent ships on the sea-lanes to Bristol.

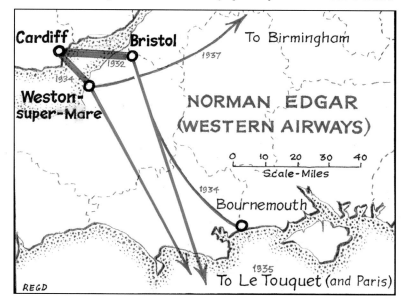

On the Fringe

NORMAN EDGAR/WESTERN AIRWAYS FLEET

Reg'n	MSN	Date of C of A	Remarks and Disposal
De Havilland D.H.84 Dragon			
G-ACAO	6001	3 Feb 33	To R.A.F. (as X9398), Apr 40
G-ACJT	6043	26 Apr 33	Crashed, 20 Dec 39
G-ACMJ	6058	7 Dec 33	To R.A.F. (as X9396), Apr 40
G-ACMP	6063	20 Feb 34	Crashed, 23 July 35
G-ACPX	6075	26 Apr 34	To R.A.F. (as X9399), Apr 40
De Havilland D.H.89A Dragon Rapide			
G-ACTU	6258	24 Aug 39	Crashed after modification as AW115
G-ADBV	6286	6 Jun 35	To R.A.F. (as X8511), Mar 40
G-ADDD	6283	8 Jun 35	To R.A.F. (as AW116), Jun 40
G-AFSO	6445	22 May 39	Destroyed by enemy in France, 31 May 40
De Havilland D.H.86B Express			
G-AETM	2353	29 Jun 37	To Finland (as OH-SLA), Dec 39
De Havilland D.H.90 Dragonfly			
G-AEDH	7510	2 Jul 36	To R.A.F. (as AV987), May 40
Percival Q.6			
G-AFIX	Q.31	13 Dec 38	Owned by A.H. White, used by Western To R.A.F. (as X9406), Apr 40

The relative success records of the trans-estuary airline projects of the mid-1930s is reflected in their fleet sizes. Pioneer Michael Scott had a single Puss Moth (see page 51); the Humber Service had only two aircraft (see page 53); as did the service across the Thames (this page). But Norman Edgar's aeroplanes constituted a fleet.

An interesting air service began on 14 April 1935 across the outer suburbs of London, to connect the two commercial airports, Heston to the west, and Croydon to the south. Several daily services were operated by **Commercial Air Hire**, under the name

ATLANTIC COAST AIR SERVICES FLEET

Reg'n	MSN	Date of C of A	Remarks and Disposal
Short Scion S.16/1			
G-ACUW	S.775	23 Aug 34	To R.A.F. as AV981, May 40
General Aircraft Monospar ST4 MK II			
G-ACCP	10	17 Mar 33	Withdrawn from service, Aug 39

SOUTHEND-ON-SEA FLYING SERVICE FLEET

Reg'n	MSN	Date of C of A	Remarks and Disposal
Short Scion S.16/1			
G-ACUY	S.777	26 Feb 35	Operated by Short Brothers
Short Scion 2			
G-ADDN	S.785	13 Jun 35	Southend aircraft. To Aircraft and Allied Enterprises, Mar 40

of **Inner Circle Airlines**, on a route that is now echoed by bus services from Heathrow to Gatwick around the M25 London Orbital Road. As the fleet record reveals, this experiment was short-lived.

INNER CIRCLE AIRLINES FLEET

Reg'n	MSN	Date of C of A	Remarks and Disposal
De Havilland D.H.84 Dragon			
G-ACCR	6011	3 Apr 33	Lost in the English Channel, 22 Jan 36
General Aircraft Monospar ST4 MK II			
G-ADIK	27	4 Jun 35	Crashed, May 36
G-ADJP	28	29 Jun 35	To R.K. Dundas, May 36
G-ADLM	30	22 Jul 35	Crashed at Croydon, 16 May 36

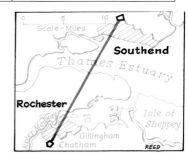

Many answered the call, few were chosen, but this was not for the want of trying. One such example of enterprise born more of amateur enthusiasm than of commercial acumen was **Atlantic Coast Air Service**. In June 1936, R.T. Boyd began operations with a daily service from Barnstaple, North Devon, across the Bristol Channel to Cardiff, and to the little Lundy Island, some 25 miles west of Barnstaple, and on the westernmost fringe of the Bristol Channel.

The granite island is only three miles long and a mile wide at its widest point, and has seldom had a resident population of more than 50. Visitors went there by air as much for curiosity as for any of the usual reasons such as a few days summer holiday. Its relative isolation gave it a history of having been occupied during the 17th Century by Turks and Spanish pirates, and later by French privateers. The landings were made at the only strip of level ground available, and all journeys were made, as the timetable stated, "at the operator's discretion."

While the Lundy traffic was sparse, there was more from Cardiff to the north Devon base, where the service to Torquay, south Devon, connected with flights by Provincial Airways (see page 72). Even so, on 26 April 1937, the name of the airline was changed to **Lundy and Atlantic Coast Air Lines**, which continued to operate with its small fleet until the outbreak of war in 1939.

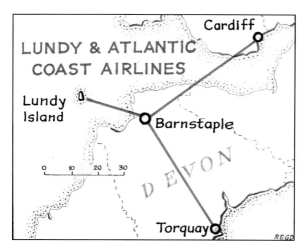

Two of the Casualties

The Maybury Committee

By the mid-1930s, the Government was becoming concerned about the proliferation of small airlines in Great Britain. Much as the spirit of free-wheeling enterprise achieved some success, this was fragmented and uncoordinated, and cool business heads were also required if competitive chaos was to be avoided. Short of direct regulation of air transport, some form of control appeared to be necessary, and this took the form of the appointment of an advisory committee, under the chairmanship of **Brigadier General Sir Henry Maybury**, who was required to advise on how the government or local authorities could assist the promotion of civil aviation in the United Kingdom, taking into account the requirements of the Post Office. The objective was a properly planned system.

The report was published on 9 December 1936 as Command Paper 5351, and concentrated on the avoidance of overlapping air routes, and particularly recommended the licensing of a single company to link the main centres of population through a central junction airport — a forerunner of what, about 40 years later, would be described as a hub system. It was clearly a carte blanche for the creation of Railway Air Services (see page 76).

Meanwhile, the struggle continued in a "survival of the fittest" environment.

Crilly Airways

One aspirant was **F. Leo Crilly**, who felt that both the railways and the other airlines were concentrating too much on London and he tried to develop a system of air routes that served the east Midlands, based at Leicester. Beginning his first services from Doncaster in March 1935, this was a brave effort, but, as the map and fleet list reveals, the operation lasted little more than a year, and on 9 September 1936, Crilly went into receivership.

Provincial Airways

Another effort was made by **H. Thomas**, who incorporated Provincial Airways on 19 March 1934, to take over the still-born route from London to Plymouth and Cornwall that International Airways had tried to establish on 24 August 1934. Although an attempt was made to emulate Crilly with a junction to the Midlands at Southampton, the airline's life was also short, ceasing operations on 23 September 1935.

One of Crilly's General Aircraft Monospars

CRILLY AIRWAYS FLEET

Reg'n	MSN	Date of C of A	Remarks and Disposal
De Havilland D.H.84 Dragon			
G-ACDN	6018	29 May 33	To Commercial Air Hire, May 37
G-ACLE	6044	5 Sep 33	To North Eastern Airways, Feb 37
General Aircraft Monospar ST25 Jubilee			
G-ADPK	55	9 Sep 35	To P.S.I.O.W.A., Dec 36
G-ADPL	56	19 Sep 35	To P.S.I.O.W.A., Dec 36
G-ADPM	57	1 Oct 35	To H.S. Ashworth, Dec 36
Fokker F-XII (All ex-K.L.M. Royal Dutch Airlines)			
G-ADZH	5284	23 Mar 36	Ex-PH-AFV, To British Airways
G-ADZI	5285	31 Jan 36	Ex-PH-AFU, To British Airways, Crashed 15 Aug 36
G-ADZJ	5292	8 Jan 36	Ex-PH-AIE, To British Airways
G-ADZK	5301	7 Feb 36	Ex-PH-AII, To British Airways, Destroyed, 16 Aug 36

	FARES — (With Transport)										
Single Fares : Light Type / Return Fares : Heavy Type	Portsmouth	Southampton	Hull	Grimsby	Nottingham	Leicester	Bournemouth	Torquay	Plymouth	Newquay	Penzance
Croydon	25/- 47/6	25/- 47/6	72/6 138/-	67/6 128/-	50/- 95/-	40/- 75/-	37/6 71/-	60/- 114/-	62/6 119/-	85/- 161/6	90/- 171/-
Portsmouth		10/- 19/-	72/6 138/-	67/6 128/-	50/- 95/-	40/- 75/-	20/- 38/-	47/6 90/-	50/- 95/-	70/- 133/-	75/- 142/6
Southampton			72/6 138/-	67/6 128/-	50/- 95/-	40/- 75/-	15/- 28/6	40/- 75/-	45/- 85/6	65/- 123/6	70/- 133/-
Hull				7/6 12/6	27/6 52/6	32/6 60/-	87/6 165/-	87/6 147/6	97/6 157/6	137/6 260/-	142/6 270/-
Grimsby					22/6 42/6	27/6 52/6	82/6 157/6	82/6 147/6	92/6 252/6	132/6 260/-	
Nottingham						10/- 19/-	65/- 125/-	60/- 105/-	70/- 217/6	115/- 227/6	120/-
Leicester							55/- 105/-	80/- 152/6	85/- 160/-	105/- 200/-	110/- 210/-
Bournemouth								35/- 66/6	60/- 71/-	52/6 100/-	57/6 109/-
Torquay									16/6 31/-	35/- 66/6	40/- 76/-
Plymouth										30/- 57/-	35/- 66/6
Newquay											
Penzance											

Door-to-Door Service Saves Money! The fare is inclusive. There are NO Tips Taxi or Car fares Meals to pay for.

N.B.—Torquay serves Exeter, Teignmouth, Dawlish, Paignton and Newton Abbot. and Penzance serves St Ives, Helston and Falmouth.

PROVINCIAL AIRWAYS FLEET

Reg'n	MSN	Date of C of A	Remarks and Disposal
De Havilland D.H.83 Fox Moth			
G-ACCF	4046	23 Feb 33	To British Air Transport (B.A.T.), May 36
G-ACEX	4056	7 Apr 33	To Pines Airways, Apr 36
G-ACEY	4057	7 Apr 33	To Crilly Airways, Apr 35
De Havilland D.H. Dragon			
G-ACBW	6009	13 Apr 33	Named Neptune. To Air Dispatch, Nov 39
G-ACDL	6016	12 May 33	To Luxury Air Tours, Jun 36
G-ACKD	6052	15 Sep 33	To League of Nations, Dec 35

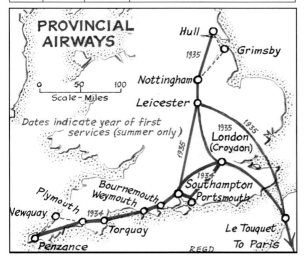

Hardy Survivor

One airline that resisted the trials of competition and efforts to restrict its marketing opportunities was **North Eastern Airways**, founded by **Lord Grimthorpe** and a group of co-investors on 4 March 1935. He was also the chairman of the Airspeed manufacturing company, and this association led to the inauguration of services with Airspeed Envoys on 8 April of that year. The daily flights from London's Heston Airport were at first to Newcastle, via Leeds, but on 27 May the route was extended to Edinburgh. But on 27 June, the airline closed down, and the assets were taken over by Alp Airline, a company also owned by Grimthorpe.

On 2 November 1936, services resumed, from Croydon to Perth, via Doncaster, Leeds, and Newcastle. The change of the Scottish terminal was because the London and North Eastern Railway (L.N.E.R.) regarded the airline as a serious competitor to its express trains, including the famous *Flying Scotsman*, and exerted pressure on the travel agents, who sold most of the tickets, to stop selling to North Eastern.

North Eastern held firm, and in 1937 survived the conflict with L.N.E.R even to extend its northern terminus to Aberdeen, including some one-stop flights from London (Croydon), via Doncaster, which became a transfer point for other flights to northern English cities. This ambitious connection had to be abandoned, however, because of the lack of suitable radio aids at Aberdeen. With Airspeed Couriers, it also operated a Humber Ferry service from Hull to Grimsby at a return fare of ten shillings.

Nevertheless, with a growing fleet of the reliable de Havilland D.H.89As, North Eastern went from strength to strength. In July 1937, it joined the prestigious International Air Travel Association (IATA) and on 21 December was once again privileged to be able to sell tickets through all the normal travel agency outlets. In April 1938 it operated special services to Glasgow, for the Empire Exhibition, and from 3 October of that year it was authorized to carry Post Office mail on the southbound flights from Scotland.

By this time, pipes of peace had been smoked and the winter 1938/39 timetable indicated that the airline and the railways were now cooperating. Passengers could exchange some air tickets for first-class rail tickets.

Together with Eric Gandar Dower, who steadfastly remained defiantly independent, even during the wartime years, North Eastern Airways claims a place in airline history for its determination, against strong corporate opposition, to cling to the right to operate an important trunk airline route.

North Eastern's first Airspeed Envoy, G-ADAZ Tyndale, at Doncaster Airport in 1935.

NORTH EASTERN AIRWAYS FLEET

Reg'n	MSN	Date of C of A	Name	Remarks and Disposal
Airspeed A.S. 6A Envoy, Series 1				
G-ADAZ	32	28 Mar 35	Tynedale	To Air Service Training, Hamble, Nov 38
G-ADBA	33	18 Apr 35		To R.A.F. (as P5778), Jan 39
G-ADBB	34	6 Apr 35	Wharfedale	To Spain, Sep 36
G-ADBZ	35	13 Apr 35	Swaledale	Leased to Air Dispatch; crashed near Croydon 22 Jan 37
De Havilland D.H.84 Dragon				
G-ACLE	6044	5 Sep 33		To Allied Airways, Dec 37
De Havilland D.H.89 Dragon Rapide				
G-ADDE	6282	31 May 35		To R.A.F. (as X9386), Mar 40
G-ADWZ	6309	9 Nov 35		To R.A.F. (as X9449), Mar 40
G-AEMH	6336	5 Sep 36		To R.A.F. (as X9387), Mar 40
G-AEXO	6368	19 Jul 37		To R.A.F. (as X8507), Mar 40
G-AEXP	6369	19 Jul 37		To R.A.F. (as X8505), Mar 40
G-AFEO	6405	9 May 38		To R.A.F. (as X8506), Mar 40
G-AFEP	6406	13 May 38		To R.A.F. (as X9388), Mar 40

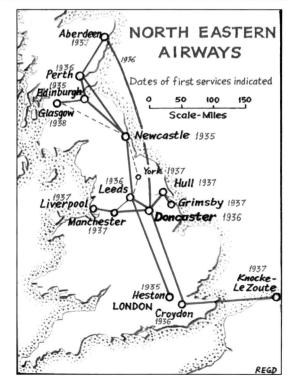

The Forces Gather . . .

As the decade of the 1930s began, the early airlines were formed mostly by bus and coach operators, who turned to the air with a pioneering spirit of adventure as well as with business objectives. But by the mid-1930s, as the airlines were losing money, the situation was serious enough for the Government to appoint a committee to look into the matter (see page 69) with the result that, if they were to survive — helped with the prospect of Post Office mail contracts, and even subsidy — they were encouraged to merge.

Whitehall Securities

The pre-war British Airways (which was later to merge with Imperial Airways in 1940 to form B.O.A.C.) began, almost in story-book fashion, after a tennis match in the summer of 1935 between **Clive Pearson**, who directed the fortunes of **Whitehall Securities**, and **Major McCrindle**, who headed **Hillman's Airways** after the founder's death.

Airline pioneers like Hillman, Sword, and Gandar Dower were extrovert personalities, but Pearson worked quietly behind the scenes, with an acute business brain and with a wealth of financial acumen and experience. Whitehall Securities had been founded in 1907, to take over all the business activities of Weetman Dickinson Pearson, who had started as a building contractor in Yorkshire in 1877. By the early 1900s, he had built docks, railways, canals, and tunnels, made a considerable personal fortune, became Baron Cowdray in 1910 and a Viscount in 1917. Clive Pearson was the younger son, and was first involved in aviation in 1925, when he formed Metal Propellers Ltd. In 1927 he invested in **Simmonds Aircraft**, which had built small three-seater Spartan biplanes.

Evolution of Spartan Air Lines

Simmonds was taken over by **Spartan Aircraft Ltd.** on 26 April 1930. The next move was, in October 1930, to take a 50% share of **Saunders-Roe (SARO)**, which had a history of building flying boats. The first Spartan aircraft was built by SARO but registered to Spartan Aircraft, and made a fast flight to Karachi in June 1932. Subsequently, the all-metal monoplane design was developed into the **Spartan Cruiser** as a comfortable six-seat passenger aircraft. To promote its own product, Spartan formed its own airline, **Spartan Air Lines**, on 2 February 1933.

These companies were all based on the Solent estuary so that Spartan's first route, from London's Heston aerodrome to Ryde and Cowes on the Isle of Wight was a natural beginning.

6 seats • 118 mph

Spartan Cruiser III

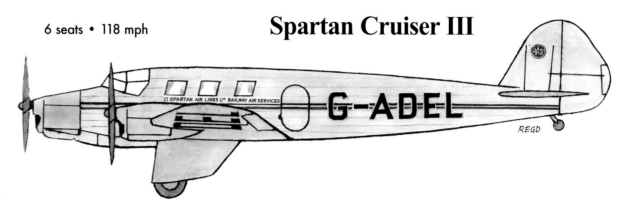

Note: The markings on this aircraft reveal Spartan's early association with Railway Air Services.

Engine	De Havilland Gypsy Major (130 hp x 3)
MGTOW	6,200 lb.
Max. Range	550 miles
Length	41 feet
Span	54 feet

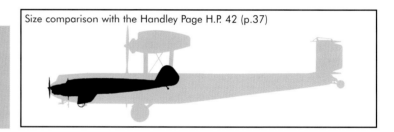

Size comparison with the Handley Page H.P. 42 (p.37)

This picture was taken on the occasion of Spartan Air Lines's service from Croydon on 1 May 1934. Faithful City *was sold to Misr Airwork for service in Egypt.*

. . . and Spar for Control

An Uneasy Truce

Spartan began its first scheduled service on 12 April 1933, and the connection to London alarmed the incumbent transport operator, the Southern Railway, and indeed was yet another perceived threat that echoed the apprehension of the L.N.E.R. and the L.M.S. companies that watched the establishment of the airlines in Scotland and the north of England. In the 1930s, the railways were a powerful force in the land, employing more than a million people, and they were not inclined to sit back and accept any encroachment on their time-honoured preserves. On 30 September, they took action and the notorious **Booking Ban** began, when a travel agent was told by the railways not to sell tickets for the new International Airlines (see page 53). Further action was more decisive which, if not a trump card, it stirred the airlines into a defensive strategy. On the basis of "if you can't beat 'em, join 'em," **Railway Air Services (R.A.S.)** was registered on 21 March 1934.

So that when Spartan began its 1934 summer season of services to the Isle of Wight on 1 May, this was operated in cooperation with the newly-formed R.A.S. The Railways soon got into their stride (see pages 76–77), and quickly developed a network to the north and to Scotland. Meanwhile, Ted Hillman went north with a route to Liverpool, the Isle of Man, and Belfast, on 16 July, and on 1 December extended to Glasgow, and played a trump card: a G.P.O. Post Office contract.

The Plot Thickens

By this time, Whitehall Securities was playing its own cards. In December, through a holding company, Channel Islands Airways, Ltd., it participated in the increased capitalization of W.L.Thurgood's **Jersey Airways**, while the Great Western and the Southern Railways also took a third of the shares. Whitehall (Pearson) and Jersey Airways then, on 4 April 1935, formed **United Airways**, which began services from Heston to the north of England. While this was going on, Ted Hillman had died on 31 December 1934, but his airline was expanding both in England and to the Continent (see map) and Fate seemed to have taken a hand with the informal meeting between Hillman's Major McCrindle and Clive Pearson, as narrated on page 74.

The First British Airways

Whether or not the agreement was a case of "choose your weapons," or whether the two tennis opponents had been nudged by the Maybury Committee (which had not yet issued its final report), a deal was made. The short-lived United may

have been a diversion, a kind of aerial false alarm. In the event, on 30 September 1935, under the supervision of Clive Pearson, the three airlines, Spartan, Hillman's, and United, merged to form **Allied British Airways**. One of the most important events in the history of British commercial aviation, the "Allied" was dropped on 29 October, and with an infusion of private capital during the next few months, **British Airways** quickly got into its stride, as will be chronicled on pages 86–88.

SPARTAN AIR LINES FLEET

Reg'n	MSN	Date of C of A	Remarks and Disposal
Spartan Cruiser I			
G-ABTY	24M	16 Aug 32	To the Hon. Mrs. Victor Bruce, Feb 36
Spartan Cruiser II			
G-ACBM	2	21 Mar 33	To British Airways, March 36
G-ACDW	3	12 May 33	Named *Faithful City*. To Misr. Airwork (as SU-ABL) April 34
G-ACDX	4	19 Jun 33	To British Airways, Apr 34
G-ACSM	10	13 Jun 34	To British Airways, Feb 36
G-ACVT	11	2 Aug 34	To British Airways, Feb 36
G-ACZM	14	13 Dec 34	To British Airways, Jan 36
Spartan Cruiser III			
G-ACYK	101	16 Apr 35	To British Airways, Apr 36
G-ADEL	102	18 Apr 35	To British Airways, Oct 36
G-ADEM	103	3 Jun 35	To British Airways, Mar 36
De Havilland D.H.84 Dragon			
G-ACNG	6069	23 Mar 34	To British Airways, Mar 36

UNITED AIRWAYS FLEET

Reg'n	MSN	Date of C of A	Remarks and Disposal
Armstrong Whitworth Argozy II			
G-AACI	A.W.364	6 Jul 29	To British Airways, Jan 36
De Havilland D.H.60 Gipsy Moth			
G-AAYY	1251	26 Jun 30	To Ceylon (as VP-CAC), Dec 36
De Havilland D.H.89 Dragon Rapide			
G-ADBU	6280	29 Apr 35	To British Airways, Jan 36
G-ADBX	6289	4 Jul 35	To British Airways, Jan 36
Spartan Three-Seater II			
G-ABTR	101	2 Jun 32	To British Airways, May 36
Spartan Cruiser II			
G-ACYL	12	24 Oct 34	To British Airways, Dec 35

A United Airways D.H.89 Dragon Rapide, lined up in front of two of Jersey Airways's D.H.86 Expresses, at Heston Airport on 30 April 1935.

Railway Air Services

Enter the Railways

The British railways had themselves become an oligopoly after the 1914-18 Great War, when the many companies, with minor exceptions, were consolidated into four systems: the London, Midland, and Scottish (L.M.S.), the London and North Eastern (L.N.E.R.), the Great Western (G.W.R.), and the Southern (S.R.) Railways. They now echoed that need for rationalization by entering the field of commercial aviation, partly as a defensive strategy against possible diversion of its rail traffic on the longer routes. On 21 March 1934, **Railway Air Services (R.A.S.)** was formed, with help from **Imperial Airways**, which held equal shares with the four railways. This was (unintentionally or independently) in line with the objectives of the Maybury Committee (see page 69), and by the time the latter's report was published early in 1936, its recommendations seemed already to have been accomplished. When Whitehall Securities formed British Airways in the autumn of 1935 (see page 71), the Railways' own airline was already well established. The combined route networks of Whitehall's three merged companies tended to run parallel, especially when R.A.S. started a trunk route from London to Glasgow, via Birmingham, Manchester, and Belfast, with the four-engined de Havilland D.H. 86, on 20 August 1934. The new British Airways promptly abandoned its domestic involvement, and concentrated on establishing routes to Europe, concentrating on destinations that Imperial Airways had ignored.

Spheres of Interest

This *quid pro quo (something for something)* appears to have worked well, as Great Britain struggled to establish a coherent pattern of domestic air routes. R.A.S. had the full resources of the railways behind it, and could withstand the financial problems that had defeated many an ambitious pioneer. British Airways was backed by the well-heeled Whitehall Securities. Understandings were reached to permit local Scottish enterprise, as long as Fresson and Gandar Dower kept north of Glasgow and Edinburgh; and similarly, the Channel Islands remained independent.

The Railway Inaugurals

The two new well-capitalized airlines, far from competing, helped each other. As stated in the first Railway Air Services timetable, for its inaugural route from London's Croydon Airport to the Isle of Wight on 1 May 1934, the aircraft were provided by Spartan Air Lines, by arrangement with the Southern Railway. Previously, when the railways had first sniffed the air in 1933 (see page 51), Imperial Airways had flown for the Great Western, so that the airline had already set a precedent for cooperation. Six days later, with its own D.H.89 aircraft, R.A.S. started a cross-country service from Plymouth to Liverpool, and on 20 August, as stated above, served notice that it was here to stay. Operating on behalf of the L.M.S., the London-Glasgow service was with the latest four-engined aircraft — and much was made of the aircraft's ability to fly even with only two engines. Also, as a valuable supplement to its revenue, R.A.S. had mail contracts on all its routes, and continuing its self-protective booking ban on the travel agents (through whom most travellers made their arrangements), the railways took to the air from a position of strength.

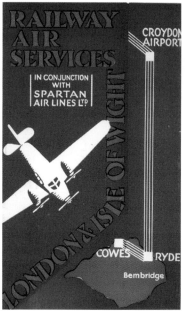

In addition to its D.H.86s and D.H.89s, R.A.S. had a fleet of D.H.84s, most of them the improved version of the famous Dragon.

De Havilland D.H.89 Dragon Rapide
6 seats • 130 mph

RAILWAY AIR SERVICES PRE-WAR FLEET

Reg'n	MSN	Date of C of A	Name	Remarks and Disposal
De Havilland D.H.84 Dragon				
G-ACHV	6035	4 Jul 33		To De Havilland Air Taxis, Dec 1938
G-ACNI	6071	28 Mar 34		Operated under Spartan Air Lines name, and passed to British Airways, Feb 36
G-ACPX	6075	Apr 34		To Western Airways
G-ACPY	6076	Apr 34		To Channel Air Ferries
G-ACVD	6084	26 Apr 34	Star of Cheshire	To Brian Allen Aviation, July 35
G-ACXI	6087	24 Jul 34		Sold Overseas, Dec 35
G-ADDI	6096	18 Aug 34	City of Cardiff	To Great Western and Southern, Jan 39
G-ADDJ	6097	18 May 35	City of Plymouth	To Australia (as VH-UZZ) March 37
G-ADED	6098	25 May 35		Crashed in the Isle of Man, 1 July 35
G-ADEE	6099	27 May 35		Crashed on Fair Snape Fell, 26 Oct 35
De Havilland D.H.86				
G-ACVY	2302	15 Aug 34	Mercury	Scapped, 1948
G-ACVZ	2303	7 Dec 34	Jupiter	Crashed 15 March 37 (operating for Imperial Airways)
G-ACZP	2321	11 May 35		To Skytravel, 1948
De Havilland D.H.86A				
G-AEFH	2350	10 Aug 36	Neptune	Lost in the evacuation from France, June 1940
De Havilland D.H.86B				
G-AENR	2352	8 Feb 37		Scrapped, Nov. 48
G-AEWR	2354	29 Jun 37	Venus	Lost in the evacuation from France, June 1940
De Havilland D.H.89 Dragon Rapide				
G-ACPP	6254	12 Mar 35	City of Bristol	To Great Western & Souther, March 39
G-ACPR	6255	18 Mar 35	City of Birmingham	To Great Western & Southern, 19 Feb 39
G-AEAJ	6320	4 Mar 36	Star of Lancashire	
G-AEAK	6324	4 Apr 36	Star of Mona	
G-AEAL	6325	25 Apr 36	Star of Yorkshire	To Isle of Man Air Services, Oct 37
G-AEAM	6326	5 May 36	Star of Ulster	
G-AEBW	6327	13 Mar 36	Star of Renfrew	
G-AEBX	6328	20 May 36	Star of Scotia	Crashed near Belfast, 3 July 1938
G-AFFF	6386	16 Mar 38	Juno	To Scottish Airways, Crashed at Milngavie, 27 Sep 46

Note: Some R.A.S. services were operated by D.H.86 G-ACPL and Westland Wessex G-AAGW of Imperial Airways

Three Score Years and Ten

As reviewed in the text on this page, the Rapide, as it became generally known, was a sturdy machine, in spite of its fabric-and-wood, metal-framed construction. Several of those built during the Second World War are still flying (G-AGJG offers joy-rides). This 1934 design has stood the test of time.

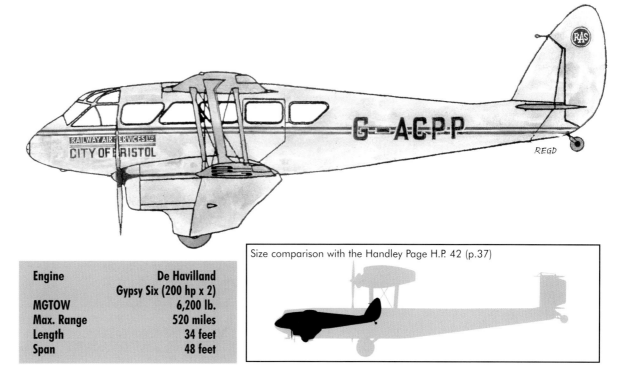

Engine	De Havilland Gypsy Six (200 hp x 2)
MGTOW	6,200 lb.
Max. Range	520 miles
Length	34 feet
Span	48 feet

Size comparison with the Handley Page H.P. 42 (p.37)

The **D.H. 89** made its first flight, piloted by Hubert Broad, on 17 April 1934. First called the **Dragon Six**, the design was a twin-engined version of the four-engined D.H. 86 Express, which was in turn a development of the D.H. 84 Dragon. The resemblance was such that it was, for several years, called the **Dragon Rapide**, but eventually it became known familiarly simply as the **Rapide**.

Although de Havilland had had problems with the D.H. 86 Express, the Hatfield company had a real winner in the Rapide. It went into service first with Hillman's — appropriately as Ted Hillman had instigated the design of the first Dragon — and was quickly followed by orders from Railway Air Services, Jersey Airways, and other domestic airlines. Significantly — and rare for the British commercial aircraft manufacturers during the 1930s — de Havilland received

orders almost immediately from overseas, and a total of 205 Rapides were delivered by the time the Second World War erupted in 1939.

The Rapide was, in spite of its partial wood-and-fabric construction, a sturdy machine, and for foreign countries where the provision of concrete runways was unknown, it was welcomed as a versatile performer that could feel at home on almost any short stretch of grass, sand, or dirt. The Royal Air Force was among the military customers which found it useful as a general-purpose aeroplane, and of the total of 730 Rapides built, 541 were military versions.

The technical stature of the Rapide did not perhaps permit it to be called an airliner. Nevertheless, many of these fine commercial aeroplanes survived the War, some for decades, and a few are still in flying condition today.

The Wake-Up Call

As the decade of the 1930s got under way, interest in aviation increased from curiosity to enthusiasm. The public followed closely the frequent breaking of records of speed, altitude, range, and endurance; and the heroes' names were as well known as those of famous footballers, jockeys, or Test Match cricketers. Songs were written about Amy Johnson, after she defied all the technical and physical odds by flying, on her own, in May 1930, to Australia in a Gipsy Moth. The efforts of **Imperial Airways** to link the Empire with air mail and passenger services was not so exciting as Schneider Trophy speed records or trans-Atlantic flights.

Imperial Struggles On

Britain's flagship airline was doing its best with the equipment available, and, as narrated in pages 29 to 48, it largely succeeded. The journeys were arduous at times, but the rest stops were pleasant, and the mail did get through. Imperial had no competition to South Africa, but it did on its route through the Middle East to southern and southeast Asia. For on 1 October 1931, the great Dutch airline, **K.L.M.**, opened a regular service from Amsterdam to Batavia (now Jakarta), with Fokker F.VIIs. These had four luxury reclining seats, and — unlike Imperial's clientèle — the passengers did not have to change aircraft. Imperial could not match the elapsed time of ten days over such a distance, and on 3 May 1933, the Dutch added a connecting service to Singapore, seven months before Imperial Airways provided any service at all.

The First American Airliners

The problem did not seem to generate decisive action. Transport aircraft were expected to fly at a good speed — something better than 100 mph — but there was little incentive to go faster (but less comfortably) than in the Handley Pages. But in 1933, across the Atlantic, the **Boeing** company had produced what later historians would regard as the world's first modern airliner. The **Model 247** was a twin-engined 10-seat monoplane that cruised at 165 mph, and was able to provide United Air Lines with a United States transcontinental schedule of 18 hours. The next year, in an effort to surpass its rival, T.W.A. sponsored the **Douglas DC-2**, which had 14 seats, was just as fast, and had a more comfortable cabin. In retrospect, the British response was inadequate. Some voices were even heard that the performances of these American aircraft were exaggerated; and the chairman of Imperial was inclined to defend the status quo. After all, Imperial could reach India far more quickly than could the ships of the P.& O. Line.

The "MacRobertson" Race

To such complacency came a rude awakening. In 1934, an Australian industrialist, **Sir MacPherson Robertson**, wishing to prove that a regular air service between Europe and Australia was technically possible and overdue, offered handsome prizes for a dramatic race. One was for the fastest aeroplane past the post, another for a handicap contest that would take into account the performances of individual aircraft.

The resultant **England-Australia Air Race** was from Mildenhall, in Suffolk, to Melbourne, Victoria. This must rank as possibly the greatest race of all time. Furthermore, it proved emphatically that American transport aircraft were in a class of their own, far superior to anything that Britain could offer. The de Havilland D.H.88 Comet won the race, but two American transport aircraft were not far behind.

The start was made, under the supervision of the Royal Aero Club, on 20 October 1934. Of the original 64 entries, only 20 started, including three specially-built Comets, and — viewed with a certain skepticism by most observers — two American transport aircraft: a Boeing 247, flown by two famous airmen, and a Douglas DC-2, entered by the Dutch airline, K.L.M., and flown by two of its regular airline pilots.

Of the 20 starters, only nine finished the course. A **D.H.88 Comet**, *Grosvenor House*, entered by hotelier A.O. Edwards, and piloted by C.W.A.Scott and T. Campbell Black, won both the speed and the handicap categories; but under the rules of the race, no competitor was eligible to receive more than one prize, so the handicap prize went to the **K.L.M. Douglas DC-2**, piloted by K.D.Parmentier and J.J.Moll.

An Amazing Achievement — and a Warning

Seventh to finish was the 20-year-old Australian Charles Melrose, whose mother had given him a D.H. Puss Moth. Of the nine that finished the course, four were de Havillands. The Douglas DC-2 had stopped at all the airfields designated by the handicap rules, and even a few more, on the regular K.L.M. route to the Dutch East Indies. It had carried three passengers and 30,000 letters; had had to turn back to Allahabad, because a passenger had been left behind; and had been stuck in the mud at Albury, not far from the finishing line. The Boeing 247 had lost time after overshooting Allahabad by 200 miles, and had had to return to the reporting point. Without hindrance, they might have arrived in Melbourne close on the heels of the Comet. If ever Britain's aircraft manufacturing industry and its airline needed a reminder of the threat of superior foreign competition, this was it.

The Outright Winner

De Havilland D.H.88 Comet
71 hr. 0 min. 18 sec.

The pilots, Scott and Black, had flown a magnificent race, but were almost exhausted at the finish.

The Honourable Second

Douglas DC-2
90 hr. 13 min. 36 sec.

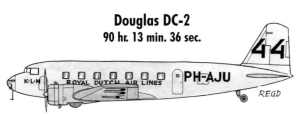

Parmentier and Moll emerged, fresh and shaved, together with their passengers; and the mail was delivered.

The Respectable Third

Boeing 247D
92 hr. 55 min. 38 sec.

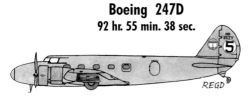

Roscoe Turner, Clyde Pangborn, and Reeder Nicholls were only three hours behind the Dutch. The registration number of the Boeing 247 reflected the slogan of its sponsor; 57 varieties.

The three drawings are on the same scale.

The "MacRobertson" Race

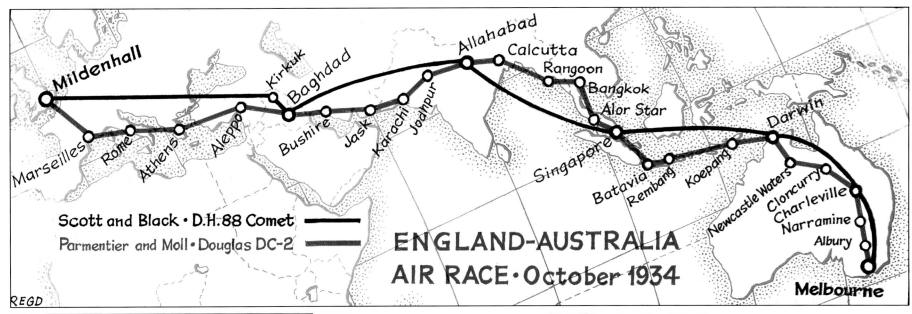

Scott and Black • D.H.88 Comet

Parmentier and Moll • Douglas DC-2

ENGLAND-AUSTRALIA AIR RACE • October 1934

Mildenhall · Marseilles · Rome · Athens · Aleppo · Kirkuk · Baghdad · Bushire · Jask · Karachi · Jodhpur · Allahabad · Calcutta · Rangoon · Bangkok · Alor Star · Singapore · Batavia · Rembang · Koepang · Darwin · Newcastle Waters · Cloncurry · Charleville · Narramine · Albury · Melbourne

REGD

Placing	Pilots (and nationality)	Aircraft	Time (hrs)	Remarks
Speed Race (based on elapsed time)				
1*	C.W.A. Scott T.C. Black (U.K.)	De Havilland D.H.88 Comet	71	In additon to the compulsory stops, also stopped at Kirkuk
2*	K.D. Parmentier J.J. Moll (Dutch)	Douglas DC-2	90	Also carried 2 other crew, 3 passengers and mail
3*	Roscoe Turner Clyde Pangborn (U.S.)	Boeing 247	93	Also carried Reeder Nichols (radio)
4*	O. Cathcart-Jones K.F.H. Waller (U.K.)	De Havilland D.H.88 Comet	108	Second D.H.88; the third Comet (Jim Mollison and Amy (Johnson) Mollison retired at Allahabad)
5*	J.D. Hewett C.E. Kay (N.Z.)	De Havilland D.H.84 Dragon	331	
Handicap Race (based on flying time only)				
1*	C.W.A. Scott T.C. Black (U.K.)	De Havilland D.H.88 Comet	66	Competitors could accept only one prize. Thus the DC-2 was awarded the Handicap Prize
2*	K.D. Parmentier J.J. Moll (Dutch)	Douglas DC-2	77	(see above)
3	C.J. Melrose (Aust.)	D.H.80A Puss Moth	79	Seventh to reach Melbourne
4	D.E. Stodart K.G. Stodart (U.K.)	Airpeed Courier	80	Sixth to reach Melbourne
5	M. MacGregor (N.Z.) H. Walker	Miles Hawk (open cockpit)	83	Fifth to reach Melbourne
6*	J.W. Hewitt (N.Z.) C.Kay	De Havilland D.H.84 Dragon	86	Last aeroplane to reach Melbourne before deadline
7	M. Hansen (Danish) D. Jensen	Desoutter Mark II	88	Eighth aeroplane to reach Melbourne

Nothing epitomized the problems facing Imperial Airways more than the performance of K.L.M.'s Douglas DC-2, seen here at a re-fuelling stop on its normal passenger and mail route. Imperial's aircraft were incapable of even entering the Race.

Imperial Struggles On

Within Great Britain, the spirit of private enterprise was in full swing, even if some casualties were sustained; but the "chosen instrument" for developing a network of air services to reach the far corners of the Empire was not making much headway. As noted on page 43, **Imperial Airways** had, almost laboriously, at last opened an air mail service to Australia. Bearing in mind that to have bought any non-British aircraft would, in 1934, have been tantamount to treason, the airline did its best with the aircraft that it could obtain. The big Handley Pages were comfortable but slow; the trans-Mediterranean segment was still a flying boat operation; the trans-Indian segment, with Armstrong Whitworth Atalantas, had to be done by Indian Transcontinental Airways; and the final leg, from Darwin to Brisbane had had to be negotiated with Australia's QANTAS, and flown by diminutive de Havilland biplanes.

To criticize, much less condemn Imperial, therefore, would be churlish. In April 1934, when it marked its first ten years of flying, its map covered almost every part of the British Empire in the eastern hemisphere, and its ton-mile traffic had grown sevenfold during the decade. The 12,750-mile London-Brisbane service was the longest air service in the world, and although the air mail took 12 days, this was 20 days shorter than by sea. England cricket teams still took a month to reach their Australian Test Match appointments.

Service to Australia
The inauguration of the through mail service on 8 December 1934 was followed by passenger service along the whole route on 13 April 1935. The one-way fare was £195, but most of the traffic was between intermediate points, especially to India. The end-to-end journey still took 12 days. But with the result of the MacRobertson Race reverberating throughout the corridors of air power in Britain, and facing the grim reality of K.L.M. setting the pace to the Orient with the DC-2, Imperial realized that stern measures were required.

Historic Air Mail Development
Something had to be done, even though the prospect of operating aircraft that would be competitive to the Douglas landplane was two years distant. Something was done, and done quickly. On 20 December 1934, the British Government announced the ambitious **Empire Air Mail Scheme**. All mail would be carried at 1-1/2d for a half-ounce letter or a penny for a postcard to all Britain's dominions overseas.

Historic Aircraft Order
To make this possible, Imperial Airways ordered 28 new high-performance flying boats "straight off the drawing board," from Shorts at Rochester; and at the same time ordered 17 large landplanes for the European services. The choice of flying boats may have seemed impractical to counter the efficient landplane service of K.L.M. But Imperial was not alone. In the early 1930s, the flagships of all the other colonial nations were following the same policy. France and Germany developed flying boats for the South Atlantic route; and the great Pan American Airways had conquered the Pacific Ocean with its Martin 130 Clippers. Landplanes still had to use grass or dirt strips (the first hard-surfaced runway in Europe, at Stockholm, was not built until 1936) and thus flying boats could be built larger as there was no weight limitation on their airfield requirement, only the need, as with the ocean liners, for unrestricted water.

Outposts of Empire
Meanwhile, Imperial continued to fulfil its mission to link almost every outpost of Empire, adhering to the then-popular slogan of "four-engined safety." For the difficult Timor Sea crossing, the Australian Government had demanded such an aircraft, to carry ten passengers, and for it to be faster than any previous type. De Havilland met the challenge with a "four-engined Dragon," similar in general appearance, with six-cylinder Gipsy Six engines. The **D.H. 86 Express Air Liner**, G-ACPL, made its first flight on 14 January 1934.

The aircraft went into service on British internal routes during the summer, and Imperial ordered 12 of them, designated the **Diana Class**. It opened a new service on 1 April 1935, from London to Budapest (see Map) and it was considered an ideal aircraft for some of the branch routes from the main-line arteries to the Far East and in Africa. On 9 February 1936, it opened the trans-Africa route from Khartoum to Kano, extended on 15 October to Lagos, and on 11 October 1937 to Accra. On 23 March of the same year, the first connection was made to Hong Kong.

On the other hand, the European routes had to face competition — or partnerships that would now be termed code-sharing — with other airlines. The biplanes of Imperial, D.H.86s, Scipios, and H.P.45s, were no match for Swissair's DC-2s, SABENA's S.M.73s, and D.L.H.'s Junkers-Ju52/3m's.

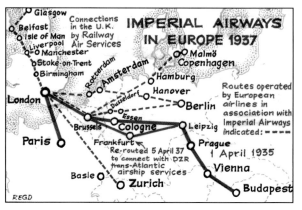

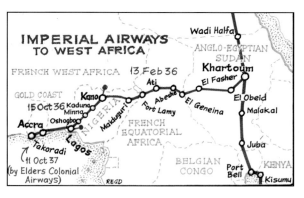

De Havilland D.H.86 Express

10 seats • 140 mph

The D.H.86 was essentially a four-engined D.H.84 Dragon, with new more-powerful engines. It was designed specifically to fly at least ten passengers on the difficult segment of the England-Australia route: across the Timor Sea, 500 miles with no possible en route alternate, and with uncertain wind and weather conditions. By agreement, Imperial Airways conceded the responsibility as a joint operation to be flown by Queensland & Northern Territories Aerial Services (QANTAS) from Singapore onwards, as **Qantas Empire Airways (Q.E.A.)**. Along with Ivan Holyman, who controlled the route to Tasmania, the Australian airline's Hudson Fysh ordered the D.H. 86, confident in the pedigree of Arthur Hagg and Frank Halford as airframe and engine designers respectively.

Inauspicious Beginning

Hubert Broad made the first flight on 14 January 1934, and after modification to the nose for side-by-side pilot positioning, two aircraft arrived by sea in October. There followed a series of crashes which did nothing to create confidence. A few days after delivery, Ivan Holyman himself was killed in a crash, and shortly thereafter two QANTAS aircraft and one of Imperial Airways's fleet were lost. A year later, another Holyman aircraft was lost and three more went down in Britain in 1936. This resulted in further modifications to produce the D.H. 86A, with a strengthened wing and rudder. Eventually, in January 1937, the D.H.86B appeared, with auxiliary fins on the tailpane.

Versatile Operational Record

Imperial Airways adopted the Express as a landplane for its European routes where the traffic did not justify 40-seaters such as the Handley Page or Scylla classes on the popular London-Paris route. They were also used initially by the new British Airways before it concentrated on faster speeds and journey times, and turned to the well-established German Junkers trimotor and then to the American Lockheed twin.

In spite of its early design shortcomings, the Express overcame its problems. 64 of all the variants, some in high-density seating up to 15 on short-haul routes, saw good service, and were still the flagships of the British internal airlines at the outbreak of the Second World War in September 1939. They were the last of the British commercial biplanes.

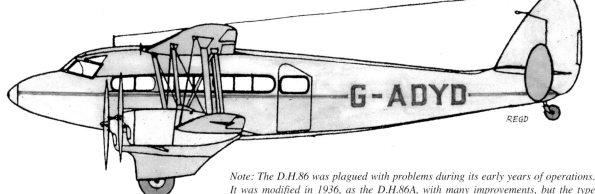

Note: The D.H.86 was plagued with problems during its early years of operations. It was modified in 1936, as the D.H.86A, with many improvements, but the type was grounded in the autumn of that year. New "Zulu shield" fins were added, to establish control in bad weather, as the D.H.86B, and all aircraft were modified to that standard, as illustrated.

Engine	D.H. Gipsy Siz (200 hp x 4)
MGTOW (D.H.86A)	11,000 lb.
Max. Range	760 miles
Length	46 feet
Span	64 feet

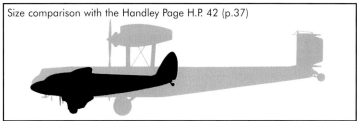

Size comparison with the Handley Page H.P. 42 (p.37)

The D.H.86 Express was immediately popular among many of the British internal airlines. This is one of Railway Air Services, which operated the trunk route from London to Glasgow. (see page 76)

Realignment in Britain

During the mid-1930s, the British internal airlines reviewed their prospects. These appeared to combine an uncertain development, because of the difficulty of balancing the books on a year-round basis, with the inevitable process of attrition. The independence that the pioneers had cherished was fragile, and a few of them did not survive. A notable casualty was John Sword's Midland & Scottish Air Ferries (pages 62–63) and there were other early departures from the airways, as listed in the tabulation on this page. Among the later entrants, **Crilly Airways** and Provincial lasted only a season or two.

Among the reasons for the difficulties were competition, even opposition, from the incumbent railways, which jealously guarded their transport territory; and the consequences of the seasonal nature of the business. Most of the traffic was in the summer, and revenues fell off abruptly at the end of the summer holidays. But the fixed expenditures remained during the winter. Some airlines simply closed down.

The vision of a future for commercial aviation in the British Isles was interpreted by some as a matter of good organization, good equipment, and above all, good finance. This last factor became dominant in shaping the course of development. The airlines needed sound management, backed by sound investment, and these emerged from the railways, which formed **Railway Air Services (R.A.S.)** (pages 76–77) and from the investment by **Whitehall Securities**, which was instrumental in establishing **British Airways** (page 75.)

The latter was a formidable force, representing the interests of Lord Cowdray's son, **Clive Pearson**, combined with the d'Erlanger bank. They supplemented the merger by shareholdings in other airlines that were natural operational partners, which, with the influx of new capital, were able to continue operations under their own names (see tabulation).

Of the fringe airlines that were not swept into the merger, some, such as Air Dispatch, Olley, and Wrightways, had specialized objectives. Norman Edgar kept his independence, against strong efforts by R.A.S.; North Eastern fought the good fight against the L.N.E.R.; and as British holiday-makers sought the guaranteed sunshine of the Channel Islands, Walter Thurgood, (who had joined up with Whitehall to manage United Airways, which, in turn, supported Northern & Scottish) watched his Jersey Airways thrive — see pages 84–85. Only one new airline appeared on the British internal scene: **Utility Airways** operated briefly from Hooton across the Mersey to Liverpool and Blackpool, with Monospars, from 14 May to 1 October 1936.

THE CASUALTIES

Airline	First Service	Terminated	Other Page Refs.
Eastern (Scott)	1931	1932	51
British Air Navigation	1932	1933	52
British Flying Boats	1932	1932	52
National Flying Services	1932		52
Great Western Rwy.	1933	1933	53
Midland & Scottish	1933	1934	**62–63**
British Amphibious	1932	1933	52
North Sea & General Transport Int	1919		53
Crilly	1915	1936	53
Provincial	1933	1935	87–88
British Continental	1935	1936	**72**
Cobham	1935	1935	
West of Scotland	1935	1937	
Utility	1937	1936	This page

Major operators shown in bold type. Whitehall Securities control or affiliation: W

THE SURVIVORS

Airline	First Service	Terminated	Other Page Refs.
Hillman's	1932	British Airways Merger	**56–57**
Spartan	1933		**74–75**
United	1934	W	75
Aberdeen (Allied)	1933		**60–61**
Blackpool & W.Coast	1933	W	67
Norman Edgar	1932		**70–71**
North Eastern	1932		73
Highland	1931		**58–59**
Northern & Scottish	1934	W	66
P. S.I.O.W.	1932		**68–69**
Railway Air Services	1934		**76–77**
Jersey	1933	W	**84–85**
Guernsey	1935	W	84–85
Wrightways	1934		102
Olley	1935		87, 102

Two major casualties were Leo Crilly (above), whose Leicester-based airline had even made a trial flight to Portugal, and John Sword (page 62), whose Midland & Scottish Air Ferries pioneered the air routes, in western Scotland.

Scottish Airways

The one area of Great Britain where the benefits of air transport were clear-cut was northern Scotland. The railways had reached the more populated eastern shores; the northernmost county, Caithness; and the western ports of Oban and Mallaig. These lines connected with ferry-boats to Orkney, Shetland, and the Hebrides, but the journeys were long and tiring, and in bad weather, arduous. The airline pioneers, Edmund Fresson (pages 58–59), Eric Gandar Dower (pages 60–61), John Sword (pages 62–63), and George Nicholson (page 66), had all done sterling work; but for mainly financial reasons, had faced the prospect of closing down. They all needed more money to establish viable fleets, to build airfields, and to create marketing organizations.

The salvation came in 1935, when **Whitehall Securities Corporation** organized British Airways by a tri-partite merger (see pages 74–75). It decided to abandon the British internal routes that it inherited, and to develop international services to northern Europe. Imperial Airways had neglected this area during the fulfilment of its main terms of reference, which were to create a route network to the far-flung British Empire. It had achieved this objective, and was in the process of modernising its fleet; but the new long-range flying boats were unsuitable for inter- or intra-European routes and services.

The outcome was a series of corporate decisions and actions that resulted in the formation of **Scottish Airways,** on 12 August 1937. In June 1935, Fresson's **Highland Airways** had merged its interests with those of **United Airways**, which had been formed by Whitehall, and managed by Walter Thurgood of Jersey Airways, another Whitehall affiliate. Then, on 1 July 1936, George Nicholson's **Northern and Scottish Airways** became a wholly-owned subsidiary of Whitehall. Both airlines had continued to operate under their own names until the spring of 1938.

The Scottish airline's ownership was N.S.A. 31.9%. Highland 18.1%, L.M.S. Railway 40%, and David McBrayne 10%. This last company operated the ferry boats to the Western Isles and was almost a public utility. The experience of the pioneers was thus backed by entrepreneurial capital and financial judgement, coupled with the advantage of inter-modal convenience. On 12 August, **Western Isles Airways** was incorporated as an associate of Scottish Airways. Service to Skye was terminated on 2 May 1938 but Tiree was included on the route to the Outer Hebrides, on which date also the two networks were linked by a route from Glasgow to Inverness (see map).

PRE-WAR FLEET OF SCOTTISH AIRWAYS

Reg'n	MSN	Date of C of A	Remarks and Disposal
De Havilland D.H.60G Moth			
G-AAWO	1235	3 Mar 30	From Highland Airways
De Havilland D.H.84 Dragon			
G-ACIT	6039	29 July 33	*Aberdeen*, from Highland Airways
G-ACMO	6062	31 Jan 34	From Northern & Scottish Airways
G-ACNG	6069	23 May 34	From Northern & Scottish Airways
G-ACOR	6073	19 Mar 34	From Northern & Scottish Airways
G-ADCT	6095	25 May 35	*Orcadian*, from Highland Airways
Spartan Cruiser II			
G-ACSM	10	13 Jun 34	From Northern & Scottish Airways
G-ACYL	12	24 Oct 34	From Northern & Scottish Airways
G-ACZM	14	13 Dec 34	From Northern & Scottish Airways
Spartan Cruiser III			
G-ACYK	101	16 Apr 35	From Northern & Scottish Airways
G-ADEL	102	18 Apr 35	From Northern & Scottish Airways
De Havilland D.H.89 and 89A Dragon Rapide			
G-ADAJ	6276	25 Jun 35	*Inverness*, from Highland Airways
G-AEWL	6367	18 Jun 37	*Zetland*, from Highland Airways
G-AFEY	6402	11 Apr 38	Delivered 7 Mar 38, Crashed at Kirkwall, 18 Mar 40
G-AFFF	6386	16 Mar 38	From Railway Air Services, 26 May 39. (Crashed Milngavie, 27 Sep 46)
G-AFOI	6450	28 Aug 38	To B.E.A.
G-AFRK	6441	8 May 39	From Isle of Man Air Services, 12 May 39

Northern & Scottish Airways first served Barra early in 1936, on a stretch of sand at the northern end of the island. This provided a firm footing for aeroplanes to land. Subject as it was to the tidal calendar, the airline could not guarantee an exact regular timetable. The pilots claimed that it was safe to land when the gulls stopped swimming and were only paddling. The beach at Barra is still being used today by Loganair, and airfield maintenance costs are reported to be extremely low.

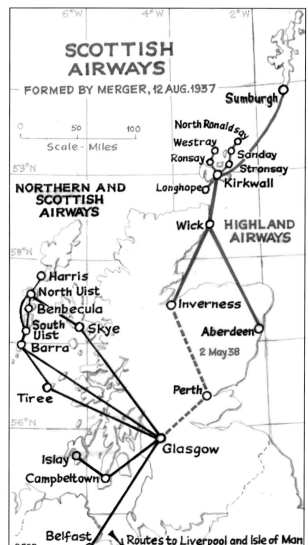

Thurgood Thrives

Another bus operator who, like Ted Hillman, John Sword, and George Nicholson, was overtaken by the rationalization of motor transport services in 1933, was **Walter L. Thurgood**, who had operated the People's Motor Coach Services, based in Ware, Hertfordshire, since 1927. Like Hillman, he received compensation for the take-over by London Transport, and, like Hillman, he recognized the opportunity for air travel where aeroplanes could compete effectively with ferry boats and shipping. While Hillman went to Paris, Thurgood went to the Channel Islands.

He quickly got into his stride. On 9 December 1933, he founded **Jersey Airways**, with an initial capital of £120,000. On 18 December, just in time for Christmas, he opened service with the first trusty D.H. 84 Dragon, on a service from Portsmouth to Jersey, using, rather spectacularly, the beach at West Park at low tide. Only five weeks later, on 28 January, he began to fly from London's Heston aerodrome, and on 21 March, extended the Portsmouth route to Southampton. During the summer, from 4 June to 30 September, a twice weekly schedule linked the popular holiday resort with Paris.

The early 1930s witnessed a determined effort by the British public to recover from the hardships of the economic depression of the 1920s. The motor coaches did a thriving business during the hot summers as Londoners and other city dwellers flocked to the seaside resorts. To follow this trend, especially in southern England, the Channel Islands beckoned, with their guarantee of wall-to-wall sunshine, and Thurgood discovered that an air service was attractive to save time and to avoid sea-sickness. During the year of 1934, Jersey Airways carried 25,000 passengers, and unlike some of the other British internal airlines, was making money,

This success was not lost in the City of London. Soon after Thurgood had formed **Guernsey Airways** on 24 November 1934, a further influx of capital came on 1 December when the influential **Whitehall Securities** joined with the Great Western Railway and the Southern Railway to make a deal with Thurgood. On that date, they formed **Channel Island Airways**, with Whitehall and Thurgood holding two-thirds of the shares, as a holding company for both airlines. Thurgood was put in charge of Whitehall's United Airways (see page 75) part of the airline empire crafted by the financial group.

With annual passenger figures averaging 30,000 a year until the outbreak of the Second World War in 1939, there was little need to expand the network. Quite often, the de Havilland Dragons, Rapides, and Expresses would fly in formation at the peak hours. On 8 January 1935, Thurgood experimented with a connection to Rennes, Brittany, to shorten the journey to France's west and southwestern coast; but this had to be abandoned on 29 March for an unusual reason: the fear of importing the Colorado Beetle pest into Jersey.

Plymouth was added to the map on 3 April 1935, and two days later, Alderney became the third of the Islands to receive air service. Landings on Jersey's beach ended on 10 March 1937 when an airfield was opened at St. Helier; and on 31 May of that year, a direct serviced from Shoreham spread the connections along the south coast of England. On 1 June 1937, the Plymouth route was transferred to Exeter, and in August 1938, a local route to Dinard made in association with Air France.

Walter Thurgood sold his shares in Channel Island Airways in July 1939, so that Whitehall Securities held 50%, with the two railways holding the balance. In the same month, this airline was of such stature that it was the launching customer for the de Havilland D.H. 95 Flamingo (see page 101), the first metal airliner built by that famous company. But the credit for such innovation was short-lived, as a few weeks later, Great Britain, including the Islands, were on a war footing, and the burgeoning holiday traffic came to an abrupt end.

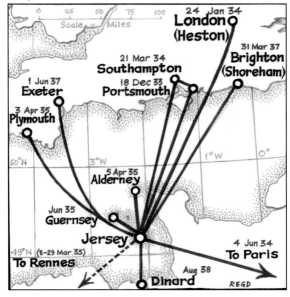

FLEETS OF JERSEY AIRWAYS AND GUERNSEY AIRWAYS

Reg'n	MSN	Date of C of A	Name	Remarks and Disposal
De Havilland D.H.84 Dragon				
G-ACCE	6010	21 Apr 33		On hire from Brian Lewis
De Havilland D.H.84 Dragon II				
G-ACMC	6053	24 Nov 33	The St. Brelade's Bay	Prototype MKII, To Airwork
G-ACMJ	6058	7 Dec 33	The St. Aubin's Bay	To Airwork
G-ACMO	6062	31 Jan 34	The St. Ouen's Bay	To Northern & Scottish, 4 July 35
G-ACMP	6063	20 Feb 34	The St. Clement's Bay	Leased to Norman Edgar, May 35, crashed near Cardiff, 22 July 35
G-ACNG	6069	23 Mar 34	The Portelet Bay	To Spartan, 27 Jun 35
G-ACNH	6070	26 Mar 34	The Bouley Bay	Sold to Northern & Scottish, 4 July 35
G-ACNI	6071	28 Mar 34	The Bonne Nuit Bay	Transferred to British Airways Feb 36
G-ACNJ	6072	27 Mar 34	The Rozel Bay	To Allied Airways
De Havilland D.H.86A				
G-ACYF	2313	6 Feb 35	The Giffard Bay	To Wearne's Air Services
G-ACYG	2314	8 Mar 35	The Grouville Bay	Impressed as AX 840
G-ACZN	2316	22 Mar 35	The St. Catherine's Bay	Leased to Imperial Airways, 8 Nov 35–22 Jan 36; crashed, Jersey, 4 Nov 38
G-ACZO	2318	9 Apr 35	The Ouaine Bay	Damaged at St. Aubin's Beach, Jersey, 17 Aug 35. To Royal Navy AX 841
G-ACZP	2321	11 May 35	The Belcroute Bay	Leased to British Airways, Dec 36. Impressed as AX 843
G-ACZR	2322	29 May 35	La Saline Bay	Leased to Imperial Airways, 11 Nov 35–18 Dec 35
De Havilland D.H.86A & B				
G-ADVK	2339	21 Apr 36		From Isle of Man Air Services, 21 Dec 38, to Guernsey Airways, 22 Apr 39
G-AENR	2352	8 Feb 37		Impressed as AX 842
De Havilland D.H.89 Dragon Rapide				
G-ADBV	6286	6 June 35	The St Ouen's Bay II	From United Airways, 28 May 35; to Jay Dade May 37.
G-ADBW	6288	27 June 35		To Isle of Man Air Services Oct 37.
Saunders-Roe A.21 Windhover				
G-ABJP	A.21/2		Windover	Guernsey Airways for service to Alderney
Saunders-Roe A.19 Cloud				
G-ABXW	A.1914		Cloud of Iona	Guernsey Airways to Alderney; crashed 31 July 36
De Havilland D.H.95 Flamingo				
G-AFUE	95001	30 Jun 39		To Royal Air Force, Oct 39
G-AFUF	95002			(Delivered direct to Royal Navy) (as X9317)

During 1935, the AVRO 642 G-ACFV
and
Short S.22 Scion Senior G-AECU
were used on hire.

Jersey and Guernsey Airways

Seeking the Sun

In the global world of the 21st Century, when Britons and northern Europeans have almost colonized southern Spain, and go to Florida's Disneyworld for a long weekend, escape from the notoriously uncertain British weather is easy and comparatively cheap. But seeking the sun in the 1930s was almost a challenge, and to choose a sunny week at the seaside was a gamble with the calendar. A whole week in the Cornish Riviera would wear out an umbrella, although, happily, there were exceptions.

But for sunbathing on the beach, the Channel Islands could almost guarantee the need for supplies of sunburn lotion. Newspapers used to print "league tables" of the hours of summer sunshine at the seaside holiday resorts. Sandown and Ventnor in the Isle of Wight were always among the leaders — much to the benefit of P.S.I.O.W. (see pages 68–69) — with Bournemouth, Weymouth, and Torquay not far behind. But none could equal the consistent figures posted by Jersey and Guernsey.

The French Riviera was still beyond the pockets of most british families; but visitors could not only feel that they were going south, they were crossing the English Channel and that was like "going abroad." The inhabitants spoke French, but they also spoke English, which was a welcome benefit.

The illustrations on this page portray the attractions of the Channel Islands for holiday-makers seeking the sun during the summers of the 1930s. The aircraft actually landed on the beach (top right), where they need not have gone far to enjoy a swim, like the lady photographed for publicity (right.) Slightly reminiscent of Copenhagen's mermaid, this was an early example of innovative promotion, other than aerial views of distant lands and cities. The aircraft (above) was one of six ten-seat four-engined de Havilland D.H.86 Express aircraft purchased in 1935 and which were leased to Imperial Airways during the Christmas week. When Guernsey Airways was formed, the timetable (right) revealed the close association between the airline and its sister company in Jersey, and emphasized the involvement of the Railways.

You'll be glad you went to THE CHANNEL ISLANDS by AIR

FROM EXETER DIRECT

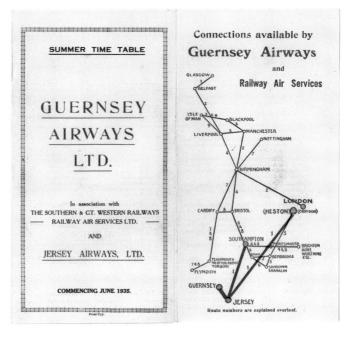

SUMMER TIME TABLE

GUERNSEY AIRWAYS LTD.

In association with
THE SOUTHERN & GT. WESTERN RAILWAYS
— RAILWAY AIR SERVICES LTD. —
AND
JERSEY AIRWAYS, LTD.

COMMENCING JUNE 1935.

Connections available by
Guernsey Airways
and
Railway Air Services

Route numbers are explained overleaf.

Inter-War Second Force

The day of 30 September 1935 was significant in the chronicle of British air transport history, comparable with that of 31 March 1924, when Imperial Airways was formed. An amalgamation of three smaller airlines, **British Airways** was founded on that date by the merger of Hillman's, Spartan, and United (see pages 74–75). First named Allied British Airways, the Allied was dropped on 29 October. It was destined to do more than follow the wishes of the Maybury Committee to rationalize the collection of internal routes. It was well-capitalized — initially for almost £250,000, a considerable sum in the mid-1930s — by the powerful Whitehall Securities investment group, which soon made its intentions clear.

With the exception of the Hillman's routes to France and Belgium, the merged airline inherited no overseas routes. But the new management took advantage of Imperial Airways's seeming neglect of northern Europe. On 17 February 1936, a four-engined de Havilland D.H. 86 inaugurated a daily service to Malmö, Sweden, via Amsterdam, Hamburg, and Copenhagen. The timetable of 1 December 1935, reproduced below, was the last "British" timetable issued by the airline.

The various amalgamations and partnerships that settled down in the latter 1930s to create an internal airline network in the British Isles are illustrated in the chart opposite.

THE BRITISH AIRCRAFT FLEET OF BRITISH AIRWAYS

Reg'n	MSN	Date of C of A	Remarks and Disposal
Armstrong Whitworth Argozy II			
G-AACJ	A.W.364	6 Jul 29	From United Airways. Cancelled, Dec 36
De Havilland D.H. 60G Moth			
G-AAYY	1251	26 Jun 30	From United Airways. To Ceylon, Dec 36 (as VP-CAC)
De Havilland D.H. 60III Moth			
G-ACGX	5029	30 May 33	From Hillman's. To London Transport Flying Club Feb 39
De Havilland D.H. 60G Moth Major			
G-ACNS	5068	10 Apr 34	From Air Hire. To South Africa, Mar 40
De Havilland D.H. 80A Puss Moth			
G-ABVX	2228	22 Apr 32	From Hillman's. Impressed (as X5044), Nov 39
De Havilland D.H. 83 Fox Moth			
G-ABVI	4004	17 Jun 32	From Hillman's. Destroyed in bombing, 6 Feb 40
G-ABVK	4005	23 Jun 32	From Hillman's. To Pines Airways, Feb 39
De Havilland D.H. 84 Dragon			
G-ACAP	6002	9 Feb 33	From Hillman's. To Commercial Air Hire, Feb 36. Crashed Lyndhurst, 26 Mar 36
G-ACEU	6022	10 May 33	From Hillman's. Sold to Airwork, 13 Jan 36, then to Spain for Civil War
G-ACEV	6023	12 Jun 33	From Hillman's. Sold to Airwork, Dec 35, then to Spain for Civil War
G-ACMC	6053	26 Nov 33	From United Airways. To Airwork, 23 Jan 36, then to Australia (as VH-UXK)
G-ACMJ	6058	7 Dec 33	From United Airways. To Airwork, 25 Jan 36, then to Norman Edgar
G-ACNG	6069	23 Mar 34	From Spartan Air Lines. To Northern & Scottish 19 Jan 37 returned to B.A. 29 Oct 37, then to Scottish Airways, 14 Jun 38
G-ACNI	6071	26 Mar 34	From United Airways. To Airwork 31 Dec 36, then to Irish Air Corps (as D.H.18)
G-ACOR	6073	19 May 34	From British Continental. To Northern & Scottish, Mar 37, then to K.Parer, New Guinea (as VH-AEA)
De Havilland D.H. 86A Express			
G-ACZP	2321	11 May 35	On loan from Jersey Airways; impressed 21 July 40 (as AX843) Returned to R.A.S., Aug 40
G-ADEA	2323	5 Jun 35	From Hillman's. To Wearnes, Malaya (as VR-SBC), Jun 38
G-ADEB	2324	20 Jun 35	From Hillman's. Crashed, 12 Aug 36, near Cologne
G-ADEC	2325	1 Jul 35	From Hillman's. To PLUNA, Uruguay (as CX-AAH), Sep 38
G-ADMY	2327	10 Aug 35	From British Continental. To Royal Navy (as X9442), Nov 40
G-ADYC	2340	14 May 36	From British Continental. To R.A.F. (as L8037), Nov 37
G-ADYD	2341	19 May 36	From British Continental. To R.A.F. (as L8040), Nov 37
G-ADYE	2346	28 Jul 36	From British Continental. To Pluna, Uruguay (as CX-ABG), Nov 37
G-ADYF	2347	2 Sep 36	From British Continental. Crashed, Gatwick, 5 Sep 36
G-ADYI	2345	26 Aug 36	To Wrightways, Mar 40; impressed (as AX795) R.A.F. May 40
G-ADYJ	2348	19 May 36	To 24 Squadron, R.A.F., Oct 37 (as L7596)

THE BRITISH AIRCRAFT FLEET OF BRITISH AIRWAYS (CONT.)

Reg'n	MSN	Date of C of A	Remarks and Disposal
De Havilland D.H.89 Dragon Rapide			
G-ACPN	6252	2 Aug 34	From Hillman's. Not used by B.A. To Airwork, then to Civil War in Spain and shot down, 27 Aug 36
G-ACPO	6253	4 Sep 34	From Hillman's. Not used by B.A. To Airwork, then to Australia (as VH-UBN), 17 Aug 36
G-ADAE	6272	17 Apr 35	From United Airways. To Denmark, 28 May 38 (as OY-DIN)
G-ADAG	6266	6 Feb 35	From Hillman's. To Northern & Scottish, 19 Aug 36
G-ADAH	6278	19 Feb 35	From Hillman's. To Northern & Scottish, 19 Aug 36
G-ADAI	6287	14 May 35	From British Continental. To Airwork, 28 Aug 37
G-ADAJ	6276	5 Jun 35	From Hillman's. To Highland, 22 Sep 36. Passed to B.E.A., then to France, evntually crashed in Laos, 20 Aug 54
G-ADAK	6281	14 May 35	From British Continental, but not used. To C. Stave, for use in Spanish Civil War, but sale banned.
G-ADAL	6263	2 Mar 35	From Hillman's, but not used. To Airwork, then to Wrightways, 4 Jun 35
G-ADBU	6280	29 Apr 35	From United. To Northern & Scottish, 11 Jun 36
G-ADBX	6289	4 Jul 35	From United. Crashed, Isle of Man, 3 Mar 36
G-ADDF	6284	8 Aug 35	From Hillman's. To Northern & Scottish, 29 Jun 36. Later sold abroad for Spanish Civil War.
G-ADIM	6293	31 Jul 35	From British Continental. To Airwork, 29 Aug 37
Spartan Three-Seater II			
G-ABTR	101	3 Jun 32	From United. To F.G. Barnard, Sep 37
Spartan Cruiser II			
G-ACBM	2	21 Feb 33	From Spartan. To Straight Corporation, Nov 37
G-ACDX	4	19 Jun 33	From United. Scrapped 9 Oct 35
G-ACSM	10	13 Jun 34	From United. To Northern & Scottish, Aug 36
G-ACVT	11	2 Aug 34	From Spartan. Crashed, Isle of Man, 23 Mar 36
G-ACYL	12	24 Oct 34	From United. To Scottish Airways, Jun 38
G-ACZM	14	13 Dec 34	From Spartan. To Scottish Airways, Jun 38
Spartan Cruiser III			
G-ACYK	101	16 Apr 35	From Spartan. To Northern & Scottish. Aug 36
G-ADEL	102	18 Apr 35	From Spartan. To Northern & Scottish. Jan 37
G-ADEM	103	3 Jun 35	From Spartan. To Northern & Scottish. Aug 36

Formation of British Airways

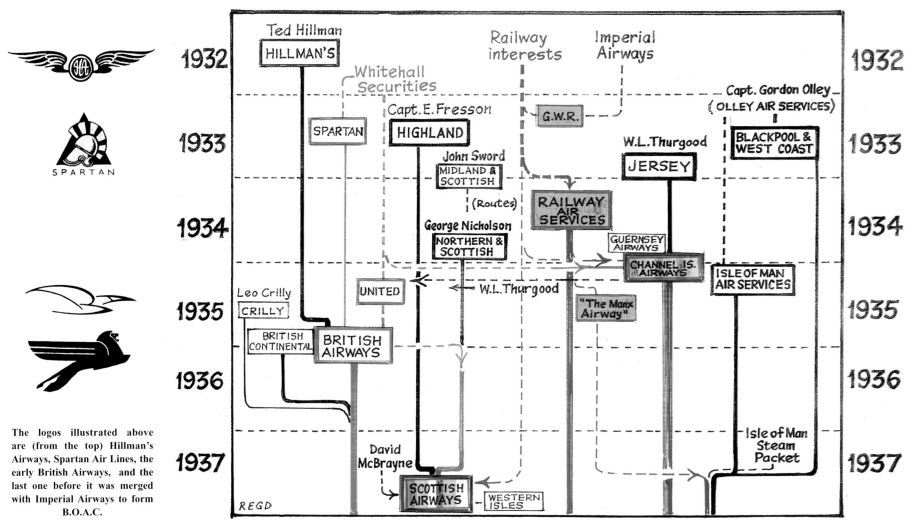

The logos illustrated above are (from the top) Hillman's Airways, Spartan Air Lines, the early British Airways, and the last one before it was merged with Imperial Airways to form B.O.A.C.

This chart illustrates the process of amalgamations that consolidated the internal British airlines into a more cohesive pattern. Most of the pioneer businessmen of the early 1930s were obliged to surrender their complete independence, but not necessarily their identity. Ted Hillman did not live to see the blossoming of his airline initiatives, and John Sword had to abandon his interest and return to Scottish Motor Transport. But Edmund Fresson, George Nicholson, and Walter Thurgood continued to play a part in the management of the Whitehall Securities interests within Great Britain. The four main railways, collectively comprising the inter-city transport incumbents, had earlier tested the market and in 1934 stepped in, coming to an accommodation with the city investors, led by Whitehall Securities. An independent group was directed by ex-Imperial Airways Captain Gordon Olley, who concentrated on services across the Irish Sea. Even the shipping companies decided to take to the air, notably David McBrayne, which was almost an institution in Scotland's Western Isles, and the Isle of Man Steam Packet service. The maritime arms of the Southern and Great Western Railways ensured their continued presence by linking with Whitehall to maintain minority shareholdings in Scotland and Jersey Airways, which was reconstituted as Channel Island Airways

Expansion in Europe

During the summer of 1936, **British Airways** made its presence felt in Europe. On 17 May, it started to fly from Gatwick, and on 1 July the Swedish terminal was extended from Malmö (see page 86) to Stockholm. To consolidate its claim for northern Europe as a sphere of influence, on 27 July, it started a night mail service to Hanover, via Cologne, using Fokker F.XIIs.

Scandinavian Rivalry

However, the airline that aimed to lead the way for a British airline foothold in northern Europe did not at first have all its own way. Another well-financed group, formed by a group of air-minded men at the Lloyds insurance company, also had its eyes on the market. Registered on 15 April 1935, with a capital of £25,000, **British Continental Airways (B.C.A.)** had begun service from Croydon to Ostend and Le Zoute on 2 July of that year, three times a day, with a weekend extension to Brussels. In October, B.C.A. also started a route to Lille, and on 1 November one to Antwerp and Amsterdam. With an increase in capital from confident investors on 11 December 1935 to £350,000, this upstart was no mean competitor to British Airways.

British Continental showed its mettle when it opened a service to Malmö, paralleling the British Airways route, on 7 February 1936, using de Havilland D.H. 86s, and emphasized its competitive spirit by an extension to Stockholm on 1 July, the same day as British Airways's. On the same date, in cooperation with K.L.M., it linked the north of England with the Netherlands with a Liverpool-Doncaster-Amsterdam route, using the Dutch airline's Fokker F.XVIIIs.

Consolidation in Northern Europe

This was all too much for British Airways, and, indeed, for the Government, which was to support the Scandinavian service with both subsidy and mail contract. It saw no reason to double up, and had to make a choice. There followed a dispute on the grounds of "who was first," and British won what today would be described as a hostile take-over. British Continental had thus operated for only a year and one month, and had been unable to challenge the strength and influence of Whitehall Securities, which absorbed B.C.A. on 1 August 1936.

Such was the strength of this network, together with an interest in the Iberian Peninsula, inherited from Crilly, that it was the basis for a complete merger with Imperial Airways in 1939. Crilly's ambitions to the south had been frustrated by the Spanish Civil War, but the idea was not abandoned.

Rather ominously, British Continental Airway's inaugural service to Hamburg was greeted by two officials giving the Nazi salute.

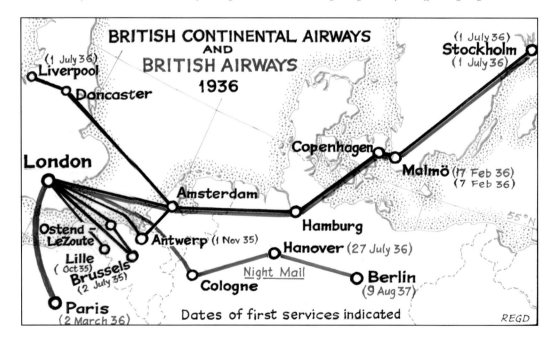

The First Foreign Aircraft

As mentioned briefly on page 81, the de Havilland D.H.86 Express, though reasonably comfortable, began its life with British Airways uncertainly as two of them crashed in the summer of 1936 and the initial 86 design had to be modified. The D.H. 86As and 86Bs were better, but the 10-seat biplane was beginning to look old-fashioned compared to the line of Fokker monoplanes used by K.L.M., and especially to the Dutch airline's Douglas DC-2s. Air France was operating the Wibault 282 from Paris, and more important, Deutche Luft Hansa had been deploying the 15-seat Junkers-Ju 52/3m tri-motor since 1933. The competition was using monoplanes of more modern design, all of which were faster, and easily serviceable at the en route stations. Except the Fokkers, already being superseded by the Douglases, they were of metal construction, which was important for maintenance, as they could be left out in the open, if necessary. The wood-and-fabric-clad de Havillands had to be kept in hangars during bad weather.

And so British Airways turned to the foreign manufacturers to augment its fleet. On 7 November 1936, Fokker F.XIIs, inherited from Crilly Airways when that airline closed down (see page 72), replaced the de Havillands on the night mail service which had been extended to Berlin on 9 August. In a far-reaching decision on 8 December, permission was granted for British Airways to purchase aircraft from Germany, and on 2 March 1937, the 15-seat Junkers-Ju 52/3m tri-motor came in to service.

These Dutch and German aircraft, however, were only interim types, and British Airways turned to the United States to upgrade its aircraft technology.

One of the British Airways Fokker F.XIIs, still in Crilly Airways colours. As noted in the table, this aircraft did reach the Spanish Nationalists, but it must have been an easy target for a fighter pilot.

BRITISH AIRWAYS AIRCRAFT FROM EUROPE

Reg'n	MSN	Date of C of A	Remarks and Disposal
Fokker F-XII			
G-ADZH	5284	23 Mar 36	From Crilly (ex K.L.M. PH-AFV); Sold to Spanish Nationalists, Aug 36
G-ADZI	5285	31 Jan 36	From Crilly (ex K.L.M. PH-AFU); sold to Spanish Nationalists, but crashed at Biarritz, 15 Aug 36
G-ADZJ	5292	8 Jan 36	From Crilly (ex K.L.M. PH-AIE); Sold to Spanish Nationalists, and shot down, Leon, 16 Dec 36
G-ADZK	5301	7 Feb 36	From Crilly (ex K.L.M. PH-AII); Sold to Spanish Nationalists, but crashed at LaRochelle, 16 Aug 36
G-AEOS	5291	3 Nov 36	From K.L.M. (PH-AID); To R.A.F., and scrapped, by BOAC May 40
G-AEOT	5300	3 Nov 36	From K.L.M. (PH-AIH); crashed, Gatwick, 19 Nov 36
Fokker F-VIII			
G-AEPT	5043	13 Jan 37	From K.L.M. (PH-AEF); Withdrawn 12 Jan 38
G-AEPU	5046	21 May 37	From K.L.M. (PH-AEI); Sold to Sweden (as SE-AHA) 25 May 39. Then to Finland.
Junkers-Ju52/3M			
G-AERU	5440	19 Feb 37	From A.B.A. Sweden (SE-AER); named *Juno*; passed to B.O.A.C.; 22 Aug 40, then to SABENA fro spares Apr 41
G-AERX	5518	7 Apr 37	From A.B.A., Sweden (SE-AES); named *Jupiter*; passed to B.O.A.C., 22 Aug 40, then to SABENA (as OO-CAP) in 1941
G-AFAP	5881	28 Jan 38	Named *Jason*; seized by the Germans at Oslo, 9 Apr 40

Life for some of the commercial aircraft during the 1930s was often adventurous. This Fokker F.XII, for example, was part of K.L.M.'s stalwart fleet that regularly flew from Amsterdam to Batavia (Dutch East Indies) — now Jakarta (Indonesia), before the Douglas DC-2s revolutionized the route to the Far East (see pages 78–79). G-ADZK was sold to Crilly Airways (see pages 72 and 82), which was planned to open a route to Lisbon. But the Spanish Civil War prevented this development, and both the French and British Governments placed restrictions on the delivery of aircraft to Spain. G-ADZK, taken over by British Airways, took off from Gatwick on 15 August 1936 "for an unknown destination." Although obviously for use in the civil war, this was never revealed, as it crashed in southwestern France on the next day.

Fokker F.VIII G-AEPT was a short-term replacement for D.H.86As in 1937 pending delivery of Electras.

A Fokker and a Junkers

Engine	**Pratt & Whitney Wasp** (420 hp x 3)
MGTOW	19,835 lb.
Max. Range	700 miles
Length	60 feet
Span	88 feet

Size comparison with the Handley Page H.P. 42 (p.37)

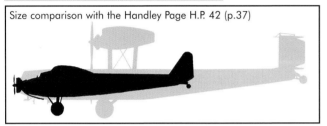

British Airways seemed to have been misnamed as it proceeded —with considerable technical justification — to replace its de Havilland biplanes with more efficient monoplanes from Europe. First came some Fokkers from the Netherlands (see also previous page) then, early in 1937, the all-metal (corrugated duralumin) Junkers tri-motors, totally reliable, and which inaugurated the night mail service to Berlin (see page 89 for fleet lists).

The mail, including small packages, is loaded onto a Junkers-Ju 52/53m (with windows blocked out) on the service to Berlin.

16 seats • 110 mph   **Fokker F.XII**

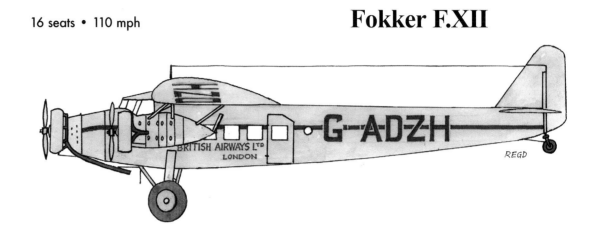

15 seats • 125 mph   **Junkers-Ju 52/3m**

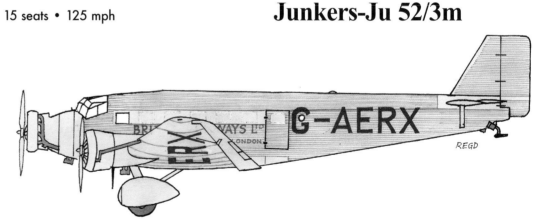

Engine	**BMW 132 H (Pratt & Whitney Hornet) (770 hp x 3)**
MGTOW	23,150 lb.
Max. Range	500 miles
Length	62 feet
Span	96 feet

Size comparison with the Handley Page H.P. 42 (p.37)

Lockheed L-10 Electra

10 seats • 185 mph

THE BRITISH AIRWAYS LOCKHEEDS

Reg'n	MSN	Date of C of A	Remarks and Disposal
Lockheed L-10A Electra			
G-AEPN	1080	12 Mar 37	Impressed, April 1940, as W9105
G-AEPO	1081	14 Mar 37	Impressed, April 1940, as W9106
G-AEPP	1082	17 Mar 37	To B.O.A.C.
G-AEPR	1083	17 Mar 37	To B.O.A.C.
G-AESY	1102	15 Jun 37	Crashed off Denmark, 15 Augh 39
G-AFCS	1025	16 Feb 38	To B.O.A.C.
G-AFEB	1122	14 Mar 38	Impressed, April 1940, as W9104
Lockheed L-14 "Super Electra"			
G-AFGN	1467	15 Sep 38	Burned out after forced landing in France, 11 Aug 39
G-AFGO	1468	15 Sep 38	Crashed in Somerset, 22 Nov 38
G-AFGP	1469	15 Sep 38	To B.O.A.C.
G-AFGR	1470	15 Sep 38	To B.O.A.C.
G-AFKD	1484	22 Nov 38	To B.O.A.C.
G-AFKE	1485	30 Nov 38	To B.O.A.C.
G-AFMO	1490	18 Mar 39	Crash-landed at Heston, 15 Jan 40
G-AFMR	1491	21 Mar 39	To B.O.A.C.
G-AFYU	1444	14 Aug 39	Lost in Mediterranean, off Malta, 21 Dec 39

No commercial transport aircraft had a greater effect on British airliner development than did the Lockheed L-10 Electra. Smaller than the famous Douglas DC-3, but slightly faster, it brought a new vision to the skies over Britain. Its all-metal construction and reliable radial engines set new levels for maintenance and dispensed with the need to park under cover or in hangars, except for major overhauls or engine changes.

Engine	**Pratt & Whitney Wasp** (450 hp x 2)
MGTOW	10,500 lb.
Max. Range	800 miles
Length	38 feet
Span	55 feet

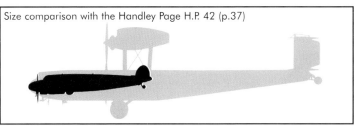

Size comparison with the Handley Page H.P. 42 (p.37)

This photograph epitomizes the revolutionary change in British commercial aviation policy in the latter 1930s: eligance, speed, and comfort.

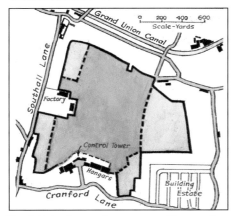

The British Airways base was at Heston, about two miles north-east of today's Heathrow Airport. The map shows the original airfield in 1935 and the 1937 extensions.

The L-14 "Super-Electra" was larger than the L-10, eight feet longer and in wing span, and could carry 14 people over twice as much range.

The Case for the Large Flying Boat

After the Second World War, when the construction of long-range landplanes had reached a high level of efficiency, and concrete runways had been built for them to operate with full loads, flying boats were regarded as obsolescent, and attempts to prolong their lives and even to develop new ones were quickly seen to be non-productive. But for the decade from the mid-1930s to the mid-1940s, an important one in the annals of air transport history, they were widely preferred for intercontinental and trans-ocean flying. Imperial Airways made its far-reaching choice for flying boats over landplanes in 1934, for several reasons. These may be summarized as follows.

1. Airfield Requirements: To serve the Empire with large landplanes would require the construction and improvement of many airfields throughout Asia, Africa, and Australasia, built to a higher standard than the fields that could accept, for instance, the Douglas twins of K.L.M. On the other hand, there was no limit to the size to which flying boats could be built, because the displacement level on any stretch of water was unlimited.

2. Level of Technology: British aircraft constructors were not yet able to build large long-range airliners, although several designs were on the drawing boards by 1938. The U.S. manufacturers, however, notably Sikorsky, had demonstrated the efficiency of 40-seat flying boats, and Britain's Short Brothers was ready to emulate them. De Havilland still specialized in wooden construction; Handley Page biplane expertise was outdated; Armstrong Whitworth designs lacked range.

3. Range Requirement: A minimum of about 900 miles with full payload was needed, so as to avoid the problem of flying through Italy or the Balkans. Non-stop to Marseilles, then across the Mediterranean to Alexandria, was needed, and no landplane could achieve this at the time.

4. Airline Precedents: On balance, world airline opinion still favoured the flying boat in 1934. Pan American Airways had conquered the Pacific Ocean with them; and both Air France and Deutsche Lufthansa favoured them for the South and Central Atlantic routes.

5. The "Buy British" Policy: (See also 3 above), Imperial was expected to support the British industry, even though it could have explored the possibility of taking aircraft off the production lines of Sikorsky or Martin in the United States.

6. Safety: A popular view was that, if in trouble for any reason, a flying boat could always make an emergency alighting on the water, either on a river, a lake, or in the sea. For a large landplane, a crash-landing, especially in mountainous territory, would be far more dangerous. Also, the undercarriage of a landplane could collapse, whereas a flying boat was built like a boat to alight on the water.

These two paintings by Ian Marshall (from his superb flying boat book, neatly sub-titled as **The J-Class Yachts of Aviation**)*, well illustrate the flying boat heritage that encouraged Short Brothers to undertake the task of modernizing the Imperial Airways fleet with the C-Class "Empire" S.23s. The top picture is of the twin-engined Short Singapore, at Port Bell, Uganda, on Lake Victoria, where Sir Alan Cobham stopped during his circumnavigation of Africa in 1931, and demonstrated that flying boats could be utilized on long-distance transcontinental routes. The lower picture shows the four-engined Short S.17 Kent* Scipio *coming in to alight at Alexandria, Egypt, Shorts wisely abandoned the biplane wings for a strong all-metal monoplane construction. Concentrating on aerodynamic cleanliness, the individual surface plates were flush-riveted.*

Short S.23 C-Class Empire

During the mid-1930s, the British aircraft industry and the British public alike tended to relegate the objective of advancing the technology of commercial air transport aircraft behind that of achieving speed records. Winning the Schneider Trophy brought a sense of pride even though the national airline flag carriers were struggling. British Airways was obliged to turn, first to Fokker, then to Lockheed, rather than continue to fly de Havilland biplanes against the Junkers-Ju 52 trimotors that Lufthansa was flying all across Europe. New faster French airliners and the Douglas twins from America served notice that the sands were running out for outdated technology.

The introduction of the big Short flying boats restored confidence. They may not have had trans-ocean range, except when specially modified, but they were more than adequate for the traditional routes throughout the eastern hemisphere. They could hold their own against K.L.M.'s Douglases to the Far East and Australia, as they were faster; on the other hand, the landplanes could maintain greater regularity, and transit stops were much quicker.

But the routes of the flying boats invoked visions of romantic places, often because the harbours and lakes and rivers en route were exactly that. Alighting on the River Nile, almost within sight of the Pyramids; or on Lake Victoria, or on the Ganges River in India, were more attractive than landing in the sweltering heat of hard-baked airports in the tropics. With the opening of the first modern flying boat services in 1937, the British national airline regained its sense of pride.

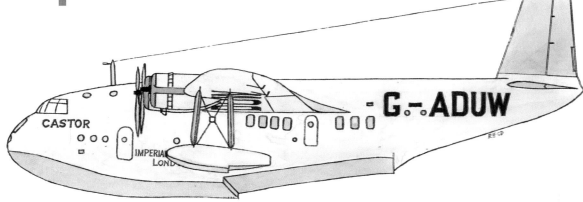

Always vulnerable to corrosion from salt sea-water, the big C-Class flying boats were painted with a corrosion-resistant solution. Contrary to the impression given by black-and-white photographs at the time, the colour was a light cream, not aluminium grey.

Engine	Bristol Pegasus (920 hp x 4)
MGTOW	40,500 lb.
Max. Range	760 miles
Length	88 feet
Span	114 feet

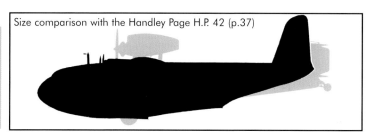

Size comparison with the Handley Page H.P. 42 (p.37)

The S.23 Capella *taxis in to the Winter Palace at Luxor, on the Nile.*

The classic lines of the "Empire" flying boat are well illustrated in this picture of Canopus, *the first one off the production line at Rochester.*

Atlantic Debut

As described on pages 78-79, the shortcomings of British commercial airliner development, compared to that of American manufacturers, was graringly emphasized by the results of the MacRobertson England-Australia Race of October 1934. To avoid further humiliation, and to counter the complacency that had been evident in Britain, the historic order for modern flying boats, able to match those of the United States, saved Imperial Airways from being completely outclassed.

The Short "Empire" flying boats were superb examples of the best that the British manufacturing industry could produce, when under pressure. Arthur Gouge's design, however, while achieving all that was desired for the Empire routes throughout Asia to Australia, and to South Africa, did not have trans-Atlantic range, at least not with a commercial payload. Pan American Airways had already started to operate Sikorsky S-42s on its South American routes in 1934, and Martin 130 "Clippers" across the Pacific in 1935. It had wished to fly to Europe but the British authorities had been reluctant to grant operating rights and installations, at least partly because it hoped to be able to match the trans-Atlantic competition when Imperial's flying boats were ready.

With its promenade deck and good speed, the Short "C-Class" S.23s were a match for the S-42s; but the American equipment had better range. Nevertheless the North Atlantic meteorological conditions were still formidable, and neither the S-42s nor the Martins could guarantee to operate with regularity against the headwinds and storms that prevailed on the critical segment of the route between Newfoundland and Ireland. After delicate negotiations, a compromise agreement was reached to inaugurate a route from New York to the mid-Atlantic British colony of Bermuda, on a reciprocal basis. The 800-mile route was well within the range capability of both the Sikorsky and the Short, and so honour was preserved on both sides.

On 25 May 1937, Imperial Airways and Pan American Airways both conducted survey flights, the former with the S.23 *Cavalier*, which had arrived by ship, and the latter with the S-42B *Bermuda Clipper*. On 16 June the airlines started a once-weekly service, increasing this to twice weekly on 25 August. Because of the danger of icing in the harbour at New York's Port Washington base, the mainland terminal was transferred further south to Baltimore on 17 November. The service continued regularly for more than a year, but *Cavalier* was lost en route, because of icing, on 21 January 1939.

SHORT S-23 v SIKORSKY S-42

Type	Year of First Service	Engines Type +hp (x4)	MGTOW (lb)	Seats	Range (st.miles)	Cruise Speed (mph)
Sikorsky S-42	1934	P&W Horner 700	38,000	32	1,200	150
S-42B	1937	P&W Horner 750	42,000	24	1,800	155
S-42B (Atlantic)	1937	P&W Horner 750	45,500	12	2,800	145
Short S-23	1936	Bristol Pegasus 920	40,500	24	760	165
S-23[1] (Atlantic)	1937	Bristol Pegasus 1,010	43,500	–	3,000	170
S-30[2]	1938	Bristol Pegasus 890	46,000	–	1,500	165

1. All-up weight increased to 52,000 lb.
2. All-up weight increased to 53,000 lb. (with in-flight refuelling)

In the north, the U.S. terminus was moved south to Baltimore because of the danger of icing in the Long Island Sound.

The North Atlantic Surveys

NORTH ATLANTIC SURVEY FLIGHTS 1937
(Imperial Airways Short S.23s and Pan American Sikorsky S-42Bs)

Date	Airline	MSN	Name	Flight	Time (hr. min.)	Remarks
5–6 Jul	Pan Am	NC16736	Clipper III	Botwood-Foynes	12.36	Crew if 7 (Capt. Harold Gray)
8–9 Jul	Imperial	G-ADHM	Caledonia	Foynes-Botwood	15.03	Crew of 4 (Capt. A.S. Wilcockson)
15–16 Jul	(Caledonia's return flight from 8–9 July)				12.05	
17–18 Jul	(Clipper III's return flight from 5–6 July)				16.29	
29–30 Jul	Pan Am	NC16736	Clipper III	Botwood-Foynes	12.33	Crew of 7 (Capt. Harold Gray)
1–2 Aug	Imperial	G-ADUV	Cambria	Foynes-Botwood	17.35	Crew of 4 (Capt. G. Powell)
7 Aug	(Clipper III's return flight from 29–30 July)				17.49	
8–9 Aug	(Cambria's return flight from 1–2 August)				12.02	
17–18 Aug	Imperial	G-ADHM	Caledonia	Foynes-Botwood	19.40	Crew of 4 (Capt. A.S. Wilcockson)
20-21 Aug	(Caledonia's return flight from 17–18 August)				11.33	
29 Aug	Imperial	G-ADUV	Cambria	Foynes-Botwood	14.20	Crew of 4 (Capt. G. Powell) Flight during same day.
15–16 Sep	Imperial	G-ADHM	Caledonia	Foynes-Botwood	15.30	Crew of 4 (Capt. A.S. Wilcockson)
23–24 Sep	(Caledonia's return flight from 13–16 Sept)				11.38	
27–28 Sep	(Cambria's return flight from 29 August)				10.36	Landing accident at Toronto. Repairs made and made record flight of the series.

As shown in the table, the Cambria *distinguished itself in the North Atlantic survey flights of 1937.*

Uunlike the American flag-carrier Pan American Airways, Imperial Airways was ill-prepared during the mid-1930s to start an airline route across the North Atlantic Ocean. Pan Am had already pioneered the world's first trans-ocean route across the Pacific which, compared to the Atlantic in meteorological terms, had lived up to its name. But although the Martin 130 Clippers and the Sikorsky S-42s, the latter in the long-range B version, with extra fuel tanks, were able to provide the range, the North Atlantic weather was more severe and uncertain. Both airlines, therefore, agreed to conduct a series of survey flights during the summer of 1937, to gain flying experience on a challenging route.

The critical segment of the route was between Ireland and Newfoundland, and satisfactory locations for flying boat operations were fixed at Foynes, near Limerick, and Botwood. These were later superseded by nearby airports at Shannon and Gander, respectively. Foynes, particularly, was to become, during the Second World War, the busiest flying boat base in the world.

The series of flights made is summarized in the tabulation on this page. Imperial made two experimental flights from Southampton to Foynes, while Pan American made one as far as Shediac, new Brunswick, one as far as Botwood, and one by the southern route, as shown on the map.

Pan American was better equipped for the tests. Its Sikorsky S-42B Clipper III was the last of a production line, with all the so-called "bugs" ironed out. Imperial's Short S.23s, *Caledonia* and *Cambria*, were among the first off the production line, and had been designed for the Empire routes in the eastern hemisphere, with long-range Atlantic operations envisaged for later development. Nevertheless, they performed well, as indicated in the tabulation, which also emphasizes the effect of the prevailing westerly winds on the flight times.

But the S.23 was clearly even less less suited for the Atlantic challenge than the American aircraft, which were never used on the route either. The two Short boats were stripped of every item except the fuel tanks. The U.S. crew included a steward, who served meals; but the British crews had to be content with sandwiches. There is a story that a good friend of the crew pleaded to accompany one of the flights, but was told that there were no seats. Volunteering to sit on the floor, if necessary, he was told "no floor."

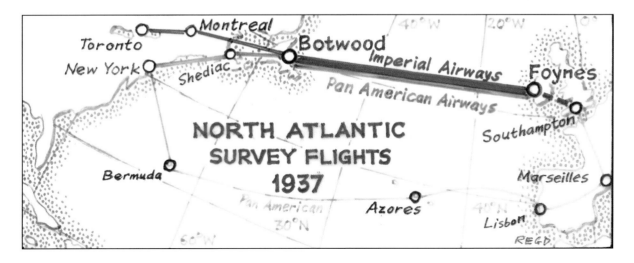

Flagships of the Imperial Fleet

Canopus, *the first S.23, rises on the step on its take-off run.*

Cassiopeia, *the seventh S.23 off the production line, at anchor while passengers disembark into the specially-designed Imperial Airways launches.*

THE SHORT "C-CLASS" EMPIRE FLYING BOATS

Reg'n	MSN	Date of C of A	Name	Remarks and Disposal
G-ADHL	S.795	20 Oct 36	Canopus	To BOAC, Apr 40. Broken up at Hythe, 23 Oct 46
G-ADHM	S.804	4 Dec 36	Caledonia	With extra tanks, made first S.23 Atlantic 1937 crossing. To BOAC, Apr 40. Broken up at Hythe, 23 March 47.
G-ADUT	S.811	7 Dec 36	Centaurus	Surveyed Far East route to New Zealand. To Australian Gout. Sept 39. Destroyed at moorings at Broome, West. Aug. 3 Mar 42
G-ADUU	S.812	25 Nov 36	Cavalier	Served on the New York-Bermuda route, crashed 21 Jan 39
G-ADUV	S.813	15 Jan 37	Cambria	With extra tanks, also used, wtih G-ADHM, on trans. Atlantic survey, 1937. To BOAC. Broken up at Hythe, Jan 1947.
G-ADUW	S.814	23 Dec 36	Castor	Made first regular fligt to Alexandria, 6 Feb 37 to BOAC. Broken up at Hythe, 4 Feb 47.
G-ADUX	S.815	25 Jan 37	Cassipeia	To BOAC. Crashed at Sabang, 22 Dec 41.
G-ADUY	S.816	16 Feb 37	Capella	Damaged beyond repair, Batavia 12 Mar 39
G-ADUZ	S.817	3 Mar 37	Cygnus	Crashed at Brindisi, 5 Dec 37
G-ADVA	S.818	16 Mar 37	Capricornus	Crashed near Macon, France, 24 Mar 37
G-ADVB	S.819	8 Apr 37	Corsair	To BOAC. Broken up at Hythe, 20 Jan 47.
G-ADVC	S.820	23 Apr 37	Courtier	Crashed near Athens, 1 Oct 37
G-ADVD	S.821	6 May 37	Challenger	Crasehd at Mozambique, 1 May 39
G-ADVE	S.822	29 May 37	Centurion	Crashed at Calcutta, 12 June 39
G-ADTV	S.838	17 Jun 37	Coriolanus	Also reg. as VH-ABG. To BOAC. Broken up at Sydney, end 47
G-AETW	S.839	30 Jun 37	Calpurnia	Crashed at Lake Habbaniya, 27 Nov 38
G-AETX	S.840	16 Jul 37	Ceres	To BOAC. Destroyed by fire at Durban, 1 Dec 42
G-AETY	S.841	26 July 37	Clio	To BOAC. Impressed as AX659, for 201 Squadron. Crashed at Loch Indal, 22 Aug 41.
G-AETZ	S.842	16 Aug 37	Circe	To BOAC. Shot down off Tjilaejap, 28 Feb 42.
G-AEUA	S.843	26 Aug 37	Calypso	To BOAC. Impressed as A18-11. Crashed at Daru, Papua-New Guinea, 8 Aug 42.
G-AEUB	S.844	13 Sep 37	Camilla	Also reg. as VH-ADU. To BOAC. Crashed at Port Meresby, 22 Apr 43
G-AEUC	S.845	25 Sep 37	Corinna	To BOAC. Destroyed in air raid at Broome, 3 March 42
G-AEUD	S.846	9 Oct 37	Cordelia	To BOAC. Impressed as AD660, for 119 Squadron. Released to BOAC, 19 Sep 41. Broken up at Hythe, 6 March 47
G-AEUE	S.847	23 Oct 37	Cameronian	To BOAC. Broken up at Hythe, Jan 47.
G-AEUF	S.848	9 Nov 37	Corinthian	To BOAC. Crashed at Darwin, 22 Mar 42
G-AEUG	S.849	8 Jan 38	Coogee	Allocated to Q.E.A., as VH-ABC. Crashed at Townsville, 1 Mar.
G-AEUH	S.850	10 Feb 38	Corio	Allocated to Q.E.A. as VH-ABD, and commandeered by Australian Govt., Sep 39. Shot down near Koepang, 10 Jan 42.
G-AEJI	S.851	26 Feb 38	Coorong	Allocated to Q.E.A. as VH-ABE. Shot down at Timor, 30 Jan 42.

Reg'n	MSN	Date of C of A	Name	Remarks and Disposal
G-AFBJ	S.876	28 Nov 37	Carpentaria	Allocated to Q.E.A. as VH-ABA. Broken up at Hythe, 19 Jan 47
G-AFBK	S.877	18 Dec 37	Coolangatta	Allocated to Q.E.A. as VH-ABB. Crashed at Sydney, 11 October 44
G-AFBL	S.878	30 Mar 38	Cooee	Allocated to Q.E.A. as VH-ABF. Broken up at Hythe, 2 Feb 47
Short S.30				
G-AFCT	S.879	27 Oct 38	Champion	First C-Class with increased all-up weight, but with Pegasus engines. To BOAC. Broken up at Hythe, 16 Mar 47.
G-AFCU	S.880	27 Jul 39	Cabot	First C-Class with Perseus engines, with 46,000 lb all-up weight. To R.A.F. Sept 39 as V3138. Destroyed in air raid at Bodö, 5 May 40
G-AFCV	S.881	7 Jul 39	Caribou	Used for in-flight re-fuelling experiments. Destroyed in air raid at Bodo, 5 May 40
G-AFCW	S.882	24 Mar 39	Connemara	Burned out during re-fuelling at Hythe, 19 June 39
G-AFCX	S.883	29 Mar 39	Clyde	To BOAC. Wrecked in a gale at Lisbon, 14 Feb 41
G-AFCY	S.884	21 Apr 39	Ao-tea-roa (originally Capt. Cook)	Allocated to trans-Tasman route. Re-registered for TEAL as ZK-AMA. Broken up at Auckland, 1953
G-AFCZ	S.885	6 Apr 39	Australia (originally Clare)	As G-AFGY, as ZK-AMB. Then to BOAC and renamed Clare. Destroyed by fire in the air, near Bathurst, West Africa, 14 Sep 42
G-AFDA	S.886	12 May 39	Awarua (originally Cumberland)	As G-AFCY, as ZK-AMC. Broken up at Auckland, 1947.
G-AFKZ	S.1003	26 Feb 40	Cathy	To BOAC. Broken up at Hythe, 9 Mar 47.
Short S.33				
G-AFPZ	S.1025	17 Apr 40	Clifton	To BOAC. Reregistered as VH-ACD. Crashed at Sydney 18 Nov 44
G-AFRA	S.1026	10 May 40	Cleopatra	To BOAC. Broken up at Hythe, 4 Nov 46
G-AFRB	S.1027	—	—	Never completed. Hull scrapped 1943.

A disadvantage of the flying boats was the need to use launches at most en route stops for passengers to board and disembark.

Shrinking the Empire

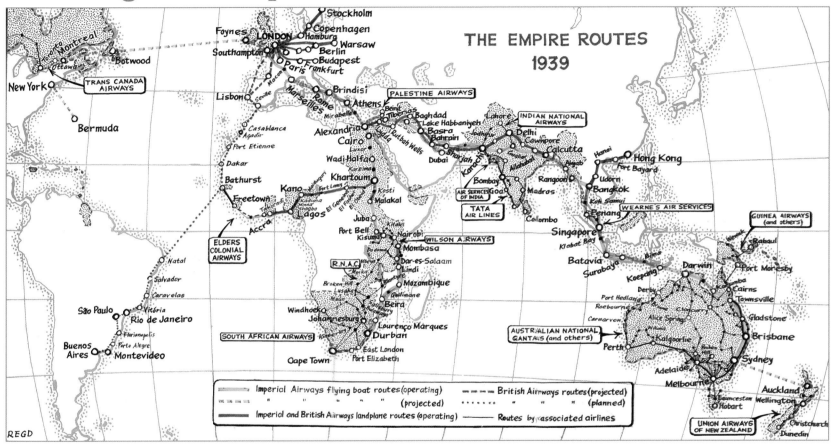

In December 1934, Imperial Airways finally extended its trunk route to Australia, and passenger service to Brisbane began on 13 April 1935. In 1936, British Airways added three more countries in Europe. The trans-Africa route and Hong Kong were important extensions to the long-distance trunk routes.

Short S.23 flying boats began to come off the production line at Rochester. First into service was *Canopus*, on 31 October 1936, flying trans-Mediterranean from Alexandria to Brindisi. On 21 December, *Caledonia* flew non-stop from Alexandria to Marseilles in 11-½ hours, but Rome was included (at Lake Bracciano) with *Castor* on 4 January 1937. *Centaurus* started scheduled service, eastbound, on 12 January. *Caledonia* flew non-stop from Southampton to Alexandria, 2,222 miles, in

13 hours. *Capella* reached Kisumu on 15 May, and *Canopus* replaced the landplanes all the way to Durban on 2 June.

The New York-Bermuda service showed the Union Jack in the United States (see page 94); the Empire Air Mail Scheme went into effect to South Africa with *Centurion* on 29 June — 1-½ d per half-ounce; while *Clio* and *Calypso* extended the S.23 service to Karachi on 3 October. On 23 February 1938, *Centurion* and *Coolangatta* took the air mail as far as Singapore, and soon the services were accelerated: 9 days to Sydney, with *Centaurus*, on 10 April, 4 days to Durban, with *Ceres*, on 13 April. The first flying boat service through to Australia opened on 26 June, with *Camilla* and *Cordelia* to Singapore, and *Challenger* to Sydney.

Flights were reported in the newspapers each day. For the Christmas mails, during the preceding seven weeks, the airline carried 240 tons of mail.

British Airways had been authorized by the Air Ministry to develop the southern trans-Atlantic route, via West Africa, on 24 March. On 7 October, a Lockheed 14 made a survey flight to Lisbon; then, on 28 December 1938, to Bathurst, in the Gambia, as a prelude to its objective. The airline also extended its Berlin service to Warsaw on 17 April 1939.

By the summer of 1939, Imperial Airways was serving almost every corner of the eastern hemisphere, except New Zealand and the Pacific islands. But all further hopes were dashed by the onset of the Second World War.

Romance of the Flying Boats . . .

Goodbye to the old — three Short S.17 Kents and a Short Calcutta, Southampton Water, in 1936.

In with the new — a Short S.23 taking off at Cairo in 1936.

On to Africa —the S.23 Capella *splashes down at Lake Naivasha, Kenya, 1937.*

To the Indian Ocean — the S.23 Calypso *at Mombasa, Kenya, in 1938.*

. . . in Faraway Places

Flying Boat elegance: the S.23 Coriolanus *coming in to Koepang, Timor, in 1938.*

The S.23 Cassiopeia *boarding passengers from the Imperial Airways launch at Luxor in 1939.*

Passengers boarding the S.23 Ceres *at Laropi, on the Albert Nile, in 1939.*

End of an Era — the S.30 Cabot *at its berth at Southampton in 1939.*

Armstrong Whitworth A.W. 27 Ensign

40 seats • 170 mph

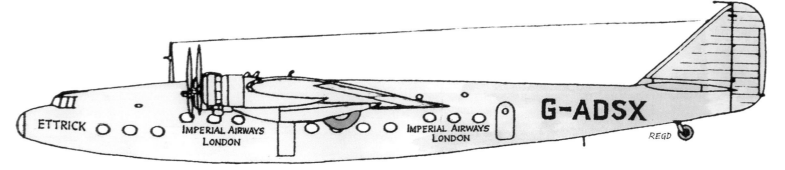

The historic order at the end of 1934 for a fleet of modern flying boats to match those of Pan American Airways was supplemented by an order for 12 **Armstrong Whitworth A.W.27 Ensign** landplanes on 29 May 1935. Similar in general layout to the Atalanta (page 41) which had won its spurs on the Empire routes, its development history was not a happy one. The large high-winged monoplane was all-metal, and had a retractable undercarriage; but this was relatively new technology for a British manufacturer. The first Ensign did not fly until early in 1938, and it was under-powered. The Armstrong Siddeley Tiger engines had to be upgraded to a higher horsepower.

The first A.W.27, *Ensign*, started service with Imperial Airways on the London-Paris route on 20 October 1938, but not on a regular scheduled basis. Four of the aircraft were intended for India, but were never delivered. Still under-powered, the type had to be re-engined with American Wright Cyclone engines, at a time when Deutsche Lufthansa and the Danish airline D.D.L. began to fly into London in April 1939 with the fine Focke-Wulf 200 Condor.

Any thoughts to cure their problems had to be abandoned because of the outbreak of war on 3 September 1939. On 22–23 May 1940, they were used to deliver food to the beleaguered troops in northern France, and one was destroyed by German air attack, as was another at Paris. The fleet list tells the story. They served honourably for trooping and logistics during the war, and deserved a collective D.F.C. But they were a disappointment for Imperial and, though their occasional accidents were never fatal, the surviving Ensigns were all broken up at Hamble in 1947.

Engine	Armstrong Siddeley Tiger 1X (850 hp x 4)
MGTOW	49,000 lb.
Max. Range	800 miles
Length	110 feet
Span	123 feet

Size comparison with the Handley Page H.P. 42 (p.37)

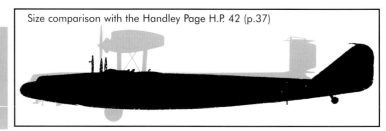

THE IMPERIAL AIRWAYS A.W.27 ENSIGNS

Reg'n	MSN	Date of C of A	Name	Remarks and Disposal
G-ADSR	A.W. 1156	29 Jun 38	Ensign	Ad hoc London-Paris service, 24 Oct 38, but withdrawn from service, and transferred to BOAC for military use. Dismantled, Cairo, Jan 45
G-ADSS	A.W. 1157	18 Nov 38	Egeria	Allocated to Indian Transcontinental Airways (as VT-AJE *Ellora*) but not delivered. Wartime service. Broken up, Hamble, 13 Apr 47
G-ADST	A.W. 1158	14 Nov 38	Elsinore	To BOAC. Broken up at Hamble, 28 Mar 47.
G-ADSU	A.W. 1159	2 Dec 38	Euterpe	(see G-ADSS) (as VT-AJR *Everest*). Dismantled at Cairo, 1946.
G-ADSV	A.W. 1160	2 Dec 38	Explorer	To BOAC. Broken up at Hamble, 23 Mar 47.
G-ADSW	A.W. 1161	8 May 39	Eddystone	To BOAC. Broken up at Hamble, 21 Apr 47 (the last Ensign, after returning from Cairo, via Castel Benito, Tripoli)
G-ADSX	A.W. 1162	12 Jun 39	Ettrick*	Abandoned at Paris, after German air raid, 1 Jun 40. Repaired and used (with Daimler-Benz engines) by Germans.
G-ADSY	A.W. 1163	23 Jun 39	Empyrean	To BOAC. Broken up at Hamble, 21 Apr 47.
G-ADSZ	A.W. 1164	30 Jun 39	Elysian*	Destroyed by German air attack at Merville, France, 23 May 40.
G-ADTA	A.W. 1165	23 Aug 39	Euryalus*	(See G-ADSS) (as VT-AJG *Ernakulam*). Damaged on supply mission to France, scrapped for spare parts for G-ADSU, 1941.
G-ADTB	A.W. 1166	19 Sep 39	Echo	To BOAC. Broken up at Hamble, 20 March 47.
G-ADTC	A.W. 1167	9 Oct 39	Endymion*	(See G-ADSS) (as VT-AJH *Etah*) Burned out during air raid at Whitchurch, 24 Nov 40.

Reg'n	MSN	Date of C of A	Name	Remarks and Disposal
G-AFZU	A.W. 1821	26 Jun 41	Everest	(Ex-G-ADTE) Delivered direct to BOAC, 1941. Broken up, Hamble, 16 Apr 47.
G-AFZV	A.W. 1822	1 Nov 41	Enterprise*	(Ex-G-ADTD) On military service, force-landed near Nouackchott, West Africa. Salvaged by French, flown to France as F-AFZV, later, F-BAHD. Used by Germans with Daimler-Benz engines.

*Wartime casualties

Seen from above the A.W.27 Ensign looked impressive.

De Havilland D.H. 91 Albatross

First delivered to Imperial Airways as its **Frobisher Class** flagship fleet in October 1938, the **D.H. 91 Albatross** was distinctive in many ways. It was the fastest commercial airliner of its time, and certainly the most beautiful. But in an age when the aviation world had turned to metal construction, it was built of wood, possibly the last airliner of its kind. It set speed records wherever it flew; but its career was cut to a bare few months by the outbreak of war in September 1939, and the type never saw airline service again.

Aerodynamic Excellence

Designed at Hatfield by Arthur Hagg, with aerodynamic cleanliness presided over by Richard M. Clarkson, it was a delight to behold; but its beauty was only skin deep. Its wooden construction was so vulnerable that one of the prototypes broke in two during a heavy landing. And one of Imperial's suffered a similar fate.

Fastest to the Continent

It made a dramatic debut by flying the 1938 Christmas mail to Cairo in December at an average speed of 219 mph. It entered scheduled service to Paris, Brussels, and Zurich on 13 January 1939, and on 10 January flew to Brussels in 48 minutes. But like all aircraft made of wood, it had to be kept in a hangar during stormy weather.

War Service

The long-range version, to be fitted with fuel tanks instead of seats, was visualized as a fast trans-Atlantic mail plane, but this never materialized. But two of this variant, *Faraday* and *Franklin*, served during the early years of the war for a fast courier service as far as India, but both of them crashed later in Iceland. The route had been opened on 22 September by *Fortuna*, and was later extended to India until Italy entered the war on 10 June 1940.

Engine	De Havilland Gipsy Twelve (525 hp x 4)
MGTOW	29,500 lb.
Max. Range	1,100 miles
Length	71 feet
Span	105 feet

Size comparison with the Handley Page H.P. 42 (p.37)

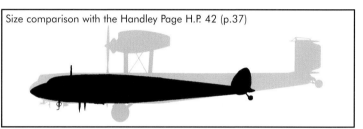

IMPERIAL'S DE HAVILLAND D.H.91 ALBATROSS FLEET

Reg'n	MSN	Date of C of A	Name	Remarks and Disposal
G-AFDI	6802	17 Oct 38	Frobisher	First flown as E-2. Destroyed by enemy action at Whitchurch, 20 Dec 40.
G-AFDJ	6803	1 Nov 38	Falcon	Scrapped Sep 43
G-AFDK	6804	6 Jan 39	Fortuna	Crashed near Shannon, Ireland, 6 July 43
G-AFDL	6805	4 Apr 39	Fingal	Crashed at Pucklechurch, near Bristol, 6 Oct 40
G-AFDM	6806	16 Jan 39	Fiona	Scrapped Sep 43

Note: Two aircraft, *Faraday* and *Franklin*, were ordered by the Air Ministry for 271 Squadron. Both crashed at Reykjavik, Iceland, on 11 Aug 41 and 7 Apr 42, respectively.

Aerodynamic Excellence — and a Thing of Beauty

Consolidation in Britain

BRITISH INTERNAL AIRLINES 1937–39 (SUMMARY)

Airline	Routes Operated	Previous Page Ref	Remarks
Air Despatch	Ad hoc flights between London aerodromes and to Paris and Le Touquet. 27 June 35	—	Associate company of Commercial Air Hire (see p. 71)
Allied Airways (Gandar Dower)	(See map, page 60)	60-61	Mail contract, Aberdeen-Lerwick, 23 Nov 37 Retained Independence after formation of Scottish Airways.
Channel Air Ferries	(See map this page)	—	Associated with Railway Air Services (see page 76). Services taken over by Great Western & Southern (see below)
Great Western & Southern Airlines	(See Channel Air Ferries)	—	Formed 5 December 1938 by British & Foreign Aviation to operate services by Channel Air Ferries and Railway Air Services (R.A.S.)
Isle of Man Air Services	(See map this page)	67	Formed by Olley Air Services, Jan 1935. L.M.S. Railway and Isle of Man Steam Packet Co. acquired interest in September 1937, and took over "The Manx Airway" of R.A.S. and Blackpool and West Coast Air Services.
Jersey Airways	(See map, page 84)	84-85	Carried 693 passengers in one day in 1938 (frequently more than 500 during the summer)
Lundy and Atlantic Coast Air Lines	Barnstaple-Lundy Island	71	Maintained services
Northern Eastern Airways	(See map, page 73)	73	Overcame Railway opposition
P.S.I.O.W.	(See map, page 68)	68-69	Maintained services
Railway Air Services	(See page 76)	76-77	Maintained services
Scottish Airways	(See page 83)	83	Formed 12 August 1937 by merging **Northern Airways** (renamed from Northern and Scottish, Sept 37) and **Highland Airways**
Southern Airways	Ipswich-Clacton, Ilford-Ramsgate	—	Formed, January 1938 by the Straight Corporation. Operated 20 June –30 September
Utility Airways	Hooton-Liverpod, Hooton-Blackpool	—	Operated 14 May–1 October only one Monospar St.12 and a Fox Moth
West Coast Air Services	(see page 67 and this page)	67	Formerly **Blackpool & West Coast** (see p. 67). Merged with **Isle of Man Air Services**, 27 Sept 37. Operated in conjunction with the Irish Aer Lingus for services from Dublin to English points (see map)
Western Airways	(See page 70)	70	Formerly **Norman Edgar**. Service extended to Swansea, 27 July 38; one night-time service, Cardiff-Western-super-Mare operated at night — first in the British Isles, 2 October
Western Isles Airways	(See page 83)	83	Maintained Services
International Air Freight	Croydon-Amsterdam	—	Fleet of four Curtiss T.32s. Started services 29 September 1937, but short-lived.
Wrightways	Croydon-Paris		Maintained services

Towards the latter 1930s, as the threat of war still seemed a distant speculation, the internal airlines settled down to routine operations. Business was brisk, as the people of Britain had recovered from the depression years, and were becoming accustomed to taking holidays more frequently and often more ambitiously, such as to the Scilly Isles. The implications of the Maybury Committee recommendations resulted in more stability, and, as the tabulation indicates, few new entrepreneurs challenged the hierarchy of the Railways. The route network of the British Isles changed little from when the airlines jostled for position in the early 1930s, and remained substantially the same as referenced in the tabulation. The main changes are shown on the maps on this page.

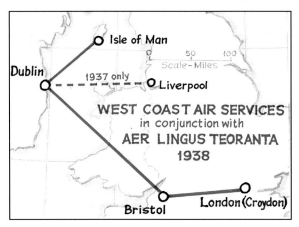

WEST COAST AIR SERVICES in conjunction with AER LINGUS TEORANTA 1938

ISLE OF MAN AIR SERVICES 1938

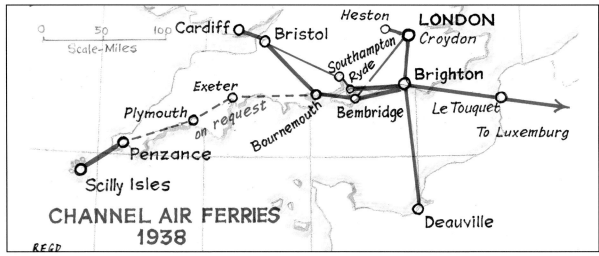

CHANNEL AIR FERRIES 1938

De Havilland D.H. 95 Flamingo

17 seats • 184 mph

After a history of building hundreds of transport aircraft, from the converted light bombers of the Great War to the fine series of Moths and Dragons of the 1930s, the de Havilland company finally recognized the need to turn to metal construction, even though the meticulous craftsmanship in wood continued, and culminated in the superb Mosquito light bomber of the Second World War.

An All-metal de Havilland

With the **D.H. 95 Flamingo**, which made its first flight on 28 December 1938, the leadership of the design team changed, as chief designer Arthur Hagg was at odds with his fellow board members and was replaced by Ronald Bishop, who was later to design the world's first jet airliner, the Comet, in the immediate post-war years. Fortunately for de Havilland, Richard Clarkson continued to ensure the aerodynamic cleanliness of the products from Hatfield.

First Services

The high-winged twin-engined airliner was, because of its speed, regarded by the Air Ministry as a potential military transport aircraft, and orders were placed for it. Two aircraft were allocated for the King's Flight, and King George VI inspected it at Hatfield on 15 August 1940. But by this time, war had been declared on 3 September 1939, and the launch customer, Guernsey Airways, had only just begun proving flights from Southampton and Heston to the Channel Islands, starting on 3 July.

A Future Denied

The D.H.95's commercial career was thus very short, a mere two months, but it had flown well. A total of 16 aircraft were completed and all saw service with the Royal Air Force, and some were delivered to B.O.A.C., which used them on communications duties in north and east Africa. But for the outbreak of war, the Flamingo would almost certainly have graced the skies of Britain for many years.

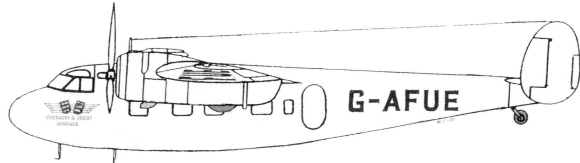

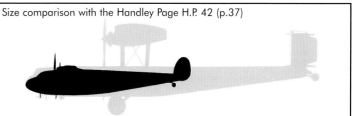

Size comparison with the Handley Page H.P. 42 (p.37)

Engine	Bristol Pegasus (890 hp x 2)
MGTOW	16,500 lb.
Max. Range	1,300 miles
Length	52 feet
Span	70 feet

THE GUERNSEY AND JERSEY AIRWAYS FLAMINGOES

Reg'n	MSN	Date of C of A	Remarks and Disposal
G-AFUE	95001	30 Jun 39	Proving flights, ad hoc, flown until declaration of war, 3 Sep 39. Impressed in Nov 39 (as T5357). Scrapped 4 Oct 40.
G-AFUF	95002	12 Jan 40	Ordered but impressed, 20 Jan 40. Withdrawn from service Oct 42.

The prototype Flamingo, G-AFUE, flying over the harbour at St. Helier, Jersey, in August 1989.

Restructuring an Industry

Imperial Airways had been the first airline to be formed, by amalgamation in 1924, as a government-supported national airline. A decade later, British Airways had been formed by another amalgamation, this time by the marriage of private enterprise and private capital. Imperial had concentrated on serving the far-flung British Empire, to the exclusion of Europe, except for Paris, Zurich, and en route points in the Mediterranean. British Airways had corrected the omission and flew to northern Europe and the Iberian Peninsula. Both airlines were receiving financial support, mainly by air mail subsidies. The British Government had, through the recommendations of the Maybury Committee (see page 72), supported the internal airlines by assistance in establishing radio and traffic controls, improving aerodromes, and encouraging pilot training schemes. But Britain was lagging behind in the world of intercontinental air transport, and something had to be done.

The Cadman Committee

More important for the future of the British airlines was the publication of the **Report of the Committee of Inquiry into Civil Aviation** on 8 February 1938. Under the chairmanship of Lord Cadman, it was announced on 17 November 1937, and began its work only on 2 December, and so had not wasted much time. Its recommendations were essentially a statement of government policy in restructuring the airline industry by merging the two major airlines. Changes should be made in management and in staff-management relations, and this seemed to be directed mainly at Imperial, leading to the resignation, on 30 June, of George Woods Humphery, who had managed Imperial since he joined it from Daimler Hire in 1924. The government should assist the aircraft and engine manufacturing industry, support research, and provide good aerodromes; but these items were marginal to the main thrust of the Report, which also recommended an increase of government subsidies to the two airlines from £1,500,000 to £3,000,000. In retrospect, some of the comments may have been a little unfair, as Imperial was expected to "buy British," but the manufacturers had not supplied the airliners that could match those from the United States or Germany; and the flying boats, though providing luxury service, were delivered late, could not cross the Atlantic, and suffered frequent delays in service. The future was with all-metal landplanes, and Imperial Airways simply did not have them.

Formation of British Overseas Airways Corporation (B.O.A.C.)

The bill to pave the way for the merger was introduced in Parliament on 12 June 1939, by Sir Kingsley Wood. Early indications were that the Whitehall Securities-controlled British Airways faction would in future guide the fortunes of the airline that carried the Union Jack to the far corners of earth as well as to the capital cities of Europe. Royal Assent was given to the Bill on 4 August and the **British Overseas Airways Corporation (B.O.A.C.)** was formally established on 24 November. The interim chairman was Sir John Reith, who had overseen British Broadcasting Corporation (B.B.C.). His deputy was Clive Pearson, formerly of British Airways.

The Short-Mayo Composite aircraft combination was an ingenious — but impracticable — attempt to solve the problem of carrying a payload of mail across the Atlantic. The project had already been rendered obsolescent by the German demonstrations of catapult-launched aircraft from depot ships stationed in mid-ocean.

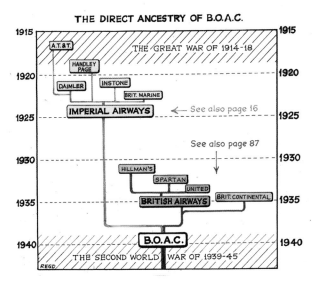

THE DIRECT ANCESTRY OF B.O.A.C.

One reason why Imperial Airways was subject to criticism was the failure to keep up with aeronautical technology. In its efforts to compete with Pan American Airways, which was on course to start passenger services across the Atlantic — which it did in July 1939 — Imperial had to improvise. Flight refuelling was not exactly practicable for scheduled commercial operations, however essential it might be for military purposes, for example, long-range reconnaissance. Another experiment was made with the Short S.20 seaplane Mercury, which made its first separation from the "mother ship," the S.27 Maia, on 6 February 1938. The idea was adopted as a way to increase the payload in the Mercury, as it did not have to use its maximum power and additional fuel in taking off and climbing to cruising height. On 21 July Mercury made the fastest crossing of the Atlantic, with 1,000 lb. of mail, but without the airborne launch, had to return via Bermuda and the Azores. It also flew from Dundee to the Orange River, South Africa, for a world's long distance record. But speed and range were worthless because passenger service was completely impracticable. The Air Ministry wisely rejected the Mayo-Composite on 31 March 1939. The experiment had lasted five years since it was first promoted. It should never have started.

The Imperial Legacy

During the twilight months during 1939 and 1940, as the necessary legislation to create B.O.A.C. went through the parliamentary and legal procedures, the historic words of Earl Grey of Falladon were recalled as "the lights went out" in Europe once again. The creation of a unified British airline coincided with the outbreak of the Second World War.

After a brief hiatus, the two companies tried to maintain "business as usual," with the landplane London bases at Croydon and Heston moving to Whitchurch Airport at Bristol, and the flying boat base moved from Southampton to Poole Harbour in Dorset. A new landplane route opened to Egypt on 22 September, then extended to India (see page 101). A British trans-Atlantic mail-only service had started with flight-refuelled *Caribou* and *Cabot* S.30s on 5 August but had to be discontinued on 30 September. The old Ensigns helped out, with casualties, at Dunkirk, and the veteran Handley Page 42s kept going in the Middle East. The staff, the new organization, and the corporate spirit were still firmly established, and the infant B.O.A.C. began to perform sterling war service as an auxiliary air transport system for the air forces.

On 30 August 1939 British Airways ordered nine **Douglas DC-5** high-winged 16-seat airliners, which would have been registered as G-AFYG and G-AFYO. The war broke out four days later and the order was cancelled.

In spite of its shortcomings in the 1930s, when it seemed to have lost its way, the British manufacturing industry was pulling itself together, and no less than four long-range all-metal landplane airliners were "on the drawing boards." Also, the D.H.95 Flamingoes showed promise. The S.23 flying boat line was transformed into military Sunderland production — two-thirds of the 1,266 big flying boats ever built were from Shorts.

But luck did not, in this situation, favour the brave. The two pictures on this page encapsulate the situation as it really was. The scene at Croydon illustrates the technical challenge, with the modern 160-mph K.L.M. Douglas DC-2 and the two British Airways Lockheed Electras contrasting with the veteran 100-mph Imperial Airways Short Scylla biplane. The sleek *Frobisher*, on the other hand, with its aerodynamic grace, seems to herald a new future.

For the first time on any of Imperial's airliners, the Lee-Elliott's timeless "Speedbird" insignia appears. It seems to point the way to the skies. And perhaps it did; for SPEEDBIRD is still the radio communications call-sign and identification code for British Airways today.

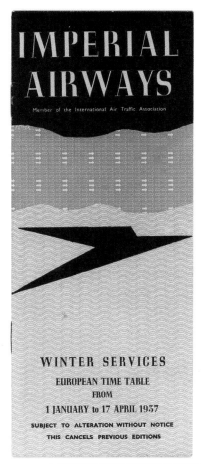

The old and the new, Croydon, 1939.

Vision of the future, Croydon, 1939.

Top Left: The "Speedbird" symbol had been a strong feature of Imperial Airways's publicity and promotion since 1932. But it never appeared on an aeroplane until 1939.

Bottom Left: This was the cheque that was paid by the new B.O.A.C. to Barclay's Bank, on the liquidation of Imperial Airways.

Bibliography

As with any book such as this, the number of reference sources are legion. The following are the ones used in seeking, compiling, and checking the facts, figures, and various data included within these pages. Those that were of premier importance are listed in bold type. All published in Great Britain, unless otherwise indicated.

Civil Aviation Annual Reports on Progress (1919–1938 inclusive).
Air Ministry

The Approach towards a System of Imperial Air Communications.
Air Ministry, 1926

Annals of British and Commonwealth Air Transport, 1919–1960 by John Stroud. Putnam, London, 1962

Aerial Transport by G. Holt Thomas. Hodder and Stoughton, London, 1920

Early Birds by Alfred Instone. Western Mail & Echo, Cardiff, 1938

Railway Air Services by John Stroud. Ian Allan, Shepperton, Surrey, 1987

European Transport Aircraft since 1910 by John Stroud. Putnam, London, 1966

British Commercial Aircraft . . . 1920–1940 by Arthur W.J.G. Ord-Hume. GMS Enterprises, Peterborough, 2003

The Triple Alliance by Neville Doyle. Air-Britain, Tonbridge, Kent, 2001

The de Havilland Dragon/Rapide Family by John F. Hamlin. Air-Britain, Tonbridge, 2003

Handley Page: a History by Alan Dowsett. Tempus Publishing, Stroud, Glos., 2003

Flying Empires — Short C-Class Empire Flying Boats by Brian Cassidy. Queen's Parade Press, Bath, 1996

Croydon Airport, from War to Peace, by Joanna Bogle. London Borough of Sutton Heritage Service, 2003

Croydon Airport by Mike Hooks. Tempus Publishing, Stroud, Glos., 1997

Croydon Airport: the Peaceful Years by Mike Hooks. Tempus Publishing, Stroud, 2002

The Seven Seas by John Pudney. Putnam, London, 1959

Britain's Imperial Air Routes 1918–39 by Robin Higham. G.T. Foulis, London, 1960

Civil Air Transport by Group Capt. W.E.Wynn. Hutchinson, London, 1945

Flying against the Elements by Peter Clegg. Peter Clegg, Godalming, Surrey, 1987

Rivals in the North by Peter Clegg. Godalming, Surrey, 1988

Wings over the Glens by Peter Clegg. GMS Enterprises, Peterborough, 1995

Sword in the Sky by Peter Clegg. Peter Clegg, Godalming, Surrey, 1990

Flying Boats: The J-Class Yachts of Aviation by Ian Marshall. Howell Press, Charlottesville, Virginia, U.S.A., 2002

De Havilland Aircraft since 1909 by A.J. Jackson. Putnam, London, 1962

D. H. — An Outline of de Havilland History by C. Martin Sharp. Faber & Faber, London, 1960

Armstrong Whitworth Aircraft since 1913 by Oliver Tapper. Putnam, London, 1973

Handley Page Aircraft since 1909 by C.H. Barnes. Putnam, London, 1976

Forty Years On . . . Handley Page Ltd.. London, 1949

Avro Aircraft since 1909 by A.J. Jackson. Putnam, London, 1965

Westland Aircraft since 1915 by Derek James. Putnam, London, 1991

Shorts Aircraft since 1900 by C.H. Barnes. Putnam, London, 1967

Boulton Paul Aircraft since 1915 by Alec Brew. Putnam, London, 1993

McDonnell Douglas Aircraft since 1920 by René Francillon. Putnam, London, 1979

Index

Notes: D = Profile drawing, with supplementary drawing showing size comparison; S = aircraft specifications; P = photograph; M = map; F = fleet list; T = tabulation (other than fleet list); E = exhibit; C = chart; A = artwork – reproduction of paintings. Major references are listed in bold type.

Index

AIRCRAFT TRANSPORT & TRAVEL 1919

Amsterdam
17 May 1919

London

Paris
25 August 1919

Scale-Miles

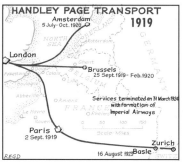

HANDLEY PAGE TRANSPORT 1919

Amsterdam
5 July–Oct. 1920

London

Brussels
25 Sept. 1919–Feb. 1920

Services terminated on 31 March 1924
with formation of
Imperial Airways

Paris
2 Sept. 1919

Zurich
16 August 1923

INSTONE AIR LINE 1920

Birmingham
(21 Feb–2 March 1921)
Cardiff (13 Oct 1921)
(S. Instone & Co Ltd. until 15 May 1920)

London

Cologne 1 Oct 1922
Prague
4 Aug 1923
(experimental)

Brussels
8 May 1922

Paris
(Private service 13 Oct.)
Public service 18 Feb 1920

Services terminated on
31 March 1924 with formation
of Imperial Airways

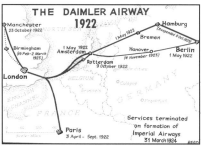

THE DAIMLER AIRWAY 1922

Manchester
23 October 1922

Hamburg
(Suspended 1 Oct. 1923)

Birmingham
(19 Feb–2 March 1923)

1 May 1922
Bremen

Amsterdam
1 May 1922

Hanover
(4 November 1923)

Berlin
1 May 1922

Rotterdam
9 October 1922

London

Services terminated
on formation of
Imperial Airways
31 March 1924

Paris
3 April–Sept. 1922

Southampton
Woolston

1923

B.M.A.N.

St. Peter Port

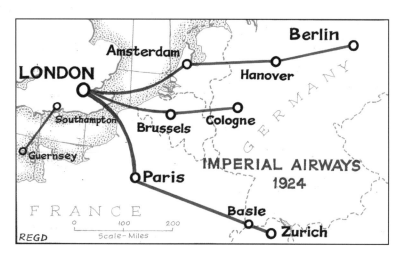

Berlin

Amsterdam

LONDON

Hanover

Southampton

Brussels
Cologne

Guernsey

Paris

Basle

IMPERIAL AIRWAYS 1924

Zurich

Scale–Miles

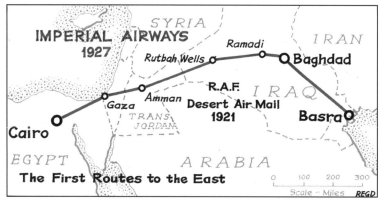

IMPERIAL AIRWAYS 1927

SYRIA

IRAN

Ramadi

Rutbah Wells

Baghdad

Gaza
Amman

**R.A.F.
Desert Air Mail
1921**

Basra

Cairo

TRANS
JORDAN

IRAQ

EGYPT

ARABIA

The First Routes to the East

Scale – Miles

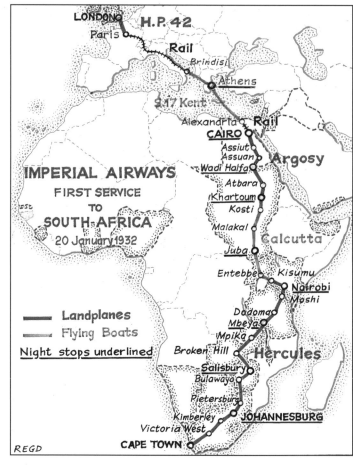

LONDON
Paris

H.P. 42

Rail
Brindisi

Athens

**IMPERIAL AIRWAYS
FIRST SERVICE
TO
SOUTH AFRICA**
20 January 1932

S.17 Kent

Alexandria
CAIRO   Rail

Assiut
Assuan
Wadi Halfa

Argosy

Atbara
Khartoum
Kosti

Calcutta

Malakal

Juba

Entebbe   Kisumu
Nairobi
Moshi

Dodoma
Mbeya
Mpika

Broken Hill

Hercules

Salisbury
Bulawayo

Pietersburg
Kimberley
Victoria West

JOHANNESBURG

CAPE TOWN

— Landplanes
— Flying Boats

Night stops underlined

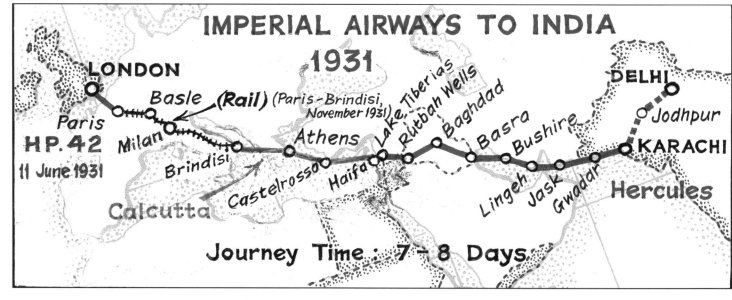

IMPERIAL AIRWAYS TO INDIA
1931

DELHI

LONDON

Basle   **(Rail)** *(Paris–Brindisi, November 1931)*

Paris

Milan

H.P. 42

Brindisi

11 June 1931

Castelrosso

Athens

Haifa

Lake Tiberias

Rutbah Wells

Baghdad

Basra

Bushire

Lingeh

Jask

Gwadar

Jodhpur

KARACHI

Hercules

Calcutta

Journey Time : 7 – 8 Days